Acclaim for
Daniel Yergin and Thane Gustafson's
RUSSIA
2010

"Invaluable.... Having spent the better part of 13 years in Moscow, this reviewer found each of the scenarios intriguing and plausible.... With this book as a guide, we can at least follow the game."
                                                                    —*The New York Times Book Review*

"The analysis is of such high quality ... remarkably insightful."
                                                                    —*Foreign Affairs*

"Excellent.... Yergin and Gustafson see the nuances. They paint a picture of a complex and volatile country. They catch its chaotic dynamism, its historical confusion, its potential.... For anyone trying to get a grasp on what could emerge from this massive, unpredictable land mass, it is just about the best place to start."
                                                                    —*Boston Globe*

"Read the book, cross your fingers, and hope for the best."
                                                                    —*Business Week*

"Extraordinarily intelligent.... Together [the authors] have applied a level of experience and acute judgment which raises *Russia 2010* to the level—rarely attained—of a book which qualifies for the accolade 'essential.'"
                                                                    —*Financial Times*

"*Russia 2010* has electrified the old and new generation of Soviet watchers with its challenging assessment of where post-communist Russia and the old Soviet Union could be heading."
                                                                    —*Daily Telegraph* (London)

BOOKS BY **Daniel Yergin**

The Prize: The Epic Quest for Oil, Money, and Power

Shattered Peace: The Origins of the Cold War and the National Security State

Energy Future (coauthor)

Global Insecurity (coauthor)

BOOKS BY **Thane Gustafson**

Crisis amid Plenty

Reform in Soviet Politics

Soviet Soldiers and the State (coauthor)

The Soviet Union at the Crossroads (coauthor)

RUSSIA
2010

RUSSIA 2010

And What It Means for the World

Daniel Yergin
and Thane Gustafson

THE CERA REPORT

VINTAGE BOOKS
A Division of Random House, Inc.
New York

When I was in Russia

FIRST VINTAGE BOOK EDITION, FEBRUARY 1995

The Library of Congress has cataloged the Random House edition as follows:
Yergin, Daniel.
Russia 2010—and what it means for the world / Daniel Yergin and Thane Gustafson.
p. cm.
Published simultaneously in Canada.
Includes bibliographical references and index.
ISBN 0-679-42995-6
1. Russia (Federation)—Forecasts. I. Gustafson, Thane. II. Title.
DK510.76Y47   1993
303.4947—dc20   93-32909
Vintage ISBN: 0-679-75922-0

Manufactured in the United States of America
10 9 8 7 6 5 4 3 2 1

To Nil and Peri, and
Angela, Rebecca, and Alexander

Contents

Contents

The scene looks eerily familiar: It is a fine spring day in Moscow, and the leaders are standing on the red-brick parapet of the Lenin Mausoleum in front of the Kremlin, waving benevolently as the military parade passes by below them. In the diplomatic stands, the Western military attachés snap pictures frantically as the sensation of the day appears; it is the latest Russian helicopter gunship, kept strictly under wraps until now.

But wait: Some things are wrong with this picture. Painted on the gunship's side is the blue two-headed eagle; more eagles glint in the sunlight from the tops of the Kremlin towers. On the parapet the civilians in business suits stand to the side, while braided military uniforms are massed solidly at the center. On the GUM *building across the street an enormous banner proclaims,* HAIL TO OUR SUPREME COMMANDER AND TO THE GLORIOUS RUSSIAN ARMY. *It is May 17, 2010, the eighth anniversary of the army coup.*

—The Russian Bear

The Russian president presses a button, and dozens of computer screens spring to life. A gigantic multicolored electronic display, filling three walls of the large hall, lights up like a pinball machine. The locations and status of all Western missiles and warheads—in real time? No—prices and trend analysis of currencies and securities at major markets all over the world. It is May 17, 2010, the date of the inauguration of a state-of-the-art trading center for the Moscow Stock Exchange, already well known to the world as the Bolshaya Doska *(Big Board), or simply, the* Doska.

The large audience, the cream of Russian government officials, corporate presidents, financiers, and the world financial media, burst into applause. Vladimir Vinogradov, chairman of the board of Inkombank, Russia's largest bank, steps to the microphone. "It gives me particular pleasure," says Vinogradov, "to announce a special present to Russia on the occasion of the opening of this center. Inkombank has just completed the acquisition of the seventh largest bank in the United States. Inkombank, which we founded a little over thirty years ago, has now joined the list of the largest banks in the world."

—Chudo

Overleaf: Map of the Former Soviet Union

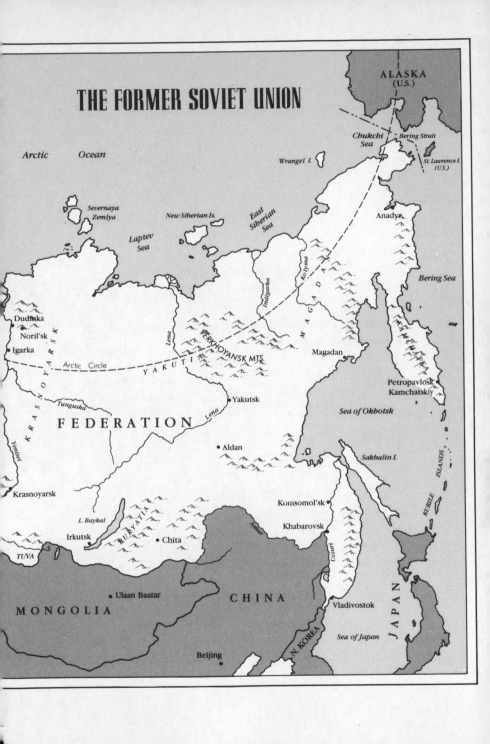

THE FORMER SOVIET UNION

Arctic   Ocean

ALASKA
(U.S.)

Chukchi
Sea

Bering Strait

St. Lawrence I.
(U.S.)

Wrangel I.

Severnaya
Zemlya

New Siberian Is.

East
Siberian
Sea

Anadyr

Laptev
Sea

Bering Sea

Dudinka

Noril'sk

Igarka

Arctic Circle

Y A K U T I A

VERKHOYANSK MTS.

Magadan

Sea of Okhotsk

Petropavlosk
Kamchatskiy

Tunguska

Lena

Yakutsk

F E D E R A T I O N

Lena

Aldan

Yenisei

Sakhalin I.

Krasnoyarsk

K R A S N O Y A R S K

Kolyma

Indigirka

M A G A D A N

K A M C H A T K A

L. Baykal

B U R Y A T I A

Komsomol'sk

Khabarovsk

K U R I L E   I S L A N D S

Irkutsk

Chita

Amur

Ussuri

TUVA

J A P A N

Ulaan Baatar

C H I N A

Vladivostok

M O N G O L I A

N. KOREA

Sea of Japan

Beijing

What we anticipate seldom occurs;
what we least expected generally happens.
                            —Benjamin Disraeli

Sometimes I've believed as many as six impossible things
before breakfast.
                            —Lewis Carroll
                            Through the Looking-Glass

Preface

Despite technology that instantaneously flashes images from around the world into our homes, the ability to anticipate change does not seem greatly improved. Surprise follows surprise; we do not know in which corner of the world the next economic, political, or social upheaval will occur. The collapse of the Soviet Union and the upheavals in Russia and its newly-independent neighbors are urgent cases in point.

In 1950 George Kennan, preeminent Sovietologist of the Cold War and great student of Russia, wrote that—in trying to understand Russia—we tread in the "unfirm substance of the imponderables." If anything, that diagnosis is even more true today. Now, at this critical juncture, Daniel Yergin and Thane Gustafson have written a brilliant book that provides the reader with a mental roadmap through—and beyond—the "unfirm substance." It is a book not only for the expert and policymaker, but also for the businessman interested in the huge market of the Former Soviet Union, and for the citizen, concerned about peace and stability and the world that they and their children will inhabit in the twenty-first century.

The objective of *Russia 2010* is to provide a framework for the "imponderables"—the possible directions and developments for the new Russian Revolution and its implications for the rest of the world. Yergin and Gustafson use the technique of "scenario planning" to get beyond the trap of simple extrapolation and to open our minds to diverse ideas and new ways of arranging our thinking about the future.

Russia 2010 does not offer the security blanket of a single forecast. Rather, it presents plausible stories for the future by building on two requirements for scenario planning—imagination and discipline. The scenario planning technique is an approach that Cambridge Energy Research Associates (CERA) has tested and applied both to energy topics and to such issues as environmental prospects; economic, political, and social change in Europe; and globalization, privatization and the international economy. *Russia 2010* grew out of the work that CERA has been conducting on change in the space of the Former Soviet Union since 1985.

It may be said that the collapse of the Former Soviet Union and communism truly marks the end of the twentieth century. Now, on the eve of the 21st century, Russia is struggling with three revolutions, each one of them immensely difficult—from dictatorship to democracy, from command economy to market, and from four-century-old empire to nation state. The consequences will be momentous.

Which future will it be? The Russian Bear or the Two-Headed Eagle? The Long Good-Bye—or "Chudo," the Russian economic miracle? Whatever the outcome, *Russia 2010* provides us with the signposts for the future and decreases the likelihood that we will be surprised by the direction of events in that critically important part of the world.

Joseph Stanislaw
Managing Director, CERA

RUSSIA
2010

1

"The World Behind the Mirror"

"We know too little about the laws of history."
—*Andrei Sakharov*

The twentieth century closes as it began, with revolution in Russia, the great landmass where Europe, Asia, and the Middle East converge. Revolution first exploded in Russia in 1905, after Japan stunned the Russian empire by sinking its fleet at the Battle of Tsushima. This upheaval was called the Great Rehearsal by Lenin; it did not succeed, but it set the stage. In 1917, in the midst of war, revolution broke out again, this time toppling the tsarist autocracy. The Bolsheviks soon captured the revolution, and the Russians were forced to reject democracy and a market economy. For the next seven decades, the Russians subjected themselves and the rest of the world to a massive experiment in totalitarian dictatorship and central planning.

Now, in the 1990s, the Russians have returned to the same fateful crossroads at which they stood more than seven decades ago. The choice that Russia made in 1917 did much to define the conflicts and the very character of the twentieth century. The collapse of communism stands as the most important development for the entire world at the end of the century. The choices Russia makes now about its future will be one of the major forces shaping the twenty-first century.

Russia does not have a free hand in making its choices. It must somehow extricate itself from the powerful grip of the Soviet past. Unlike Japan and Germany in the late 1940s, the former Soviet Union is not a defeated country. The old factories still stand. While new people are entering the lists of power, many of the rulers of yesterday are still present today, even if they wear different labels and even if they disavow the past. And, although the ideology of communism is gone, the mind-set of socialism is still very much alive. Moreover, the formerly Soviet lands that now are fourteen other sovereign republics are still deeply bound to Russia, and both sides must come to terms with a new, complex, and difficult relationship. Defeat in war sometimes enables people to bury the past and start anew. But that option is not open to the Russians, or to most of their former subjects. The past is still very much in place.

Yet, truly, there is no going back. The core of the Soviet system has been obliterated. The Communist ideology and its center of power, the apparatus of the Communist Party of the Soviet Union, have been destroyed. Above all, what has collapsed is the Communist ideal itself. Even though its utopianism turned out to be a cloak for a brutal system of power, this ideal has not yet been replaced by another strong ideal that commands broad allegiance. That new ideal could well prove to be nationalism, which can manifest itself in many different forms. A battle over the soul and character of Russian nationalism has already begun. Will the result be a constructive, unifying principle that brings the past and the future into alignment and provides a foundation for a democratic political order, or will it become the tool of extremists filled with anger and resentment and hungry for authoritarianism? The "market" and "democracy" are, in varying degrees to various people, enticing ideas, though frightening at the same time. To others, these are foreign ideas, abominations, with no place in Russia and unsuited to the Russian people. Yet what must be measured against the potential for extremism is the widespread yearning for "normality" and "civilization" after the Bolshevik experiment. That desire was summed up with simplicity by a minister in the current government when he quietly said, "We want Russia to be a normal country."

THE TRIPLE TRANSITION

In such circumstances, Russia faces an immense agenda, trying simultaneously to make three very difficult transitions. The first is from dictatorship to democracy. The second is from a command economy, which was run by planners at the center, and in which money did not really count, to a free market. And the third is from a four-century-old empire to a nation-state.

The possibilities before Russia are very broad. The nation could move toward democracy and toward what we call "Capitalism Russian-

Style." Or it could be captured by the "Red-Browns," a coalition of Communists and fascists, who would carry Russia back to dictatorship. Some fear that Russia could be swept up in chaos and a series of ethnic and regional wars; this dark vision has become known as "Yugoslavia in eleven time zones." Yet Russia's situation is quite different from that of the former Yugoslavia. While intense racial and ethnic hatreds dominate the new states along Russia's southern border, they are for the most part absent from Russia itself. One consequence of the breakup of the Soviet Union is that the Russian Federation is relatively homogeneous—80 percent Russian—which is one factor in favor of stability.

Internationally, Russia might well reemerge as a Great Power, a partner in a more peaceful world. Or, on the contrary, humiliation at Russia's loss of status, distress at the collapse of living standards, and resentment at the breakup of the Soviet Union—all of these could combine to lead to a rebirth of a virulent nationalism and a Russian imperialism, intent on reversing the course of the last half decade. If there is truly a protracted economic collapse and Russia does fissure, the results could be chaos and even war, both on and within Russia's borders. This, in turn, could not only loose a massive flood of refugees on the world, but also entangle the Western countries in ways we do not now imagine. The world could be caught up in the convulsions shaking the former Soviet empire. Certainly, upheaval within Russia and the rest of the former Soviet Union will threaten the stability of Europe, Asia, and the Middle East.

This specter is made more alarming by the blunt fact that, while the Soviet Union is gone, its weapons are not. The breakup of the Soviet Union increases the risks of nuclear proliferation. About thirty thousand nuclear weapons remain in Russia, along with a vast arsenal of chemical and conventional weapons. (There are several thousand more nuclear warheads in Ukraine and Kazakhstan.) No one really knows the degree to which the chain of "command and control" in Russia has survived the extreme stress of the breakup of the USSR nor the degree to which the "warning system," which governs the launch of nuclear weapons, has degraded. The accounting system for weaponry is not reassuring. How well are those weapons minded, how many could end up for sale to terrorists and other governments, how many could fall into the hands of rogue commanders? What happens to those weapons, and to the large stocks of fissile material, if government weakens further and Russia becomes more chaotic?

Yet we cannot lose sight of two facts. The first is how much has already and so quickly changed in Russia. Not long ago, Boris Fedorov, the former Russian finance minister, was asked whether he thought Russia could ever achieve a "functioning market economy."

"Why not?" he replied, only somewhat facetiously. "We already have a malfunctioning market economy."

The second fact is that, after four decades of a dangerous and costly global rivalry, the Cold War has ended without a hot war, opening up the opportunity, at least, for a more peaceful and less endangered world. What can the United States and the other countries of the West, all preoccupied with their own political and economic problems, do to support Russia's move toward democracy, free markets, and international cooperation? It is a paramount question. For this is a unique time of opportunity, both for Russia and for the rest of the world. Nevertheless, the difficulties and risks of the Russian transition will prove enormous; they will last the better part of a generation; and they will be felt by peoples all over the world.[1]

THE OBJECTIVE

These issues—and Russia's struggle to make the transition to democracy, a market economy, and a nation state—form the core of this book. In 1950, George Kennan wrote that, in trying to understand the Soviet Union, we tread "in the unfirm substance of the imponderables."[2] Much the same can be said of Russia at this moment, when the old is discredited and the new has not yet been built. The objective of this book is to help provide a framework for understanding the possible developments and directions of the new Russian revolution and its implications for the rest of the world—in short, to bring some clarity to the unfolding process.

The need is certainly there. So much that has happened, and is happening, in Russia and the rest of the former Soviet Union is astonishing, confusing, dramatic. Communism itself, which seemed to be the gray constancy of the twentieth century, imploded. Then, with the lifting of the Communist grip, ancient and not-so-ancient ethnic rivalries erupted in various parts of the former Soviet empire. Russia's official gross national product has plummeted by 40 percent since 1990. In the meantime, a fierce battle for power, property, and revenues is taking place. Everyone is involved—old commissars and new entrepreneurs, ex-KGB men and former dissidents. Government officials serve at the same time on the boards of private companies. Recent émigrés, who left under the scornful eye of the secret police, are going back to help start biotechnology companies, while generals who spent their professional lives preparing to fight the United States are now making telecommunication deals with American investors. Former members of the Communist apparatus have become enthusiastic converts to capitalism and are running private businesses. Sometimes, it seems, every Russian has at least three different business cards.

Even after the loss of its empire, Russia retains a huge army. But that army is embittered by its own humiliations and its loss of status. Many officers and their families, returned from bases in Eastern Europe, are now living in tents. By some estimates, as many as 150,000 Russian officers are currently homeless. Some are waiting restlessly and uneasily for the new military housing that a united Germany is helping to build for them as part of the price of troop withdrawals from the former East Germany. The future of Russia's formidable armed forces is uncertain even to those who command them.

In its Russian translation, *Through the Looking Glass* (the sequel to *Alice in Wonderland*) is titled a little differently: *Alice in the World Behind the Mirror*. And that is how Russians describe the situation in which they find themselves today with the end of communism and the collapse of the Soviet Union—"behind the mirror." Everything they took for granted—economic security, the dictatorship of the Communist party and the control of the KGB, the predictability of life and the delivery of food by the enterprise that employs them, the stupefying cant of Marxism and safety in the streets, a yearly holiday in the Crimea and the Soviet Union as a superpower—it's all disappeared. Crime, in one form or another, has become widespread. Life "behind the mirror" is confusing and disorienting, and it can also be terrifying. And it all came so quickly, without any time to prepare—a surprise of momentous proportions for the Russian people, given their entire life experience, and also for the rest of the world.

"THE FATAL LAP"

Indeed, the collapse of communism and the rebirth of Russia will stand as a classic example of "surprise" in history. And so often, great events do come as a surprise. In the spring and early summer of 1914, Europe had seemed more at peace, and war further away, than had been the case for many years. British naval units were even making courtesy

7

visits to German ports. Yet in August 1914, less than six weeks after the assassination of the Austrian archduke Franz Ferdinand in Sarajevo, Europe was at war. Thirteen million people were to die before it was over.

The attack on Pearl Harbor, which brought the United States into World War II, was the worst shock in American history. It, too, came as a complete surprise. Before the Second World War was over, fifty million people would die around the world.

In September 1973, the Japanese prime minister said an energy crisis might come within ten years. Instead, it came within ten days, with the unexpected outbreak of the Yom Kippur War and then the 1973 oil embargo. The consequences of these events dominated the international economy in the 1970s.[3]

The fall of the shah of Iran in 1979 was also a great surprise, at least for most people, including senior officials in the West. Only a year before, the President of the United States had described the shah's regime as "an island of stability in one of the more unstable parts of the world."[4] The abrupt disappearance of that government dramatically altered the strategic balance of the entire Middle East. But the effects did not end there. The consequences of the regime's collapse helped destroy the administration of Jimmy Carter, and the shah's fall also tempted the Soviet Union into what proved eventually to be the disastrous decision, from Moscow's point of view, to invade Afghanistan.

What unexpected developments lie ahead? In his old age, former British prime minister Anthony Eden looked back at the failure of nations to anticipate crises earlier in the twentieth century. "It is impossible to read the record now and not feel that we had a responsibility for always being a lap behind," he said. "Always a lap behind, the fatal lap."[5] At the end of the century, we can try to make up that lap so as not to be left behind, and caught unprepared once again.

THE LIMITS OF FORECASTING

But how are we to envision the year 2010? What will Russia and the world be like then? As so often happens at a time of great change, events seem to outrun our capacity to grasp them, to make sense of them, to be prepared for them. At such times, there are two requirements for clear thinking. One is imagination. The other is discipline.

Both are basic to the approach that we use here. It is called "scenario planning," and it is a structured, disciplined method for thinking about the future. We believe that it is an effective technique for tackling questions about the future and reducing complexity. It seeks to open the mind to diverse ideas and to get beyond the tradition and trap of simple extrapolation. It can facilitate an earlier recognition of change, thus promoting flexibility. If successful, it makes "surprises" less surprising and, as such, helps one to "look around the corner."

We apply scenario planning to the future of Russia. It can also be usefully applied to a wide variety of questions in very different realms, as people struggle with the shape of the future and decision making in the midst of uncertainty.

Inattention and the almost inevitable preoccupation with the here and now are often the culprits that prevent people from focusing on the developments that turn out to be significant in the future. The tragic spectacle of Sarajevo could at least have been anticipated. But the West was a lap behind.[6]

Scenario planning does not, of course, tell us the future; only fortune-tellers can do that. Rather, it encourages the judgment and engagement of the decision-maker or, in this case, the reader. Indeed, at the end of this book, we hope readers will have grappled with the scenarios, joined in the debate, and come to their own conclusions.

With startling regularity, more conventional processes of planning and forecasting have proven to be inadequate; they often get their users into deep trouble. They tend to reinforce the consensus and established thinking—and dogmas—in organizations. The people at the top think "this" or "that"; their careers, their positions and power, are rooted in these established beliefs. There is no window through which to admit new ideas or information that might challenge established ideas. Anyone who tries to do so—to ask "What if?"—runs the risk of being treated like a maverick, a crank or, even worse, a court jester.

Conventional forecasting may be called "corporate planning" in companies, or "intelligence and analysis" in governments. In any case, it has its difficulty in identifying the points of inflection, the changes in the trends, the major shifts. In the words of James Schlesinger, former director of the CIA, and former U.S. secretary of defense and of energy: "Intelligence is pretty good at monitoring continuing or patterned activities. Its great weakness, not surprisingly, is in discerning the turning points." Yet it is exactly those turning points, the big changes, that matter the most, for they take us into a different world—"behind the mirror"—in which new perspectives and new responses are required.

"THE UNTHINKABLE"

In the mid-1970s, General Motors failed in its forecasting to take seriously the possibility that Japanese cars would sell in large numbers in the United States. In other words, it refused to imagine how drastically the competitive arena could change from what it knew and was comfortable with. Japanese cars, it thought, would flunk the market test in America on quality, styling, and size. Yet the massive onslaught of Japanese autos on the American market was already beginning; the consequences for Detroit were disastrous.

In the late 1980s and early 1990s the same thing happened to another American corporation—IBM. It also failed to imagine how drastically technology and markets could shift, altering its competitive position.

The reasons for IBM's fall are complex, but a significant element was the company's failure to anticipate and prepare for the forces of change. IBM's motto was "Think!" but it failed to think seriously about the unthinkable—in its case, that its highly profitable mainframe computer business could be successfully challenged by personal computers and networking. Its forecasting process gave management the answers that management wanted. The company paid a heavy price. It has already laid off almost 200,000 people, and its stock price is only 25 percent of what it was three years ago.[7]

A third example, this one from government, demonstrates how failing to conceptualize the future—and being locked into the axioms of the past—helped cause the United States government to miss the tremors of the earthquake that destroyed the Soviet Union. Although there were analysts and voices within the intelligence community saying that change was coming, they were not taken as seriously as they might have been. The year after Gorbachev came to power, one senior official dismissed projections of "fundamental change" as idle speculation. But what might be dismissed as "idle speculation" can, in fact, be a powerful tool. As the then CIA deputy director said in 1991, "We've all learned some important lessons from the events of the last three or four years in terms of thinking the unthinkable."[8]

SCENARIO PLANNING

"Thinking the unthinkable" and "idle speculation" are essential to scenario planning. Contrast the experience of a group that did use scenario planning, Royal Dutch Shell, in anticipating the forces of change in the Soviet Union.

Scenario planning was, in fact, developed in the early 1970s by planners at Shell, who had run headlong into the inadequacies of conventional forecasting. The oil industry operates on very long-term investments, the viability of which can be dramatically affected by political, economic, social, and technological changes. Simple extrapolation might have worked in the 1960s, when each year simply meant more growth over the previous year, but it looked like a prescription for disaster as the 1970s began. Seeking an alternative, these planners built upon the scenario technique that Herman Kahn and other strategists had developed at the RAND Corporation to think through issues involving nuclear weapons and the nature of nuclear warfare.[9]

The result was scenario planning, which offered a way to evaluate strategy, test investment decisions—and clarify risk and uncertainty. As part of preparing for the future, the Shell planners applied scenario planning not only to the energy business but also to larger global political, economic, and social trends. The Soviet Union was one subject.

In 1984, the year before Gorbachev came to power, "no change" and "more of the same" were the conventional diagnoses around the world on the Soviet system. But a small group at Shell, with the help of a few outsiders, decided to ask the "what if?" questions. Could radical reform come to the Soviet Union? And what might be the results? The answer, after a year's work, was the "Greening of Russia" scenario, in which a younger leadership would come to power and begin to make decisive economic and political changes.[10]

To have discussed the scenario publicly would have invited ridicule, given the general attitude at the time toward the prospects for the Soviet Union. Yet, within the scenario process, there was no penalty for "playing" with the unthinkable. Events since have demonstrated that the "Greening of Russia" was a better road map than many others to the "new Russian Revolution."

"STORIES OF THE FUTURE"

We at CERA (Cambridge Energy Research Associates) began applying scenarios in the middle 1980s, both on energy subjects and on broader political and economic questions. The subjects have included oil and natural gas prices, and electricity; the future of Mexico and Latin

America, and the Middle East; environmental policies; political, economic, and social change in Europe; and privatization and global economic prospects.

As our colleague Joseph Stanislaw, CERA's director of research, has put the matter: "It's very difficult to plan and think ahead when change is at hand. Sometimes, even if you think the unthinkable, events move before you've finished your thought. The habit, and the risk, is to impose the rules from the old order. Scenario planning does not offer the security blanket of a single forecast. What it does do is create plausible 'stories of the future.' These enable one to pick up the signals and search out the clues to the future. They also identify the key signposts to look for along the way."

The objective of the scenario approach is not to decide which scenario is right, but rather to provide a language for talking about the future—and a way to join in the game. There is no "right" answer. Scenarios are learning stories, and the process of working through them, experiencing them, is as important as the conclusions.

THE NEWS IN MOSCOW

By this point, it should be clear that we have no intention of offering a single forecast of what Russia's future will look like. Probabilities and rankings of likelihood are to be avoided at all costs, because they will immediately close down the gates on creative thinking and open debate. Rather, we hope to provide a group of persuasive, plausible scenarios that together offer a framework for interpreting the confusing flow of information coming out of the Russian revolution. In the 1940 movie *Comrade X,* Clark Gable complains to Hedy Lamarr, "Let's face it, baby. There ain't no news in Moscow." Now, there's much too much news, and it is very hard to get that news into perspective and to understand its importance.

CERA began its work on change in the former Soviet Union in 1985, when it began to be apparent that Western companies might be able to become involved with the Soviet economy as something more than just trading partners.

As the Russian revolution unfolded in 1990 and 1991, we were asked by a group of international companies to develop scenarios on the future of the former Soviet Union and its energy development in the form of a multiclient study.[11] That study's objective was to help firms that are considering major business and investment decisions in Russia

and the other republics, in a situation in which there are no precedents, no framework, to guide such decision making. *Russia 2010* now represents a further stage in an ongoing research effort that includes our colleagues. The project has involved many trips to Russia and other parts of the former Soviet Union over the last two years, and hundreds of discussions and interviews. We have also had access to extensive public opinion surveying.

OUR STORY

We have chosen the year 2010 as the focusing point for the scenarios. It will have been exactly twenty-five years since Gorbachev came to power, starting the process that led to the new Russian revolution. By then, the multiple transitions will be very far along and many of the uncertainties will be resolved. And, of critical importance, by then a wholly new, post-Communist generation will be active in Russian life.

Our story begins, however, with the 1970s and early 1980s, and with the question of how did it get from "there" to "here"?—that is, from the seemingly immutable Soviet Union of Leonid Brezhnev to the new Russian revolution. The answer lies, more than anywhere else, in the failure of central planning and the command economy.

The second part of the book is composed of the "building blocks" for the scenarios. We identify three driving forces. The first is political: the tumultuous repercussions of the collapse of communism. The second is economic: the shock waves from the breakdown of the centralized "command economy." The third is the Russian quest for identity both as a nation and in the world, following the breakup of the Soviet Union. Our prime movers at this point include Boris Yeltsin, as well as many groups and institutions. Among them is the FSK, whose initials are not yet very well known in the West but which is the successor to the KGB.

The political constraints arise from the difficult process of creating democracy in a society that has always known, except for fleeting moments in the past, authoritarianism and dictatorship. The economic constraints derive from the difficulties inherent in trying to "build capitalism in a day"—or even a decade. Other constraints range from a rigid industrial system, built to meet the needs of a centrally planned economy, to a culture that brands as pathological and criminal what would be regarded as normal commercial behavior elsewhere.

Another decisive constraint is the environment. The collapse of the

Soviet Union has laid bare decades of environmental abuse on a massive scale. This will be one of the lasting legacies of communism, and one that Russia will have difficulty dealing with, owing to its economic difficulties. The scenarios have major implications for the future state of the environment in Russia and whether the leaders will have the will —and, more important, the financial resources—to address the debacle that exists there.

We present each of our scenarios in two sections. The first consists of a story, written as we might find it in some future history book. The second is an analysis of the elements of each scenario, elements in which the story is embedded and out of which it grows.

The first scenario, Muddling Down, picks up from today. It is the scenario of a society and an economy that are running down. Lawlessness is increasingly a fact of life. Nostalgia for the old order and the politics of resentment and humiliation can become potent political forces. But it is also the scenario of the emerging market economy, developing more rapidly than many people think. And Muddling Down could become Muddling Up.

The future points in three possible directions. One looks toward the emergence of a stronger political middle, which would stabilize and reinforce the weak central government. This we call Two-Headed Eagle. It is the alliance of the "red barons"—the defense industrialists and industrial managers—with the army and the police. It aims to restore self-respect, but reimposes the state on the economy.

The second path leads in the opposite direction, toward ever-greater loss of central control, producing varying degrees of chaos—and reaction against it. We call this the Time of Troubles. This is not a single scenario, but rather a "family" of scenarios, out of which we develop two. In the benign version, Russia could go toward the Long Goodbye, the further weakening of the formerly centralized Russian state. The Russian Far East and Siberia would move into the orbits of Japan and China and perhaps be caught in a tug-of-war between the two. St. Petersburg and the Russian northwest would orient themselves toward Scandinavia and Germany. Sooner or later, however, any period of chaos is likely to be followed by a reaction, a "recentralizing" response, a "regathering of the Russian lands." If the chaos is severe, it could give way to the reactionary Russian Bear: a highly authoritarian and aggressively nationalistic state, hostile to the outside world and intent on reimposing Russian domination over the other new states of the

former Soviet Union. In this scenario, defense spending in the West would reverse direction, and start going up again.

Yet Muddling Down might also go in a direction that seems wholly unlikely now; it might muddle up toward what we call the *Chudo* scenario. *"Chudo"* is the Russian word for "miracle," and this is the scenario of the Russian economic miracle. Looks unlikely? Yes. Impossible? No. But in order to grasp the potential of a *Chudo,* one must recognize that other famous modern economic miracles—including the German and Japanese—did not happen overnight. Rather, they emerged out of very unpromising beginnings and unfolded over a decade, in very difficult, even treacherous conditions. Unlike those two countries, Russia does not have a commercial tradition or a preexisting base of private property. It does, however, have a highly educated and technically adept population, enormous pent-up demand for goods and services of every kind, an eager and hungry younger generation, and extensive resources. Also, integration into the world economy and the application of "enabling technologies"—computers and communications—could accelerate economic change, much more so than generally expected.

Finally, we believe that at the end of the road lies Capitalism Russian-Style. We are confident that Russia will arrive there; but the character of Capitalism Russian-Style will be shaped by the path to it.

RUSSIA AND THE WORLD

In the final section of the book, we use the perspective of the scenarios to examine the new Russia and the world, and the fundamental questions that arise.

Will Russia be a cooperative partner in world affairs as a national state? Or will it again be driven to imperialism? Russia's long imperial tradition predates by four centuries the assault on the Winter Palace in 1917. Resentment and humiliation will surely be potent political forces in Russia. Russia still has a large military establishment, which has yet to find a new mission. Russia's role in the world will be determined not only by Russia itself, but also by events in the "Near Abroad," the neighboring nations that were once part of the former Soviet Union. Instability in these countries could inflame security anxieties and draw Russia into conflicts that will reverberate far beyond the Near Abroad. This risk is made even more palpable by the "Russian diaspora," the 25 million ethnic Russians who live in the other states. At the same time, there will be strong economic forces—in particular the economic difficulties within each of the now-independent nations—driving efforts to reintegrate the fractured former "Soviet space."

The biggest danger of all is conflict between Russia and Ukraine. Owing to the way Moscow deployed its weapons during the Soviet days, independent Ukraine is at least for the time being the third-largest nuclear-weapons state in the world, behind Russia and the United States but ahead of Britain, France, and China. The nature of the Soviet Union's breakup has created many contentious issues between Russia and Ukraine, any one of which could take fire. Ukraine itself is far from settled. There is also a complex relationship ahead between Germany and Russia, and this could include a competition between them for spheres of influence. In northeast Asia, there will be a competition involving Russia, China, Japan, and possibly a unified Korea.

What role will there be, in a new Russia, for Western business and investment? Foreign companies are trying to decide whether investment in Russia will be a prudent bet on the future, or money thrown down a black hole. What strategies are available for the foreign investor, and what kinds of risks will an investor encounter? The answers depend on how quickly Russia can create the legal, financial, and institutional bases for foreign investment. Foreign investors will certainly encounter one fundamental obstacle: Russians themselves are unsure whether they really want Western investment, and are struggling among themselves over this question.

We turn to Russia and the West. For over forty years, treasure and willpower and technology were poured into the Cold War. What should the policies of the West be now? To what degree can it help support the transition? Can the West help in some way to build a better life for the Russian people, and, at the same time, better and safer lives for its own and other peoples of the world? Understandably, the focus of Western policy today is on aid. Within a few years, however, the critical focus may well shift to trade—that is, to what kind of access Russian exports will have to global markets. While the aid questions are difficult, trade will be more difficult for Western countries to deal with because of the possible effects on businesses and jobs within Western countries.

The interests of the West, and much of the rest of the world, are vitally engaged with what happens in Russia. Yet, finally, what Russia chooses, in terms of democracy or authoritarianism, and in terms of its economic system, depends on the Russians themselves. In the end, it is Russian actions, Russian votes, Russian capital that will determine Russia's fate. If Russian energies and capital are unleashed, it will be because Russians themselves have created the economic and political institutions that make it possible. The West can help, but that is all.

Russia will be a nation and a society in transition for many years. The obstacles to the development of both modern capitalism and democracy are many and formidable—not the least of which is the absence of any market or democratic traditions over the last three quarters of a century. So long as Russia remains in this transition, the authority of the government will be limited, its power divided.

Disorder will be a central preoccupation in the midst of social turmoil, economic insecurity and degradation, impoverishment and rising crime. Russians will fear that both their economic life and personal security are increasingly in the hands of the underworld. With the sharp contraction of the old and inefficient Soviet economy, unemployment—until now virtually unknown—could rise dramatically, adding greatly to the difficulties, creating potentially dangerous pressures, and posing one of the greatest challenges to the new political order. Demagogues and authoritarians will seek to channel this discontent for their own political ends.

As they live through the transition, Russians will be ambivalent about capitalism and the outside world, particularly the West, skeptical of foreign business, and suspicious of other nations' intentions. There will be a longing for the certitudes of life, however mediocre, as they were in the Soviet era. If things do not go well, Russians could end up blaming "outside forces" for the collapse of the USSR, for their own current difficulties, and for their loss of status both at home and in the world. Any Russian government that pursues cooperative policies with the West will run the risk of being accused of kowtowing to the West and the international bankers, and of selling out "Russian interests." This will take on major political importance if living standards do not rebound.

In the last several years, under both Gorbachev and Yeltsin, there has been a strong aversion to the use of force as a political instrument—in very marked contrast to the first seven decades of Soviet rule. Such self-restraint is not likely to last in the face of increasing lawlessness, ethnic conflict, separatism, and the very scale of the stakes, both political and economic—as well as the dissatisfactions of the military and security services. Indeed, the confrontation between president and parliament in the autumn of 1993 marked the return of force as a factor in Russian politics.

All these themes emerge out of the scenario process. Yet our work on these scenarios leads us to other themes as well, and to see things somewhat differently from the views that are dominant today.

We find reasons to be optimistic, if cautiously so, about the future of Russia, despite the pessimism that seems to be the order of the day. Russia has many resources, including an educated, creative, and technologically proficient population. We do not underestimate the enormously difficult problems Russia faces and the pressures and conflicts that constrain choices. But we do not think that Russia is necessarily poised to break up; at least, strong forces exist that will counteract a movement toward dissolution. It is not inevitable that Russia will sink back into authoritarianism, except in reaction to prolonged chaos. Nor are hostility and confrontation inevitable between Russia and the West over geopolitics. The private market economy, though hardly measured, is already moving fast. We think that a Russian economic miracle is possible, at least when measured against today's expectations. And, by 2010, if not before, there will be "Capitalism Russian-Style," a market system, but one distinctively Russian, partly shaped by Russia's forced inheritance from its Soviet past.

It is to that past that we must now turn. For all these questions and themes, and the scenarios themselves, derive from the same starting point—the great "surprise," the crumbling of the monolith, the end of communism, and the birth of Russia as an independent state. Bringing into focus the recent past—the collapse of the Soviet Union and Russia's experience since—is the first step toward the scenarios, and that is where our story begins.

PART I

After the Fall

2

The New Russian Revolution

"At the end of the 1970s, we knew the economy would fall apart. We had exhausted all our resources. But I thought it could go on for another ten years, until the end of the century."
— *Russian economist*

"Today, Russia does not change every year. It changes every month."
— *Government minister*

It was the great anticlimax of the twentieth century. On December 25, Christmas Day, 1991, Mikhail Gorbachev, president of the Soviet Union, went on television to announce that the Soviet Union itself would shortly cease to exist. After twelve minutes, Gorbachev concluded his valedictory and faded into the ether. Six days later, on December 31, 1991, the Soviet Union followed suit, disappearing into the night. There was no great celebration, no honking of horns or ringing of bells, just a great silence in the dark, and uncertainty as to what the dawn would bring.

The Soviet Union was gone. Born of revolution; created out of a civil war that took millions of lives; shaped by Stalin's campaign of harsh industrialization, collectivization, and mass terror, which together claimed at least twenty million lives; allied to America and Britain in the struggle against Nazism; leader of the Soviet bloc; nuclear superpower—the Soviet Union was gone. The people were still there, and so were the buildings, the ligaments of economic life, the weapons. But, after seventy-five years, the Soviet Union, earthly expression of Marx's utopian ideas and the concrete embodiment of Lenin's drive for power, was finished.

Today, the inheritors, led by Boris Yeltsin, Gorbachev's great rival, confront an awesome challenge—to develop a new pluralistic political system in a country that has known only totalitarianism for three generations; to build a market economy out of a command economy; and to adapt to the loss of an empire that was centuries in the making. These changes and the turmoil that surround them, triggered by the end of the Soviet Union and the collapse of communism, constitute the new Russian revolution.

The fall of Gorbachev and the struggles of Yeltsin and the other politicians since independence demonstrate the difficulties Russia faces in making its transition—and show how hard it will be to govern the country through the upheaval. Hope and despair will, no doubt, alternate. This revolution is still in such an early stage, the forces are so many and complex, and the passions so bitter, that no one can know what course the new Russian revolution will ultimately take—whether it will be contained by moderate forces or, as happened once before, it will turn radical and "devour its own children."

As with all great historical events, there is no single explanation for what has happened and is unfolding. Yet the essential elements can be identified.

The starting point is the decay of the Soviet economy. More than three decades ago, one student of the Soviet command economy described its essence as "totalitarianism harnessed to the task of rapid industrialization and economic growth."[1] Economic growth was the raison d'être, critical for justifying the system.

So long as the system delivered growth, it commanded loyalty. But poor economic performance would undermine its rationale, corrode its mystique, and destroy its self-confidence and, ultimately, its legitimacy. Already, in the 1970s, it had begun to stagnate, unable to find the additional labor and resources to propel growth as in previous decades. It was ill-equipped to take advantage of the technological changes that were driving growth in the West. In the 1950s and 1960s, it had boasted of its "heroic" capacity to produce ever more steel and cement. But those were the heroes of an earlier age of industrialization. By the 1970s and early 1980s, when computers and electronics became the real heroes, the Soviet Union was falling behind. It still continued to direct an enormous part of its economic activity to supporting its vast war machine, further distorting and damaging the economy in the process. To make matters worse, the Soviet Union increasingly found that it could no longer bear the costs of its empire in Eastern Europe.

Meanwhile, political life was suffocating, and the political system was ossified. Marxist-Leninist ideology had long since turned into what one Soviet official once described as "stale bread." The decrepit condition of the leadership was a metaphor for a system that was itself dying. Leonid Brezhnev, general secretary of the Communist party, died, infirm and incompetent, at age seventy-five in November 1982. He was succeeded by Yuri Andropov, former head of the KGB, who himself then proceeded to die, aged sixty-nine, in February 1984. Andropov in turn was succeeded by Konstantin Chernenko, a Brezhnev sycophant, who lasted only thirteen months, dying in March 1985 at seventy-three.

This system was regarded by increasing numbers of people with cynicism, contempt, and ridicule—not expressed publicly, to be sure, but "in the kitchen," where Russians could safely discuss the important things of life. As a senior official under Yeltsin put it, "The last seven or eight years under Brezhnev were already ridiculous. Everyone knew it, and was laughing at it, not in public, but in their home or where they worked. Brezhnev would give a speech on television, and his jaw would be hanging out, and sometimes he would read the same page twice."

The system appeared, to those who could look closely, to be in a downward spiral. So it seemed to Mikhail Gorbachev, energetic and vigorous, who succeeded Chernenko in March 1985. He was only fifty-four, the "baby" of the Politburo, and he had a generational perspective quite different from the others', as well as a professional perspective that contrasted with a leadership dominated by engineers and industrial managers. He had been a law student at Moscow State University in 1953 when Stalin died, and a rising apparatchik in 1968 when Brezhnev snuffed out the Prague Spring and threw "socialism with a human face" on the dust heap of history.

The system was degenerating, Gorbachev believed, but somehow it could be reformed, the "human face" recovered, and the real core of the system restored. The political system would have to change. So would the economic system. It was an immense task, and prospects were not good. Success had eluded would-be reformers for thirty years.

Gorbachev may not have had a grand plan for reform in mind, but he was determined to break with the Stalinist past. He began to purge the Brezhnev hacks. He started to loosen controls on the media, allowing fresh and somewhat more varied views to be aired. Already, for instance, by the spring of 1986 the unthinkable was happening on the Moscow stage: a play about a family emigrating from Odessa that portrayed the would-be émigrés in a sympathetic manner. And, at the same time, Gorbachev initiated the first steps in the "new thinking" in foreign policy—a shift away from the concept of irreversible class-based conflict with the West, and toward cooperation.

THE ACCIDENT OF CHERNOBYL

Then occurred an unexpected, but decisive event. On April 26, 1986, operators lost control of a nuclear reactor at Chernobyl in Ukraine. The reactor was consumed in a partial nuclear meltdown, and clouds of radioactive emissions spewed forth and were carried by winds across vast stretches of the European continent. The initial reaction of the Soviet government was denial, the customary response. (Airplane crashes and other disasters were never reported; the population was not to know that Soviet technology could fail.) Instead, reports of a nuclear disaster were denounced as a creation of the malevolent Western media. Two Westerners, visiting a senior energy official in early May 1986 for what was otherwise a friendly discussion, innocently asked the official an economically oriented question: Would the nuclear accident lead to increased demand for Russian natural gas, both in the Soviet Union and Western Europe? The official exploded in a rage: This talk of a nuclear accident, he said, pounding his fist on the table, was the invention of the filthy, slandering Western press. All the while, rumors were reaching Moscow: riots at the train station in Kiev, of people fighting for space on trains to get as far away from Ukraine as possible; mass evacuations in the region of Chernobyl; deaths and disaster.

For seventeen days, the official denials went on. Then, on May 14, Gorbachev appeared on television and gave a speech that was wholly uncharacteristic of Soviet leadership and represented a sharp break with the way the Kremlin had traditionally communicated with its own people and the rest of the world. Instead of propaganda, he delivered a serious, somber admission that a grave accident had occurred.

Gorbachev's speech and the relative openness that followed it ran so counter to the familiar mode of communication that some Muscovites speculated that the accident must have been even worse than acknowledged, to have occasioned such uncharacteristic forthrightness. (And it did turn out to be worse.)

In addition to the huge human and financial costs from Chernobyl, there were also grave political costs. The Brezhnev system that Gorbachev had inherited was deeply shaken, discredited not only to the public but also to those within the governing system. Beyond the disaster itself, Chernobyl would become the symbol of an arrogant production system that did what it wanted to with little concern for the people and their health and well-being, and that could destroy the society it was meant to serve. Some in the Soviet leadership would later say that Chernobyl was a major turning point for reform—for what Gorbachev would call *perestroika,* or "restructuring," and *glasnost,* or "openness." Certainly Chernobyl gave a major boost to both.

The expansion of glasnost, after Chernobyl, engendered consequences that ultimately had a major impact on the entire course of the Gorbachev years. Increased environmental coverage in the national media encouraged people at the local level to create "informal" associations and, since they could not trust the party bosses, to take environmental issues into their own hands. The informal associations soon crossed the boundary from protection of nature into politics. In non-Russian areas, environmental policies became nationalist politics, directed against Moscow. In response, local politicians moved quickly to jump on the bandwagon. In places like Kazakhstan, Estonia, and Armenia, Communist party officials actually succeeded in stealing the environmental issue and using it to reinforce their own power at the expense of the Union government. Within Russian areas, some local politicians also managed to identify themselves with environmental concerns. (This was the first hint that Communist politicians would survive after the Communist system itself had disappeared.) Throughout the Soviet Union, polluting power plants and factories were shut down by an increasingly powerful "green" movement at the grass roots.

Thus did Chernobyl and environmentalism undermine the credibility of the system, stimulate change in local politics, and accelerate the weakening of central power.

WHICH MARX?

Yet Gorbachev still thought he could ride the tiger of reform and that the system could be revitalized and renewed—yet also preserved. One day in the late 1980s he was visited privately by a group of senior Western statesmen. When they insisted that socialism was a failure,

Gorbachev vigorously argued back. After the statesmen left, Gorbachev continued his arguments in favor of reformed socialism, although his audience by this time was reduced to nothing more than two of his own aides. "We couldn't figure out why he kept on making his case," recalled one of the aides, "since the Westerners were gone. Then, after five minutes, we understood—he believed what he was saying."

During Stalin's Great Terror in the 1930s, one of Gorbachev's grandfathers was sent away to a prison camp that produced timber. His sin: failing to "fulfill" the sowing plan for 1933. The other grandfather was imprisoned for a little over a year and then branded for the rest of his life as "an enemy of the people." "When I was up for a membership in the Communist party, I had to answer for all this," Gorbachev later said. "It was a very painful moment."[2]

Whatever the pain, Gorbachev was still a true believer. He was part of the ideology, and part of the generation that would be bound to the Soviet past, however difficult, by the shared suffering of the Second World War. Gorbachev had risen from a two-room mud hut to become the leader of a superpower. For him, the socialist system was flawed, but remediable, and its essential grandeur remained. Socialism was still his "banner." What he did not comprehend was the cynicism of so many in the younger generation, who had grown up with more information and less fear and on whom, ultimately, the system would have to depend if it were to be reformed.

For those members of the younger generation, the glorious Marxist-Leninist system was not grand but banal—nothing more than empty ritual, black comedy, and endless "promises." A decade ago one economist from this generation (now a member of the government) was completing his doctorate. In order to finish, he went to the index of Lenin's works and came up with twelve quotes from the "great" Lenin. They had no relation at all to his own themes, but they would do. He had to have Lenin quotations. He stuck them into the text. It didn't matter where, since they were only part of the ritual and no one would take them seriously anyway. At his oral examination, he was questioned about Friedrich Engels's tract *Anti-Dühring*. He spoke fluently about it for half an hour, even though he had never read it. If his examiners had read it, they had forgotten it. He passed brilliantly.

In 1979, in the late Brezhnev period, another young scholar (also now a key government adviser) found himself almost automatically made a member of the party. He invited a group of colleagues out for a drink at a café near their institute. Over Soviet champagne, he raised a toast, paraphrasing Marx, but in this case Groucho rather than Karl: "To the Communist Party of the USSR. It is doomed if they make the likes of me a member."

"CABBAGE SOUP"

Glasnost was proceeding, as Gorbachev himself would regularly say. The economy, however, was not recovering. But then, aside from banning alcohol, Gorbachev had undertaken little in the way of new economic initiatives in his first two years. That changed in 1987, when laws were enacted reducing central control over enterprises and permitting private shops and kiosks (initially called cooperatives), as well as joint ventures with Western investors. The monopoly of the state bank was also broken. These reforms only confused the sputtering economy, removing controls without changing the irrational pricing system or breaking up the monopolies. Economic conditions actually worsened, and new shortages appeared. Absurdly enough, soap and detergent disappeared from the shelves even though manufacturers swore that there had been no decline in output. On summer days, ice cream vendors would say *"Morozhenogo net"*—"No ice cream." Such was life under the command economy.

Politically, Gorbachev found himself battling against both the proponents and the opponents of reform. In the autumn of 1987, Boris Yeltsin, then the Moscow party boss and a junior member of the Politburo, was intent on reform and cleaning up corruption. Blocked by conservative opponents, Yeltsin angrily castigated and denounced Yegor Ligachev, a leading conservative. For that sin, and for being too rebellious, Gorbachev expelled Yeltsin from the Politburo and stripped him of his position.

Yet at the same time, Gorbachev condemned much more vigorously the repression practiced by the Soviet state and raised for the first time the possibility that the Communist party would lose its all-important "leading role," its monopoly of power. Gorbachev also challenged the traditional relationship between state and society in Russia. The state, Gorbachev proclaimed, should be bound by its own laws—should become, in Russian, *pravovoe gosudarstvo,* a "state of laws." Such a doctrine provides no guarantee that the state will not adopt tyrannical laws. But Gorbachev's doctrine was an enormous step forward compared with what any previous Soviet or Russian ruler had done, because it broke with the tradition of arbitrary state power.

All this was too much for conservatives. They became increasingly outspoken in declaring that perestroika and glasnost were going too far. In the summer of 1988, at the first Party Conference convened since 1941, the conservative Ligachev won warm applause when he derisively castigated Gorbachev and his style with the ringing declaration, "Politics is not the same thing as slurping down cabbage soup."[3]

Gorbachev concluded that there was no other way to improve the economy and, at the same time, defeat the conservative opposition in the party, than by taking the most radical step: He dismantled the machinery by which the party had controlled the economy. He also had himself elected president by the Supreme Soviet, thus transferring his base of authority for running the country from his position as party leader to the position of president of the country. What this all meant, however, was that Gorbachev had weakened the central institution of the Soviet system, the Communist party, without having any real alternative to put in its place. To make matters even more difficult, the continuing economic decline was eroding his popularity.

THE RETURN OF NATIONALISM AND THE LOSS OF EASTERN EUROPE

The non-Russian nationalities were also becoming more assertive and defiant of Moscow. Perhaps because, unlike all his predecessors, he had never worked in the republics outside Russia, Gorbachev was less alert to this issue than they had been. Or perhaps simply the deep-seated resentment of Russian domination was so strong that, once the hand of control began to lift, nationalism became an even more potent force, one that captured more and more people.

Nationalist passions were strong even among those who had benefited most from the Soviet system. In May 1989, Foreign Minister Eduard Shevardnadze did something unheard-of in Soviet-American relations—he invited U.S. Secretary of State James Baker to his apartment for dinner. Baker was startled to find that Shevardnadze's wife was a fervent Georgian nationalist, who declared that "Georgia must be free!"[4] Throughout the republics, nationalist movements were agitating with increasing vigor for autonomy and "sovereignty," however ill-defined. At some points, they were met with military repression, which, whether ordered by Gorbachev or not, weakened his authority among reformers.

While Gorbachev struggled with political problems at home, the Soviet empire in Eastern Europe slipped away. The Soviets might well have prevented the loss, had they been willing to use force. But by now they were questioning the value of holding onto Eastern Europe. The costs of empire had been too great. With grave economic problems at home, how could they continue to subsidize the likes of Erich Honecker in East Germany? In addition, force would have jeopardized Western economic aid and arms-control agreements—both regarded as essential if the Soviet economic decline were to be reversed. And Gorbachev may well have thought that socialism with a human face would be the choice of the peoples of Eastern Europe. If so, he would quickly be proved wrong.

Poland held an election in which the Communists were humiliated and the Solidarity union, until recently illegal, triumphed. The Hungarians staged a public barbed-wire-cutting ceremony on their border with Austria, and the Communist party of Hungary turned itself into a socialist party that would compete in a multiparty system. But all those changes paled compared to what happened in November 1989, when the Berlin Wall came down. The very symbol of the Iron Curtain —and of divided Europe and of the entire Cold War—was no more. A linchpin of the Soviet Union's European policy—the preservation of a Communist-run, subservient East Germany and prevention of German reunification—was gone.

TWO GOVERNMENTS IN "ONE SPACE"

At home, perestroika was turning into something more than reform. It was nearing the edge of revolution. Power was flowing from Gorbachev to Boris Yeltsin, who, beginning in 1989, accomplished the once unthinkable, a political comeback by a man who had been exiled from the Politburo. He seized the opportunities opened up by Gorbachev's expanding reforms; he ran for a seat in Parliament in 1989 and 1990, and was elected speaker of the Russian parliament in 1990. Yeltsin set out to create an alternative government. In June 1990, the Russian parliament asserted its "sovereignty." Now there were two competing governments occupying the same Russian space. One year later, in June 1991, Yeltsin became the first freely elected president of the Russian Republic.

Yeltsin and Gorbachev engaged in increasingly bitter rivalry, poorly masked by occasional attempts at cooperation. In the summer of 1990, Gorbachev joined with Yeltsin to jointly sponsor a radical program of economic reform called the Five Hundred Days—a rapid dash to the market that would also redistribute power to the provinces. But, almost as quickly as he had endorsed it, Gorbachev—prompted by the conservatives who had so much to lose—disavowed it. Meanwhile, the Russian Federation was winning the battle it had initiated against the Soviet government for tax revenues. By mid-1991, the Soviet government was running out of money, a fact that played no small part in its collapse.

Day by day, the existing system was failing. All of the republics, each with its own national identity, declared that their own laws took precedence over those of the USSR. Nationalism was fatally undermining the authority of the Soviet state.

"THE RETURN OF HISTORY"

Something else no less profound, which some have called the return of history, was also causing the system to lose all authority and the most basic legitimacy. Stalin's lasting monument may well have been the terror itself. In his paranoia, he had purpose: "Who's going to remember all this riffraff in ten or twenty years' time?" Stalin once said during the 1930s, while reviewing a list of people to be executed. "No one. Who remembers the names now of the boyars Ivan the Terrible got rid of. No one. . . . The people had to know he was getting rid of all his enemies."[5] The history was meant to be buried in the unmarked mass graves.

But, in the early Gorbachev days, isolated individuals began to dig into the state-imposed secrecy to recover the names of some of the millions and millions who had been arbitrarily killed and forgotten. As the soil was being turned over, the past in all its horror was coming into view, far more clearly than ever before.

Sergei was one of those diggers. His story, one of millions in Russia, is illustrative. His father was arrested in Moscow in 1938, a few months before Sergei's birth. His mother, eventually exiled from the city, never knew what had become of her husband. She settled in western Siberia. Sergei grew up in Siberia and became a journalist. For twenty years he crisscrossed the tundra of the oil- and gas-rich area. He got to know nearly everyone, it seemed, who counted.

In 1990, when the Soviet Union started breaking up, Sergei resolved to discover what had become of his father, the father he had never known. He simply went to the local office of the KGB. There he finally learned the truth: His father had been shot in the basement of the Lubianka prison, the headquarters of the secret police in Moscow. He died within days of his arrest, even as his wife stood outside the building with packages of food for him, one of thousands of wives carrying little bits of hope when there was none.

Sergei resolved to write a book about the local victims of the purge in Siberia. From KGB records and family interviews he was able to assemble documents and photographs. He toured prisons and camp sites throughout western Siberia.

In January 1993, he took a Western friend to the infamous Siberian prison of Tobol'sk, where Dostoyevsky had once been confined, and which had been a killing factory during Stalin's terror. The prison had closed only three years before. It was twenty below zero in a Siberian winter. After walking about for a bit they ended up in a small courtyard. Sergei turned to his friend.

"Beneath your feet are twenty-five hundred people," he quietly said.

He explained that, in the late 1930s, the guards marched prisoners into this courtyard in batches of several hundred, then fired on them from the balconies above. When everyone had been killed, other prisoners would be marched in, and the same process repeated. A small plaque marks the spot. Sergei had arranged to have it placed there. The process had required lengthy negotiations with the local mayor.

As glasnost continued, the cumulative effect of all the Sergeis was becoming a major political factor. The rivulets turned into great rivers of revelation—of everything from the fates of relatives who had been arrested in the middle of the night, never to be seen again, to the secret protocols of the Nazi-Soviet Non-Aggression Pact. Leading the official commission that was exposing the secrets was Alexander Yakovlev, who had been Gorbachev's chief adviser and ideologist in the first years but had left Gorbachev over the latter's unwillingness to break more fully with the past.

A system based on such pervasive cruelty and such fundamental lies lost its authority. Even the myths of the Great Patriotic War could not survive against the flood. A young man, now an entrepreneur in Moscow, went into the army in the late 1980s as a Komsomol leader. He was the boxing champion of his regiment. In an earlier time, he would have been tagged for advancement in the party, just as a young Mikhail

Gorbachev would have been. But no longer. "Nothing serious had happened before I went in the army. But 1990 was the turning point for me. When I returned, I could see real perestroika, not economic, but political. I had the opportunity to have plenty of information, and I learned what Stalin had done to our soldiers returning from the war. When I served in the army I believed. Afterward, I understand that this system was completely wrong." The number of believers was dwindling.

THE WRONG TARGET

Gorbachev could now see that reform was rushing toward a destination far different from what he had intended or indeed comprehended. Wanting to stop events from going "too far," he relied increasingly on conservatives, alienating in the process those who had been his strongest supporters. But by 1991, the conservatives were plotting against him, sure that he was leading the Soviet Union to disaster and that force was the only option left. On August 18, 1991, they struck, arresting Gorbachev as he vacationed in the Crimea. But the supreme irony was that they had concentrated their efforts on the wrong target. By mid-1991, their real enemy was Boris Yeltsin.

The plotters quickly found that their organization was not up to the task of successfully carrying out a counterrevolution. Resistance was widespread. They were not able to cut communications, or did not think to; factories in St. Petersburg stayed in contact with Yeltsin by fax machine. The military itself was divided, and the would-be powers-that-be were not at first prepared to order force sufficient to turn the tide.

When the plotters finally did decide to use force, they found that key commanders and units would not obey them. General Pavel Grachev prepared his paratroopers, on orders, to storm the Belyi Dom —the "White House"—where Yeltsin and his supporters were barricaded. But, at the same time, he maintained constant telephone contact with the people inside. Three hours before the scheduled attack, he informed his superiors that the paratroopers would not move against Yeltsin. And they didn't.*

Moreover, fear was no longer a pervasive part of people's lives; six years of perestroika meant that there was a generation of young adults

---

* Grachev is now defense minister.

who had grown up without dread of the secret police. Fathers and sons, divided by generations, were reunited on the barricades.

And the police, going by mistake first to Yeltsin's apartment in the city rather than his dacha in the country, were a half hour too late. Though the Soviet Union officially died at midnight, December 31, 1991, it really perished in August 1991 when, while Mikhail Gorbachev was being held incommunicado by his own erstwhile allies, Boris Yeltsin, donning a bulletproof vest, eluded his would-be captors and stood defiantly on a tank outside the Russian White House.[6]

"I PAID DEARLY"

Mikhail Gorbachev can claim a great achievement; he had done what would have seemed inconceivable at the beginning. Even Boris Yeltsin, who would call Gorbachev "my perpetual opponent, the lover of half measures and half steps," would also say that "what he has achieved will, of course, go down in history." Gorbachev had initiated glasnost, attempted democratization, introduced the beginnings of a market economy, and destroyed the myth of the "hero party." He had brought the Soviet Union a great distance and manipulated the system so as to wind it down, and in a largely peaceful way. But it was simultaneously not enough—and too much. Gorbachev catalyzed the destruction of the old order, but never seemed to grasp fully the forces he was unleashing, or how to control them.

"I misjudged the situation," Gorbachev would reflect at the time. "For all the importance of strategy, it is important in politics to make the right decision at the right moment. It is like a battle in war. In that situation, I should have forged a common front with the democrats."

"I missed that opportunity," he added, "and paid dearly for it."[7]

"THE BUILDER": BORIS YELTSIN

In the immediate aftermath of the failed coup, the Russian government under Yeltsin, who had been elected president of Russia by popular vote earlier in the year, moved hastily to turn itself into something more than a shadow government. It was not organized to govern, and it quickly sought to build up its ministries and its staff. Gorbachev's decisions had undermined the old system, but he had been unable to develop a replacement. Yeltsin had no choice but to try to construct a new one.

Yeltsin brought to the task something that Gorbachev did not have. Gorbachev was a lawyer by training, and he thought that he could revive the system by introducing law and legality into it, avoiding bloodshed and civil war in the process. But the system could not be reformed. By contrast, Yeltsin was, literally, a builder. That was a basic point of reference for him all through his life, and the skills of a "builder" would be needed in constructing a new state and a new system.

Yeltsin was born in 1931 and grew up in what he was later to call "a fairly joyless time . . . hard times, very bad harvests, and no food." The family of six, plus a goat, slept huddled together on the floor of a hut. Yeltsin hardly had a childhood; by age six, he already had responsibilities in the household. Nor did he have much opportunity to develop illusions about human nature. "Gangs of outlaws roamed at large," he recalled, "and almost every day we saw shootouts, murders, and robbery." He never had any sweets or treats. "We had only one aim —to survive."[8]

Yeltsin graduated from Zaporozhye Polytechnic with a degree in civil engineering, having written a thesis on how to construct a television tower, which received a grade of "Excellent." He brought ferocious intensity to whatever he did, whether it was practicing his particularly aggressive style of volleyball for hours a day, or deciding single-mindedly, after graduation, to master every one of the twelve basic building trades, beginning with bricklaying. Construction even dominated his dreams. Once, as a young engineer, he left the gear in the wrong setting on a huge construction crane. He was sleeping in the building next to it. He awoke in the middle of a terrible storm to see that it was about to topple over in the wind. He ran outside in his underwear and regained control of the gears just in time to prevent the crane from going over. For years afterward, he had nightmares about the episode. Now, as president, he tried to manage the gears of the Russian Federation, which so often seemed about to topple over in the storm loosed by the collapse of communism.

Yeltsin was always a builder. When he looked back on the decade he had spent as party leader in Sverdlovsk, what he was most proud of was a 220-mile road he had commanded into existence, linking two parts of that province through very difficult terrain. He was also more independent than other apparatchiks, more willing to challenge and not bend. He wanted to do things his way. "Even a conformist system will sometimes produce a rebel," one of his ministers said.

Yet it must be remembered that Yeltsin had also succeeded brilliantly as an apparatchik within the Communist system. He had become a section chief of the party in Sverdlovsk province, then a secretary; then he was quickly promoted to party boss in Sverdlovsk. In 1985, he had been abruptly called to Moscow, first to take charge of construction for the Central Committee, then to head the critical Moscow party apparatus. In fundamental ways, the party had defined who Boris Yeltsin was and had given him his purpose.

Thus, the worst times of his life were after he was thrown out of the Politburo in 1987. He suffered a physical breakdown and spent months in a hospital. He was a pariah, rejected by the system into which he had thrown himself, to which he was committed, and which had done so much to shape him. It was as though his identity had been taken away. He was in "a void, a vacuum," he would say.[9] The single most difficult moment was when Gorbachev forced him, against his wife's and doctor's protests, to get out of his sickbed to attend the plenum of the Communist Party of the City of Moscow, only in order to hear himself vilified, denounced, and summarily expelled.

Out of the months of humiliation, abnegation, and self-examination, he found a new use for his formidable energy and resoluteness. It was no longer to reform the Soviet system and save it from itself. Rather, it was to obliterate that system. But a new system for Russia would have to be built to replace it. This was one construction job for which there was no precedent.

CAPITALISM IN A DAY?

After the defeat of the August coup, Yeltsin appointed a young economist, Yegor Gaidar, as prime minister. Gaidar's government launched a radical drive to dismantle the command economy and move to the market as fast as possible. The Soviets had tried to build socialism virtually "in a day." Could capitalism be built in a day? As a result of "shock therapy," money acquired real meaning for the first time in decades. But "shock therapy" could not easily work in so disordered and unsettled a time. The legal and institutional bases for a market did not exist; the basic logistics of the economy had been disrupted by the breakup of the Union; and Russia did not have control over its own currency, since Ukraine and other former Soviet republics could also print rubles. Moreover, despite the support of the president, Gaidar was not strong enough to carry out his program in full. He decontrolled many prices but he could not free all of them. He could not break up the monopolies, nor could he restrict their access to cheap credits and subsidies.

Thus, Gaidar could not build capitalism "in a day," any more than anyone could have. But he did decapitate the command economy, with stunning effects. The Gaidar program, applied to an economy already weakened by six years of uncertain reforms and the simultaneous collapse of the Soviet "economic space" (i.e., the integrated economy of the fifteen republics), threw the Russian economy into a seizure. Investment dropped by half, industrial production plummeted, high inflation took over, people's savings were wiped out, and popular resistance and anger quickly mounted. Between January 1992 and the summer of 1993, prices jumped nearly a hundredfold. As early as May 1992, Yeltsin was forced to back away from the more radical elements of shock therapy. The government rushed to the rescue of heavy industry with subsidies and cheap credits. It managed to avert a tidal wave of plant closures and unemployment, but at the cost of even higher deficits and more inflation.[10]

The politicians and industrial managers who had emerged out of the Communist system and who were still the backbone of the economy regarded Gaidar and his associates with disdain, dismissing them, as Aleksandr Rutskoi, Yeltsin's then vice president, put it, as "these kids in pink shorts."

That was not the way they saw the man who took over from Gaidar as prime minister in December 1992. Viktor Chernomyrdin was one of the most successful industrial managers in the country. He had directed the buildup of the Soviet natural-gas industry in the 1970s and the early 1980s, an extraordinary accomplishment on a huge scale; and his appointment reassured the industrial managers.

Chernomyrdin had made his career up till then in energy, and that remained his first love. He recalled that his happiest days were when he headed a gas processing plant in Orenberg, in Siberia, in the mid-1970s. "I was delighted with my work," he said. "It's like when you don't want to go home when your working day is over."

But now Chernomyrdin had responsibility for the whole economy. Under him, reform continued, but at a more measured pace, with greater attention to production and employment. Most of the radical features of the Gaidar reform program were slowed. One key program, however, remained on course—privatization. Under the privatization scheme, all citizens received vouchers valid for ten thousand rubles.

Managers and employees could purchase between 40 and 56 percent of enterprises. The vouchers could be sold or traded. Tens of thousands of small enterprises, mainly restaurants and shops, quickly passed into private hands. Many larger enterprises soon followed, although at a less rapid pace. Privatization proved to be the most popular reform. Opinion polls so indicated. So did the hit parade; for months, one of the top songs was "Wow-Wow-Voucher!" Despite all the uncertainties and struggles and the very haziness of the concept in Russia, private property was becoming a reality.

But the controversy over reform and economic shock therapy fueled a bitter battle between Yeltsin and the Russian parliament. The struggle was complex: at stake was the choice between a strong president and a strong parliament; the balance between the center and the regions; the character of economic policy.

The conflict produced a virtual gridlock. Yeltsin won enough support in an April 1993 referendum to summon a constitutional convention to replace the patchworked-over constitution from the Brezhnev era. This effort, however, was soon stalemated by the contending forces.

The country itself seemed in danger of unraveling, as Russian provinces and cities took to declaring themselves independent republics for the very purpose of gaining privileges granted to so-called "autonomous" regions. By the summer of 1993, announcing "independence" suddenly seemed almost the fashionable thing to do. Even some deputies from the Moscow provincial soviet tried to promote an independent republic of "Moskovia," formed out of the region around the city of Moscow.

The battle among the regions slowed down the job of drafting a new constitution. The real problem was the absence of a consensus on the fundamentals of the political and economic order. The parliament launched a legislative offensive aimed at taking control of the whole reform program, removing it from the president's hands. It tried to rescind privatization, launch spending programs that would have increased inflation, and restrict the president's power and perogatives.

Once again there were effectively two governments in one space, as had been the case in 1991. But now, instead of Yeltsin's Russian Federation closing in on Gorbachev's Soviet Union, it was Yeltsin's executive stymied by a parliament that had once elected Yeltsin its speaker but was now dominated by his former allies turned bitter enemies. The root of the struggle was the old constitution that made both president and parliament sovereign, but without providing a mechanism to resolve the inevitable conflicts between them.

By September 1993, the parliament seemed determined to enact a whole menu of anti-reform measures and to reduce Yeltsin to a figurehead. But Yeltsin moved first. On September 21, he dissolved both the Supreme Soviet and the parent Congress of People's Deputies. He admitted that the existing constitution did not provide for his action. "Being the guarantor of the security of our state, I am obliged to propose a way out of this deadlock," he explained. "I am obliged to break this ruinous, vicious circle."

The parliament—led by Vice President Aleksandr Rutskoi and Speaker Ruslan Khasbulatov—vowed resistance. It "deposed" Yeltsin as president and "installed" Rutskoi. Yeltsin replied by throwing a ring of troops around the parliament building, the "White House," to force its evacuation.

The siege of the White House in September–October 1993 was an eerie replay of August 1991, abounding in ironies. Many of the people inside the building were the same ones who had defied the plotters of twenty-five months before—but the principal resistant, the man who had become a symbol of embattled Russian democracy the world over by standing on a tank in front of the White House, was now on the other side, directing the operation.

Who would resort to violence first? The answer came when Khasbulatov and Rutskoi sent armed supporters to seize the mayor's office and then to capture the television tower at Ostankino. In so doing, they seemed to confirm that they had fallen completely under the sway of extreme right-wing paramilitary groups and hard-line communists. Their blunder proved fatal. The government hastily mobilized much greater military force, sending tanks through the streets of Moscow to the White House and setting the huge parliamentary building on fire with cannons, forcing the total surrender of the occupants.

This second siege of the White House brought to an end the opening phase of the new Russian revolution. During the previous twenty-five months, force had been practically suspended as an instrument of domestic politics. But in the future no political question will be decided without at last the implicit threat that one side or the other will use coercion, and the loyalty of the security forces at all levels will become a pressing everyday concern for politicians.

In the aftermath of the battle, Yeltsin seemed to be firmly in command—until the ballots were counted in the December 12 election.

The results shook the nation. Yeltsin had concentrated his efforts on pushing through a new constitution, based on the French model, with a strong presidency. And that new constitution squeaked through.

What was not generally anticipated was the outcome of the vote for the State Duma, as the new parliament was called. The communists did well; the reformers did poorly. But the real shock was the almost 25 percent of the vote received by the woefully-misnamed Liberal Democrats, the extreme rightwing fascist party. Its leader, the demagogic Vladimir Zhirinovskii, harped on Russia's "humiliations", called for Russia's retaking of the other former republics, and launched a host of bizarre threats, including the advance of Russian troops to the Indian Ocean and the retaking of Alaska, sold by Russia to the United States in 1867. He cavorted with ex-SS men and neo-fascists in Western Europe. He continually attacked—and continues to attack—the impact of the outside world, particularly the United States, on Russia.

Yet the election did not mean that the Russian people had embraced extremism again. Rather, the vote appeared to be a vote against crime and chaos and against the squabbling reformers. Russians were voicing their economic distress and fear for what the future would hold. In short, it was a protest vote. The election also marked the emergence of parties as a force in Russian politics. It established television and private campaign contributions as critical elements for the first time. And the campaign brought some important new players into the Russian political arena, notably the Women of Russia party.

The election had immediate impact on Russian foreign policy. Almost all politicians, reading the results, hastened to become more nationalist and critical of the West. Russian foreign policy itself became more assertive, particularly in terms of neighboring nations.

Yet if Zhirinovskii was a clear winner from the election, so was Prime Minister Chernomyrdin, who has gained steadily in stature and power. He consolidated his centrist government and proclaimed the end of "market romanticism." Yet, after some hesitation, he renewed the commitment to reform. He even went so far as to call for the privatization of land, despite the opposition of entrenched interests. Meanwhile, the State Duma, sitting in its "founding session," faced an enormous task in creating the laws and regulations required for a market economy.

The decline of the old Soviet economy continued. By 1994, gross national product was 40 percent lower than it had been in 1990. Investment had fallen by even more, while inflation remained high. Yet a market economy was also developing faster than many would have expected. By the spring of 1994, over 80 percent of small enterprises had been privatized and almost half of larger enterprises. An estimated 40 percent of the working population was now in the "privatized" economy.[11] Much of this process occurred spontaneously from below, despite the lack of a coherent economic policy from the government. As one of President Yeltsin's economic advisers, Evgenii Yasin, commented, "Unlike socialism, one doesn't have to build capitalism. It builds itself."[12]

Yet, whatever the degree of privatization, the old economy had not yet faced its greatest challenge—the winding down of the huge, inefficient, polluting military industrial enterprises, for which markets no longer exist. Their closing will, inevitably, precipitate a serious unemployment problem, if not an outright crisis, which, in turn, could fuel demogogues and severely test the political system.

The other major threat to the new Russian Revolution lies on Russia's borders—whether issues between Russia and the other newly-independent states will turn into conflicts, which would disrupt progress toward reform. There are few things less settled in the world today than Russia's relations with its newly-independent neighbors. When Crimea, officially part of Ukraine but 70 percent ethnically Russian, reset itself to Moscow time, rather than Kiev time, one could not but wonder if that was the sound of a ticking clock.

What does seem inevitable is a reassertion of Russian influence in its neighborhood and some economic reintegration among the nations of the former Soviet Union. Meanwhile, the struggle goes on within Russia—over resources, property, and political power—as the revolution continues to unfold.

PART II

The Building Blocks

Having described the events of the epic collapse of the Soviet Union and the emergence of an independent Russia, we turn to the "driving forces" that will shape and reshape the future of Russia. We will identify three key driving forces —powerful manifestations that, like electricity or energy, will be channeled or harnessed in some form or another in the coming years. The first of these is the political collapse and its consequences. The second is the collapse of the command economy, and the shock waves that follow. The third is the struggle for Russian identity that results from the disintegration of both the Soviet empire and the Soviet identity.

3

The Battle for Power

"You are blind, like young kittens," Stalin told his lieutenants shortly before his death in 1953. "What will happen here without me?"[1] In fact, his successors managed to hang on for nearly another forty years. But they never managed to solve the problem the old tyrant bequeathed them: How could a regime founded in revolution, conquest, and terror win the lasting loyalty of its people? Perhaps it could have done so, had it continued to deliver the economic performance of the 1950s and '60s. But it did not, even with the improvisations of perestroika at the end. Thus it could not finally hold its people's loyalty. When the Soviet Union fell apart in 1991, the political collapse was total: It destroyed simultaneously the state, the ruling party, and the ideology.

The political "driving force" in Russia is the massive and tumultuous repercussions of this collapse, and the political void it has left behind. The new problem it poses for those who would rule Russia today is this: How can a stable and effective government be built, when there is nothing left on which to base authority, and the entire country is in the midst of a free-for-all over power, revenues, and property?

Certainly, as a result of the collapse of the old Soviet system of power, Russia is freer than ever before in its history. But, at the same time, there is no individual or group in Russia today with the power, legitimate or otherwise, to develop and implement constructive policy. And there is little prospect that the crisis of power and authority in Russia will be resolved soon.

WHO HAS AUTHORITY?

One of the fundamental questions about any society is this: "What makes people support or obey the government?" The reasons, of course, vary. Sometimes they fear it. Sometimes they profit from it. Sometimes they are just used to it. And sometimes they accept it as legitimate. A government that enjoys such acceptance has what is called authority.

The Soviet regime claimed its authority as the architect of the "shining heights"—the bright Communist future of mankind. It never managed to make the claim stick with more than a part of the Soviet population. But the collapse of the Soviet system leaves a vacuum in Russia. There is no widely shared principle available today on which a new authority—legitimate power—can be based.

The list of once official beliefs, now defunct, reads like so many tombstones: "Soviet internationalism," "dialectical materialism," "democratic centralism," "leading role of the Communist party." Nothing has yet emerged to replace them, except a vague and sometimes superficial commitment to their perceived opposites—democracy, capitalism, and "civilization." And that commitment is shared only by a limited number of people. It has yet to establish deep roots.

There is currently no movement of faith, whether religious or secular, that a smart and determined leader (such as Lenin) could harness. People in Russia are now suspicious of ideologies. There is little in the way of tradition or custom available to invoke, since the bulk of recent history is overwhelmingly rejected by the population, and the more remote traditions are only distantly remembered. The Russian Orthodox church, though increasingly active, is in an ambiguous position because of its previous dependence on the state. Constitutional authority is popular among many in the reformist intelligentsia, but its values are borrowed mainly from the West and are not widely or deeply shared by the population.

There remains a collection of popular attitudes that one might call broadly socialist. Many people are still dubious about private property, especially when it comes to the land. Most Russians still tend to prefer to think in groups, and are suspicious of individualism. Many people feel vulnerable to the kind of personal risks that markets bring. Real markets (as opposed to underground contraband and barter) are altogether foreign to their life experience, and they continue to look to the state for solutions. They are hostile to privileges based on private gain rather than state service. To be sure, polls suggest that these attitudes are not uniformly shared, and that they may be evolving fast.

FAITH IN PROMISES

In such a vacuum, the only authority that can be built in the foreseeable future is of a vastly weaker sort: an authority based on faith in promises, and belief in a leader's capacity to deliver. But this is a contingent and fragile form of authority. It disappears as soon as the leader proves himself unable to perform.

Boris Yeltsin's own position illustrates this problem. Until the fall of 1993, he had "the moral authority" of a victim of the previous system. Yeltsin was also the hero of August 1991—the man who stood on the tank. But in the eyes of many Russians that moral authority weakened with the dissolution of the parliament in September 1993 and the shelling of the White House two weeks later. Yeltsin's own distant and sometimes erratic behavior affects his stature in popular eyes.

On the other hand, Yeltsin's authority is now bolstered by the new Russian Constitution, which was approved by popular vote in December 1993. Yeltsin had previously gained a measure of "legal authority" when he was elected Russia's president by universal suffrage in 1991. But there was no constitutional basis for that election, and Yeltsin's status was still open to challenge. Now, the president's powers and responsibilities are fully spelled out, in a document that gives the president a very strong role.

But few Russians yet place much faith in the new constitution. It was passed by a thin margin—only about 60 percent of the eligible voters turned out, and only a little over half of those voted for the constitution, so that only a little over 30 percent of the electorate actually approved it. A slim basis indeed for a country's founding charter.

Given its weak legal and moral basis, Yeltsin's authority is ultimately based on promises—promises that, in view of the overwhelming problems that Russia and Russians face, cannot be quickly or easily fulfilled.

Yeltsin's successor will inherit the same problems. It may be that a candidate with real charisma will emerge in the next few years, someone whose personal stature will reinforce the authority of both the constitution and presidency. Dark horses sometimes grow into great presidents. But that is a matter of faith and luck.

It is more likely that over the next critical years the authority of future Russian presidents will not be based on strong moral or legal authority, but instead will rest dangerously on their ability to deliver policy successes, a difficult thing to do in a weak government. Russian leaders, as has happened elsewhere in the world, may be tempted to seek "quick" successes in foreign affairs.

EIGHTY PERCENT RUSSIAN

In these circumstances, loyalty to family, clan, or nation is reemerging as the only strong principle. Here and there in Russia, people are starting to look to local Tatar, or Chechen, or Kalmyk leaders. One of the oddest cases is that of the self-made Kalmyk billionaire, Kirsan Ilyumzhinov, who made his money in raw materials trading. He was recently elected president of the "autonomous republic" of Kalmykiia, on the lower Volga, with the pledge of turning the republic into a corporation. Every resident would be a shareholder, and, of course, he could be the CEO.[2]

Faced with such non-Russian allegiances, Russian nationalism has been slow to develop in response. Prior to the breakup of the USSR, many Russians had long resented what they perceived as the privileged status of non-Russians in the Soviet system, and they felt increasingly threatened as their share of the Soviet population dropped toward the 50 percent mark and seemed headed below that. But since the breakup of the Soviet empire, the Russians have inherited a space in which they make up over four-fifths of the population (and in which many in the remaining fifth are strongly Russianized).

The fundamental importance of this fact has not yet been fully grasped in the West. Despite many non-Russian enclaves inside the Russian Federation, the fact is that the population inside Russian borders today is more homogeneously Russian than at any time in the last four hundred years. This could mean that Russian nationalism may indeed provide a powerful authority principle in years to come, but in a less aggressive form than in the pre-1917 Russian empire, which was driven to absorb and russify (albeit with uneven consistency and success) the non-Russians it had conquered. In any event, Russian nationalism is not yet a strong binding force today.

That will not prevent some Russian politicians from trying to whip up Russian nationalist sentiment. Wounded national pride, hostility toward foreign influences, solidarity with the orthodox Serbs in Yugoslavia, concern over the fate of Russians outside Russian borders—all these are ample fodder for right-wing politicians. Russian nationalism became a factor in the federal parliament as early as 1992. Nationalist parties began to emerge strongly in 1993. And appeals to nationalist sentiment accounted for a large part of the success of Vladimir Zhirinovskii and his Liberal Democratic Party in the elections of December 1993. But it is doubtful that Russian nationalism alone could provide a strong basis for the authority of the Russian state.

In sum, we believe that the authority of any Russian government will tend to be weak for some years to come. It will also lack power. To see why, we look first to the Soviet past.

"WHIP AND CAKE"—POWER IN THE OLD SYSTEM

Power in the Soviet Union, especially in more recent decades, relied only partly on fear. The core of the system of power was an elaborately graduated system of carrots and sticks that officially allocated benefits and privileges, as well as penalties. The Russians called it *metod knuta i prianika*—"the whip and cake method." The economic system made certain goods scarce; the political system then distributed them to the favored and reliable few or withheld them, as required. These "goods" extended into a wide range of benefits—from advantages in education, careers, apartments, and foreign travel, down to access to ballet tickets and inside information. The list was very long.

The chief characteristic of "whip and cake" was that the system was based not on money, but on official position. Political power was the currency, the medium of exchange, through which one scarce good was traded for another. As one rose in rank in the state or party, all the other advantages came along too. Cash alone bought very little in the old Soviet system, except in the underground economy. Only as the system decayed in the Brezhnev period, especially in the southern provinces and republics, did money begin to intrude as a source of power in its own right, as the wealthy invested gains from the black market by buying scientific degrees and institute directorships, or even positions in the local Communist parties.

Taxation played a minor role as an instrument of state power. Indeed, the old Soviet system did not have a real system of taxation. It would be more accurate to say that the state collected "rent" and "value added" revenues from its enterprises, harvesting them as a bee-keeper gathers honey from beehives, by making direct levies against their accounts in the State Bank or by absorbing the difference between wholesale and retail prices.

The most important mechanism through which official position was translated into power was control of personnel, especially in the professional apparatus of the Communist party. This control of "cadres" was the hallmark of the system. Naturally, patronage ties and personal friendship networks reinforced one another. The powerful appointed their friends and protégés to powerful positions and opened up for them the perquisites of rank.

One last characteristic of the system was control over information. All media were in state hands, and controlling the media was one of the principal functions of the Communist party apparatus. "I used to call the party Central Committee on the telephone before planning a new issue," recalled one former journal editor. "And a young man from the propaganda department, very smooth and very polite, would 'advise' me on the current party line."

But control over information involved much more than censorship. Information, tightly compartmentalized and doled out on the basis of rank, was one of the most important carrots of the system. The higher you rose, the more you had the right to know. Only the senior members of the Politburo had full access to knowledge. But as the fax machine and videotape penetrated Russia in the 1980s, they undermined the ability of the Soviet regime to use information as an instrument of power. The global village brought down the hermit kingdom.

"FAMILY CIRCLES" AND BLACK MARKETS

Some power resources the Soviet state never did bring under control. These were networks of personal friendships, typically within bureaucracies or local regions—*krugovye poruki* or "family circles." In the southern republics "family circles" shaded into covert clan loyalties. Local officials or enterprise managers in their "family circle" looked out for one another, knowing well that the only way to survive was to cut corners and beat the system—together. In a Soviet joke, an enterprise director was interviewing candidates for the job of chief accountant. He asked each one the same question: "How much is one plus one?"

The man who got the job was the one who answered, "How much do you need, Comrade Director?"

The state also never quite managed to control the black market. In one way or another, the entire Soviet population was involved in informal, semi-illicit ties, which the Soviet government increasingly tolerated as time went on. In part, these provided an essential lubricant, oiling the wheels of the official state economy. In part, senior officials were themselves on the take. The most spectacular case, which came to light early in the Gorbachev period, was a scam that extended over many years, in which Uzbek government officials pocketed literally billions of dollars from the sale of nonexistent cotton to the state. One of the beneficiaries was Brezhnev's son-in-law, Yuri Churbanov.

The old Soviet system of power was unusual. Most of the resources commonly used in the game of politics in other countries could not be "cashed in" in Soviet politics. What counted was the apparatus of the one-party dictatorship. But now that this dictatorship is gone, how does power work in the new Russian politics?

THE OLD TRUMPS

Since the breakup of the Soviet system, the old resources for power, based on the state, have weakened but have not disappeared. What remains of those "old trumps" has been partly inherited by the Russian federal government, partly dispersed into the hands of local governments. New resources for power are emerging from society, but are not yet dominant in political life. And there are no settled rules. No one knows now exactly how much power he or anyone else has; and, with political resources in flux, and no agreed-upon rules, everyone is testing everyone else.

During his brief tenure as minister of energy in the Gaidar government, reformer Vladimir Lopukhin became famous for meeting Western delegations in his office at one A.M., or sometimes at six A.M. It would always seem that he had had no sleep. "My ministry is eighty percent understaffed," he would explain. "No one can afford to work for the government."

With the collapse of the Soviet system and the Communist party apparatus, government service and politics have indeed become less attractive careers. Government pay is low, especially when measured against the private sector, and perquisites have dwindled. There isn't much in the way of "cake" at all. The famous "Kremlin ration" (*kremly-*

ovskii payok), a monthly supplement of scarce food and goods for party and government officials, is only a memory. Many of the cadres of the previous Communist system have scattered, often into the new private sector as businessmen. As the army and KGB have shrunk, many former officers have joined the expanded customs service and the tax inspectorate. But even more have joined the rapidly growing network of private security firms, hired by private businesses to defend themselves against the mafia.

It is no longer clear who has the power to hire and fire, and consequently battles over senior personnel appointments are frequently prolonged and bitter, full of unexpected reversals. At lower levels, most industrial managers and politicians hang on to their jobs because their status is cloudy and there is no one clearly empowered to replace them. Gradually, through their control of their jobs and the assets that go with them, these people are becoming independent of higher authority.

The Russian federal government, starting from a very weak position in 1991–92, has managed to reclaim some of the powers of the Soviet government, although it will never have (nor does it aspire to have) the "totalitarian" control of its predecessor. It has gradually improved its ability to collect taxes. Its previously underdeveloped ministries have absorbed some of the personnel and activities of the former Soviet bureaucracy. And it is struggling to consolidate the military and the police. The government retains de facto control over central television, and it subsidizes most of the print media. But, overall, the Russian state is still struggling for control over the basic functions of government.

The Gorbachev and Yeltsin years have seen a strong reaction against the use of force as an instrument of politics. This aversion to force was a powerful cause of the breakup of the Soviet empire. But, as the events of October 1993 demonstrate, such idealism is not likely to last much longer in the face of rising crime, ethnic violence, political separatism, and the attempts to use force in politics.

The role of coercion will grow again, we may be sure, as all sides mobilize to protect themselves and secure their objectives. The key questions are whether Moscow will retain its fraying monopoly of the means of coercion within the Russian Federation, and to what extent the use of state coercion will be restrained by public opinion, or regulated by laws and legal procedures, or deterred by violent responses and the threat of separatism.

Finally and most crucially, personal friendships and family loyalties are more important than ever. A popular saying in Russia today is, "We may not have a market, but we have friends." Especially if they are friends in high places. Patron-client relations have always been at the core of Russian politics and are likely to remain so.

THE NEW TRUMPS

The most important new resource for power is money—especially hard currency. As the old planned economy dies and the role of money grows generally throughout the Russian economy, so does its importance as a political instrument. This can take legitimate forms, such as taxation, credit and monetary policy, budgets, and political contributions, or illegitimate ones, such as bribery, graft, and tax evasion.

Creating new institutions and training people to manage money is so new and complex a task that Russians are only beginning to get the hang of it. For three crucial years, from 1991 to 1993, the federal government lost control of money in all its forms—banking, credit, taxes, and foreign exchange. What had been a state banking monopoly —the USSR Gosbank—exploded into over 2000 private banks, and for a time credit and the money supply both mushroomed. And whereas until 1986 the state controlled foreign trade and all hard-currency receipts, the break-up of the foreign-trade monopoly allowed Russians to export practically anything they could get their hands on. The result, beginning around 1988, was a phenomenal tidal wave of wealth into private hands.

By 1994, the chief "money agencies" of the Russian government, the Russian Central Bank and the Ministry of Finance, had regained basic control over credit and the money supply. The ruble has become almost entirely convertible, at least within Russian borders, and hard currency, though still prized, has not displaced the ruble as the main currency of the country, as it threatened to do in 1992–93. Inflation, which ran as high as 20% a month in 1992 and 1993 and nearly spiralled into hyperinflation, has been brought back under 8% a month.

But in those brief years, a revolution of ownership took place. The private banking sector is already the most dynamic part of the new Russian economy. There are several Russian dollar billionaires, and probably several thousand millionaires. The three crucial years during which there was practically an open season on the state's wealth has produced overnight a new upper class—a class based on wealth, not on political position.

The flood of transfer of wealth continues, but now mainly through the one gaping loophole that the Russian government has been unable to close—the collection of taxes. If control of tax revenues is the *sine qua non* of political power, then the Russian government is still a weak state.

Property is already emerging as an important resource for power, although in the absence of legal protections the de facto possession and enjoyment of the fruits of property—for example, control of exportable oil—are more important than formal title. In other words, "property" really means access to assets. The most attractive new "properties" are the ones that enable their owners to siphon off resources at low state prices and resell them to the private sector at high prices or export them. These new owners have protection because they are themselves members of local clans and political "mafias," or offshoots of large state enterprises.

Money and property are emerging as independent political resources in their own right. Here and there, they are the "currency" with which all other resources, including political position, are bought. But the "old" and "new" political styles tend to run together. Much of the new money and property are still, directly or indirectly, an outgrowth of political position. This is what Russians have in mind when they speak of "nomenklatura privatization." But now private money and property are taking on a life of their own, and increasingly it is political position that depends on private power, not the other way around.

The nomenklatura élite were the several tens of thousands of people who, under communism, held the key jobs and in sum ran the country. Communism is gone, but the nomenklatura remains largely in place; and its members are carving out their position in the new society. A typical example is the former Communist party official who forms a joint-stock corporation, with some of his ex-colleagues, who are still in government, as stockholders. He obtains from them a license to export timber; this he buys at low state prices from another ex-colleague and stockholder, who happens to be the director of the local paper and pulp combine. All of them get rich together, in a modern-day reenactment of the old "family circle."

Votes have become an important new trump in politics. Under the old Soviet system, people dutifully turned out for parliamentary elections—they were required to—but they knew that their votes were practically meaningless. All that changed under Gorbachev. The elections of 1989 and 1990 were important events in speeding the destruction of the old system, and the popular election of Boris Yeltsin as president of Russia, in June 1991, was the final nail in the coffin of the Soviet order.

But Russians, especially in the big cities, seem to have lost faith in the power of their votes to make a difference. With each passing election, they turn out in smaller and smaller numbers. That favors the handful who do vote—the extremists and the conservatives. In the December 1993 election, for example, farmers trooped to the polls and voted as the farm bosses told them to—for the pro-communist Agrarian Party. The same thing happened in the big factories, which benefited the communists. Meanwhile, Vladimir Zhirinovskii's television appeals brought out in droves the votes of the malcontent and the bitter.

The result is a paradox: the anti-democratic forces in Russia today are the ones most eager for early elections, while the democrats are in no hurry to hear the voice of the people. Yet the importance of votes is bound to keep growing. In today's Russia no politician can expect to build or win power without using votes as a resource—unless he is willing to take the authoritarian path.

A second and related potential resource is publicity. The print media in the major cities, despite their dependence on state subsidy, are relatively free, and they provide exposure to political news of all kinds and at all levels. But whether large numbers of people are attentive outside Russia's two larger cities, Moscow and St. Petersburg, is another question. The circulation of the major newspapers and magazines has fallen sharply in the last two years, as their prices have risen.

The impact of the media could be more polarizing than consensus-building, since much of the new press is highly partisan and not always careful about its facts. Television has become the prime media resource, since practically all Russian families have a TV set and watch it assiduously. It is much more closely controlled by the central governments than the print media. But so far the government has not used its control over television to close off the opposition. In December 1993, television was crucial to the success of the communists and the nationalists.

At the local level, the media are much more vulnerable to political and financial pressure from the local rulers. Since most of the provinces are dominated by conservative politicians, the democrats in the regions have a hard time getting their message heard.

A third potential resource is direct local participation, such as membership in neighborhood groups, social-action committees, benefit funds, and the like. In contrast to the enforced pseudo-participation of the past, local participation is the voluntary decision of individuals. When harnessed, it is a constructive resource for peaceful political power. Unharnessed, it can bolt into the streets.

In the late 1980s, an explosion of "informal" associations, such as environmental-defense groups, appeared to herald the rise of civil society and promised the early development of political parties. The promise is still there, but the energy of constructive local participation has weakened, as people are more preoccupied with survival.

What has begun to grow, in contrast, is "street power": the unorganized power of the mob, fueled by the emotions of angry and frightened people. In the north Caucasus and in a handful of other places in Russia, this energy has been exploited by nationalist demagogues to settle old scores, whether with Moscow or with neighbors. In the rest of Russia, mob anger has already become a factor in politics, and there are would-be leaders ready to exploit it. Much depends on how widespread such anger really is, especially among idle young males, the typical tinder of revolutions.

Finally, the law is potentially a crucial new political resource, not only because it prescribes the rules of the political game, but also because it embodies the new relationships of power, revenue, and property. This last point helps to explain the striking paradox that while the judicial system remains very weak, making law (chiefly the process of legislation) is a subject of feverish concern among all political players. Yet writing the law one's own way, while it reflects one's power from other sources, does not yet add to power directly, because in most cases the law is not implemented or is easily sidestepped.

Recourse to the courts by individuals against the state is theoretically possible, but is still rare in practice, although some Russian politicians have been quick to discover the uses of libel suits, brought in compliant courts, to intimidate their critics, especially newspapers. Political connections and the right friendships are still the best protection for property and contracts. So long as these things remain true, the law will remain a minor political resource, and a weak element in the growth of a true market economy.

The old Soviet system of power and authority has been destroyed, but a new system has not yet evolved. The old trumps for power—control of official position, personnel, and perks, political friendships and patron-client relations within a small political class—are too weak to run the country. The new trumps—money, votes, publicity, and law—are of uncertain effect. In the old days, power lay in a few hands. Nowadays power is in many hands, but nothing makes those hands work together.

The collapse of the Soviet system has detonated an intense and far-reaching struggle at all levels to define the new political system and gain control over power, revenues, and property. Given the high stakes of the contest and the absence of stable political rules or structures, it will be a long time before a stable political system evolves. The repercussions of the collapse of the Communist system of power, then, are the first of the driving forces shaping the scenarios.

4

The Big Engine That Couldn't

"They pretend to pay us, and we pretend to work."
—*Anonymous*

Russia is in the midst of a great economic depression. But this depression has nothing in common with a Western-style, business-cycle depression. Instead, this crisis is the shock wave of a system that has collapsed, and it is one of the fundamental driving forces for Russia's future.

The old Soviet economy was, by the mid-1980s, like an ancient steam pump. In its day, it had been a wonder of the world—admired by some, criticized by others—and a model for designers elsewhere for more than three decades. Its engineers had tinkered endlessly with the pump, trying to improve its lumbering speed and make it more efficient. Yet at the end of their efforts they had to face the truth: The basic design of the engine was stretched to its limits.

The old engine was dependable enough, and its operators were used to its quirks. But it used too much fuel, and it polluted badly. It could probably have been patched up for another generation. But a new management tried to raise its boiler pressure and get the engine going faster. Instead, it blew up.

The image of a pump is appropriate. For, at bottom, the Soviet economy was precisely that: a political pump for the distribution of resources by bureaucratic means. It was not supply and demand that ran the system, nor people's preferences and desires, but rather what the political leaders wanted. It was frequently called a command economy. This in contrast to the capitalist "market" economy, in which "demand" is built up out of tens and tens of millions of individual decisions. The aim of the command economy's inventors, back in the 1920s and '30s. was precisely to replace the market. All of the major functions of a market—allocating supplies, labor, and capital; setting the level and type of production; establishing prices—were performed by state agencies. That engine is now gone.

For the next several years, if not longer, the Russian economy will be traversing a no-man's-land that is neither command system nor market economy. The state economy is continuing to wind down. Many people are still leaving low-paying jobs in the government and the state enterprises to take the plunge into the private sector, while others keep their state jobs but moonlight. The few remaining political controls continue to dissolve. The state sector is being broken up and privatized, each day a little bit more. And despite the fact that state enterprises are receiving such emergency care as the government can dispense under the oxygen tent of state subsidies and credits, output from the state sector continues to go down.

But Russia is still far from a modern market economy. In the Wild West atmosphere of the new Russian private sector, property and contracts have only the weakest basis in the law or in practice. There is no solid financial, budgetary, or fiscal system. A good deal of the private sector's activity, insofar as it consists of profiteering from the decay of the state sector, is a passing thing and will eventually have no place in a mature Russian economy. Corruption and crime prey on honest enterprise, although in the present moral and legal void it is hard to say just what "honest" means.

"THE STATE CIRCUS"

Under the command economy, instead of the alphabet soup by which government agencies are named in Washington, people in Moscow used words that all began with one abbreviation from the Russian word for "state"—*gos.* Thus "Gosplan" set the plan, and "Gostsen" the prices. "Gossnab" distributed supplies, "Gostrud" decided labor and wage policy, and "Gostekhnika" directed research and technology. Another essential part of the system was "Gosbezopasnost," better known as the KGB. It supplied security. Cynics captured the bureaucratic irrationality of the whole *gos* system when they called it "Gostsirk," the State Circus.

The essential innards of the system was the apparatus of the Communist party. This was the machinery of power that drove the command economy at all levels, enforcing the plan, correcting minor malfunctions, keeping the engine running.

And this is the system that Gorbachev and his reformers destroyed by seeking to save it. The entire basis of the command economy has disappeared. The political leadership that drove it no longer exists. The institutional mechanism and the Marxist ideology that supported it are gone. And the party apparatus that enforced the command economy at the local levels has disappeared.[1]

To make matters even more difficult, the integrated economic space within which the command economy operated—the Soviet Union—has disintegrated, and with it the economic ties that knit production and markets together. Cotton is a classic case. The output of cotton cloth in Ivanovo province, where much of the Russian textile industry is located, is down to the level of 1947, only half that of 1991, which itself was not a good year. At any given time, only four of the forty-six factories in Ivanovo are working. Half of Russia's total supplies for cotton were to come from Uzbekistan (and the rest from abroad). But Uzbekistan, now independent, has cut back on its plantings of cotton and is selling what it can at higher prices on the world market.

The result of the breakup of the State Circus and its command economy has been a dizzying drop in economic output in nearly every category. Official GNP has shrunk by more than one third in three years. Agriculture, industry, and trade have all declined. And though the decline has slowed recently, it has not yet halted. Experts are divided on where and when the Russian economy will bottom out, but it is likely that the low point has not yet been reached.

WHY HASN'T IT BEEN WORSE?

Still, if the entire command economy has collapsed, then why hasn't the decline been even worse? While "official unemployment" is less than two percent, surveys indicate it could actually be closer to ten percent. That is high, but no worse than current rates in many countries of the West. Very few enterprises have closed. Heavy industry has been able to defend itself politically and continue to extract subsidies. Most Russians appear to be getting by, if at a lower standard of living than before. What is the explanation?

First, the old economy itself is far from dead, even though the central command mechanism is gone. Like a dinosaur, it always had both a central brain and a local nervous system. The central brain was located in all of those *gos* agencies in Moscow. The local system consisted of a vast network of negotiated relations among enterprises. In addition, there was a large black market in goods and services, which the political authorities simultaneously repressed and tolerated.

Much of the central brain is now defunct. The "local" part of the system survives. The thousands of state enterprises continue to operate, selling to one another on credit, or simply not paying their bills. Most of these enterprises own housing and run municipal services, and are often more powerful than the local city and county authorities. State farms, tens of thousands of them, soldier on, still selling most of their produce to the state, to which they are linked through a complex system of subsidies. Privatized distribution organizations are actually thinly repainted state trading bodies. They remain in business, often holding monopolies in their area or product.

The remnants of the State Circus, the central agencies in Moscow, understaffed and underfunded, struggle to continue performing some of their old functions. Since Russia still lacks any real market system to replace the old order, these lingering agency functions have helped prevent the old economy from collapsing altogether. But they, in turn, exact a high price. The ministerial bureaucrats fight to retain control and to block change.

Lately the local part of the command economy has begun to run down as well. A vivid example is the Vladimir Tractor Factory, one of the largest industries in Russia. Until the end of 1993 its Soviet-era management fought to keep production lines going and workers employed, and to maintain the factory's welfare system—22 kindergartens, three collective farms, and a small city's worth of housing. But the factory was not being paid for its output. The only way it could keep producing was to borrow money at increasingly high interest rates. By the end of the year its back was to the wall.

In March 1994 the end of the Soviet era finally came to the Vladimir Tractor Factory. The company was taken over by a young Russian graduate of the Harvard Business School, Iosif Bakaleinik, backed by two private investment companies that had managed to acquire a controlling block of the company's shares. Bakaleinik promptly began shedding labor, cutting production, and divesting the company of its farms and kindergartens. The workers took the changes calmly, especially the loss of the farms. They said that they were finding more variety in the regular stores, and at better prices. The money economy is coming to Russia.[2]

All over Russia the experience of the Vladimir Tractor Factory is beginning to be repeated, as the last of the command economy grinds down to a halt.

A NEW ECONOMY ALONGSIDE THE OLD

The second reason the economic decline has not been worse is that a new economy is quickly growing up alongside the old. Private entrepreneurs are appearing all over—making telephones in their homes, setting up travel agencies, establishing software companies, manufacturing eyeglasses, selling seeds and plants from private greenhouses. Many of these are supplying the long-denied wants of Russian consumers, providing goods and badly needed services that the state never cared about. Other new entrepreneurs are parasitic, stripping the state enterprises of their assets, extorting bribes and protection money, exporting anything that can be moved—oil products, fertilizers, precious and nonprecious metals of all sorts. Many of these people are essentially feeding off the corpse of the dying command economy.

Eighty percent of small and medium enterprises have now been privatized. The privatization program, which has been strongly supported by the Yeltsin government, has moved on to large enterprises. By early 1994, over 7000 large state enterprises (half the number eligible for privatization) had been turned into joint-stock companies and sold to private shareholders. Less than two years after the death of the Soviet Union, perhaps as much as one-half of Russian economic activity is already private in one way or another.

In fact, most Russians today are better off than official statistics might lead one to think. GNP (gross national product) numbers mostly measure the output of the state economy. They leave out most of the new private activity, much of which is unreported. Agricultural production and services are especially underestimated in the official statistics.

In the old Soviet economy, managers had an incentive to exaggerate their production. They were rewarded on the basis of their total output. Thus, in the oil sector, the more feet you drilled, the more you were paid. It didn't matter whether you found oil. In heavy industry, the more steel you turned out, the higher your bonus, whether or not there was a market for your steel, and whatever its quality. Today, managers have the opposite incentive: They underreport output, to avoid high taxes.

For such reasons, official Soviet statistics overstated GNP in the old days. Now Russian statistics understate it because of their failure to account for the private economy. And that makes the decline seem even steeper. Consequently, official GNP is an inadequate, incomplete, and increasingly misleading measure of people's actual welfare.

All that being said, the majority of people are worse off than they were three years ago—but not as badly off as the numbers indicate. Virtually everyone complains of hard times. One revealing sign among many: The Russian daily *Izvestiia* reported recently that in former years the popular beaches of the Black Sea had up to twelve million visitors each year. By 1993 the number was down to two million or less, an 85 percent decline. Some of that drop, no doubt, results from the civil war in neighboring Georgia and tensions with Ukraine over the status of Crimea, but most of it is due to the fact that most people can no longer afford to travel. In the old days, people received holiday passes from their factories and institutes, rode on subsidized planes and trains at very cheap fares, and stayed free at enterprise-owned resorts. Now the tourists are more likely to be the new rich and middle class, and Sochi is starting to assume a little of the air of Saint-Tropez. But the average Russian can no longer afford to go there.

The impact of the economic decline has been highly uneven. Those with jobs, connections, family members working in the private sector, are managing to get by. But those who fall outside the support system of enterprise and family and who cannot seize the new opportunities—pensioners, refugees, migrant workers—have been badly hurt.

"EVERYTHING WAS SO CHEAP!"

Many Russians today feel increasingly nostalgic about the old command economy. "It didn't work well," they say, "but at least it worked." It didn't produce much wealth; at best, it generated a shabby sort of welfare state. The quality of goods was generally poor. Not only was there no true domestic market to demand higher quality, but insofar as the Soviet Union exported manufactured and finished goods, it did so to "soft markets," such as its Eastern European satellites or third-world countries, in barter deals. The lack of competition and choice meant that there was no incentive, no need, no pressure to attend to quality.

Still, jobs were secure, most of the basic necessities of life were virtually free, inequalities were not so glaring as they are today, there was less corruption and crime, and the streets were much safer. For the elite, the state-subsidized welfare system could be comfortable indeed. "Every Friday afternoon," a prominent heart surgeon recalled, "my driver picked me up outside my Moscow institute and took me to the airport. I flew from Moscow to my beachfront home on the Black Sea every weekend. Everything was so cheap!" Today, that surgeon earns the equivalent of twenty dollars a month from the state at current exchange rates. He's earning a good deal more practicing private medicine, but he certainly no longer flies to the Black Sea every weekend.

Those Russians who have lost out, especially older people and those who occupied privileged positions in the old system, would be tempted to try to go back. But the political and ideological underpinnings of the old command system are not there. In the final analysis, it was ultimately Lenin's ideology and Stalin's dictatorship that built the command economy, and those are now gone forever.

It is true that a strong central government could return to some elements of the command economy. This might take the form of state orders and targets for the largest state industries (especially defense-related), wage and price controls, state allocation of the most important commodities, and state controls over foreign-currency operations and foreign trade. Indeed, the Russian government over the last year has tried to do some of this, and if conservative Russian economists and politicians have their way, even more controls may be on the way.

But they will not work. The fact is, a return to the command economy is impossible precisely because, at the end, that system did *not* work any longer. It produced the wrong output: a lopsided "basket of goods" (as economists say) that was too heavy on military and construction goods and much too light on consumer goods and services, and which the Russian government is no longer able to buy. This destroyed ordinary people's incentive to work. Moreover, the old command economy was incurably inefficient and sluggish. It was so wasteful that the only way it could keep growing was to keep using more and more raw materials and manpower every year. But these were no longer available, except at higher and higher cost.

In addition, the command economy was incapable of innovating except on a very limited basis. Russian science, excellent in theory, was poor at translating its discoveries into new technologies and innovations, except where political pressure drove it to do so. This was particularly true from the 1970s onward, when the Soviet Union failed to keep pace with global technological advances in computers and electronics.[3] The only solution is to reward people for innovation and efficiency, and create an environment that encourages both. Only market systems seem to have learned the secret of doing that.

Any attempt to return to the old ways would mean a return to the old dilemmas. The Soviet economy was starting to slip inexorably backward well before it started to collapse. Whatever people's attitudes toward the command economy, one conclusion is clear: There is no going back to it.

5

The Implosion of Empire

It is hard for a Westerner to imagine what the sudden collapse of the Soviet empire must feel like for a Russian. It is as though the entire American sphere of influence in the world had abruptly collapsed, the NATO alliance had disappeared, and the western third of the United States had declared independence.

But it is not just the "outer space" of the Soviet empire that has disappeared; so has the "inner space." The high walls carefully built by the Soviet dictatorship to keep the West out and keep Soviet citizens in have also disappeared. Madison Avenue materialism has taken over from dialectical materialism. It brings with it—at a price, of course—the goods and opportunities that the West takes for granted, but that until now have been unattainable for Russians.

Suddenly Russia is exposed to a flood of Western influences of all sorts. Countless Western businessmen and officials, and even no small number of rock stars, crisscross the country, visiting at least the big cities, advertising the Western way of life and business—all of them, in one way or another, latter-day missionaries for capitalism, the market, and the Western way of life. Right alongside them are the real missionaries, Western evangelical groups holding revival meetings and proselytizing on street corners.

The shock of the collapse of the Soviet empire and Soviet identity, followed by the massive opening-up to the West, constitutes a powerful force that topples all the assumptions that Russians grew up with, increases their insecurity, and obliges them to rethink their place in the world and in their own country. Russians today wonder anxiously what it means to be Russian. The insecurity about identity and the absence of shared values or ideology will make for instability until answers to these questions gradually evolve.

As Russia's economic and intellectual barricades come down, the impact of the outside world—the West—will become evident in every part of Russian life. Will this be seen as a net plus, as a way to accelerate the reconstruction of Russia? Not necessarily. The flood of Western influences might also feed the politics of resentment and humiliation, stirring sentiments against the very presence of Westerners, against being "colonized." Ultimately, if things go badly, Russians might end up blaming "outside forces" for the collapse of the USSR and the consequent degradation and loss of status of the Russian people.

THE BISHOP

Last winter, a visitor sat in the austere eighteenth-century study of a Russian Orthodox bishop in Siberia, gratefully sipping hot Georgian tea as the subzero wind howled outside. The bishop—a still-youthful man who had completed training as a highway engineer before entering the clergy—was proud of the church's revival since the fall of the Communist regime. At one point, he drew back a curtain, revealing a large Sony television set and a cassette recorder. He put in a cassette. It showed him standing deep in snow, surrounded by a resonant Russian choir, blessing the waters of the powerful river that runs through town. Many decades ago, the Communists had banned the ritual, which is part of the Russian Orthodox Christmas. Now the bishop had revived it. He was very proud.

But the bishop was not at all happy with the arrival of the West. He spoke disapprovingly of Westerners' attempting to adopt Russian children and said he backed legislation to prevent it. After all, he insisted, Russia was not some third world country. Then he stepped over to a closet and pulled out a thick manila file labeled "Sects."

"These evangelicals," he said, "are financed by the CIA to come here and put strange ideas into people's heads."

How, he was asked, could he be so sure about the CIA?

"Isn't it obvious?" the bishop replied. "The aim is to destabilize Russia."

Such attitudes are not unusual in Russia today. A poll in 1993 found that four out of ten Russian respondents worried that Russia might be attacked by a foreign country within the next five years. The same poll showed that most Russians are much more concerned about problems at home, but it suggests that they hardly view the outside world as benign or safe.

THREE LAYERS OF EMPIRE STRIPPED AWAY

To the minds of Russians, it is not just one empire that has collapsed, but three: the outer tier, Soviet clients and allies (Cuba, Afghanistan, Ethiopia, Iraq, Vietnam, etc.); the middle tier, the Soviet bloc (mainly Eastern Europe); and the inner tier, the non-Russian republics of the Soviet Union.

Russians do not grieve equally about all three losses. The loss of the outer tier nullifies the gains of the "Soviet internationalism" of the 1960s and after. These clients were never securely held, and they were never a source of pride, wealth, or psychic security for most Russians; quite the contrary. Russians never particularly liked or trusted them, and resented the money the Kremlin was spending on them. Consequently, their loss is not deeply mourned today. Of the lot, only Afghanistan remains an active concern for Russians, but for quite a different, and ironic, reason: Afghan mujaheddin, mobilized by Russia's invasion, are intervening in the politics of a former Soviet republic, Tajikistan, and may become a wider threat.

The shedding of the middle tier of empire is a more serious matter. It cancels the gains of World War II and eliminates the security zone the Soviets had built in the west. These gains, mainly in Eastern Europe, were paid for in Russian blood, and Russians feel regret for their loss, even though they had few illusions, at the end, about the region's allegiance to communism or affection for Russia.

But it is the loss of the inner tier that is the real shock for Russians. The breakup of the former Soviet Union strips away the gains of Russian colonists and soldiers—and indeed culture and language—over the last four centuries. This is so radical a loss that many Russians still refuse to believe it is real or accept it as permanent. Moreover, it leaves around 25 million Russians "stranded" outside Russia, in states that were formerly part of the Soviet Union—an incendiary situation.

There are few examples in the modern world of such a dramatic loss of imperial "space," and it is much too soon to know what the reaction will be. Russia is huge; even without its lost western marches it stretches across eleven time zones. In conversations with Russians, one does not get the sense that they feel naked. Yet they do talk about the need to find a new basis for their national identity and their national security. This would seem essential for coherence of the state. The Soviet "internationalist" idea is dead. Russia sits in an uneasy void amid four civilizations to which it does not belong: the European-American, the Muslim, the Chinese, and the Japanese.[1] It would seem that the only real choice is between an attempt to join Europe, and a turning inward to defend Russian "uniqueness." Thus Russians are thrust back to dilemmas familiar from their earlier, pre-Soviet history —dilemmas they will be struggling with for a long time to come.

One evening last spring at a dacha near the old town of Sergiev Posad, north of Moscow, Alyosha was hosting a Westerner, a friend of twenty years, going back to the time when the Westerner had been an exchange student. Alyosha thumbed through well-worn manuals from his days as a Pioneer (the Soviet equivalent of a Boy Scout) in the early 1950s. Bright-eyed Russian boys and girls with red kerchiefs marched toward communism under the benevolent gaze of Stalin, resplendent in his white marshal's uniform. In the manuals it was perpetual summer. Alyosha, who went on to become one of the earliest and most active environmentalists in the Soviet Union in the 1970s, shook his head, partly in amusement and partly in nostalgia. "That was our world, and we believed in it," he said. "Even now, we are not Europe. We must find our own way."

"HAVE A GOOD DAY!"

If "Tverskaia Ulitsa" seems slightly unfamiliar, that is because it is the new name of Gorkii Street, the increasingly fashionable main boulevard that sweeps north from Moscow's Red Square. But more and more the street seems like home—to Westerners, not Russians. On the right, a billboard in Russian touts a candy that melts in your mouth, not in your hand. On the left stands McDonald's gleaming new office building, built with ruble profits from the company's flagship restaurant on Pushkin Square, a few yards farther along. Familiar Western names in cosmetics and high fashion line the boulevard. Bright red kiosks in the shape of large Coca-Cola cans do a brisk business in front of the Intourist Hotel, while nearby an Austrian firm is renovating the storied old Natsional' Hotel.

Western companies by the hundreds are setting up offices in Russian cities, establishing settlements for expatriate workers throughout the country, and lodging their executives in the Western-style hotels that are opening in downtown Moscow and St. Petersburg. The suspicious scowl of the *dezhurnaya,* the dour key lady who stood guard on every floor in the old Soviet hotels, is being replaced by a cheery "Have a good day!" from the well-trained and multilingual Russian staff. Russians, as they sit in Western-style traffic jams, look out at Western cars and tune in to new Moscow rock stations broadcasting in French and English. They can also read Russian-language editions of *The New York Times* and the *Financial Times.*

For the well-heeled Russian who can buy a Western car or pay for a dinner at the Balchug Hotel (currently the most luxurious in Moscow), the changes are heady. For some, they are more like an invasion of home by foreign carpetbaggers. These people fear that this is only the beginning of loss and humiliation, as foreign companies develop Russian resources and as Russian enterprises collapse, allegedly at the insistence of Western financial institutions. They see and hear the invasion of foreign music and media, and they fear that Russian culture will be swept away by Western pop and pornography. In such circumstances, any Russian government that pursues open policies toward the rest of the world will always run the risk of being accused of selling out Russian "interests" to foreigners, especially if living standards are not improving.

THE TURN TOWARD THE WEST

But one should perhaps beware of exaggerating the impact of the latest influences from the West, or the incapacity of Russians to assimilate them. The fact is that the West has been the main source of example and competition for Russia for a long time, ever since the Russian élite turned decisively toward Europe at the beginning of the seventeenth century. French and (later) German were the languages spoken at the tsarist courts. Bolshevism itself was a version of Marxism, a Western doctrine. Stalinist industrialization borrowed heavily from American technology. But Western influences did not fully reach the Russian masses until late in the Soviet period. Since the death of Stalin, Western influences of many different kinds have been a major driving force in the evolution of Russian life at all levels, and remain so today. In many ways, the Western tidal wave now washing over Russia began in the 1960s, with the first homemade recordings of Western jazz, bootlegged by Russian fans on X-ray film purloined from hospitals.[2]

The attractions and challenges from the West have been of five main kinds:

Economic Competition

The failure of the Soviet command economy to keep up with the West in growth rates and technological dynamism was perhaps the single greatest force undermining the legitimacy of the Soviet system. The command economy did manage to compete effectively into the 1960s, so long as the arena was "coal and steel"—that is, traditional heavy-industrial output. In the 1970s, however, as the arena changed to computers and microelectronics, it became increasingly evident that the command economy was lagging further and further behind. The success of Japan and other resource-poor East Asian economies only highlighted the weaknesses of the Russian command economy, at least in the eyes of those Russians who were alert to what was happening in the outside world (including those who were among the best informed, the KGB).

The state of the world economy will have great impact on Russia's future evolution. Good economic growth in the rest of the world will provide larger markets for Russian goods and facilitate more investment, technology transfer, and aid. Asian economic development—particularly involving China, Japan, and Korea—will be much more important for Russia's own development than is now generally recognized. A weaker global economy, on the other hand, will have the opposite impact, making the transition more difficult. The "success" or "failure" of the global market economy will do much to determine the extent to which capitalism establishes long-term legitimacy as the models for Russians to emulate.

Military and Technological Competition

No less devastating to the performance and viability of the Soviet system was the steady pressure of military competition with the United States. From its beginning, the Soviet command economy was always a war machine. But it was smaller than the American economy and less able to generate wealth to begin with. The burden of sustaining an all-out arms race with the world's largest technological and military power—especially as the relevant technology changed dramatically—ultimately sapped the ability of the command economy to devote itself to any purpose but war. It was not Star Wars itself that did in the Soviets. Rather, it was the steady application over the last half

71

century of Western resolve and technological advance, of which Star Wars was among the most recent elements.[3]

The military competition with the West, and in particular the United States, should be a far less significant force for Russia in the future than it was for the Soviet Union in the past. A permanent end to the arms race would permit the overgrown military sector to shrink. This would free resources and skills for economic development.

The Postindustrial Technological Revolution

Wave after wave of economic revolution swept over the world during the Soviet period: the consumer revolution, modern agro-industry, the rise of computers and telecommunications, and the like. Not only was the Soviet system unable to keep up with these revolutions, but also they all contributed to undermining it. Thus the regime, which devoted enormous energy to controlling its borders, airwaves, and airspace, proved in the long run unable to do so, as satellite communications, portable radios, tape players, and VCRs all enabled Russian citizens in growing numbers to rope in the outside world. It became technically impossible for the Soviet system to keep them out. The fax machine was on the front line during the 1991 coup, undermining the plotters' attempt to seize control over information and communications during the critical coup hours.

Such "enabling technologies" will in the future help unlock the technical and scientific and commercial talent of the Russian people. As they are absorbed and diffused through society, communications technologies will be a very powerful force for innovation and creativity in a society long straitjacketed. The newest technologies, such as cellular telephones and cheap personal computers, may enable the Russians to leapfrog over some of their infrastructure gaps and technological lags. These capabilities will also decentralize and democratize information, counteracting the forces trying to restore hierarchy and controls.

Western Intellectual Movements and Pop Culture

Beginning in the 1960s, every successive intellectual and social movement that swept through the outside world eventually, if circuitously, seemed to reach the Soviet Union: environmentalism, energy conservation, Islamic fundamentalism and political Islam, neo-liberal economics, fundamentalist Christian religions, nationalism, and the "New Age," to mention some. But far more devastating in its impact on Soviet values was Western pop culture, especially jazz and then rock, followed by Western tastes in clothes, the youth revolution, and the drug culture. The Soviet élite, which had managed from the mid-1930s to create an austere Victorianism based on late-nineteenth-century European values, found itself subverted from within, by its own children. In the end, the idols of Marxism-Leninism were mocked and ignored long before they were toppled.

The Consumer Society

The small streams of the 1960s have now turned into a flood of images and fashions of a global culture. The flood will continue to rise in the years ahead. It will change incentives and promote acquisitiveness. Not only will people desire goods, but the goods will also be visible and attainable. The materialism of the West will submerge whatever remains of dialectical materialism. The appeal will be very powerful in a society that has been starved of consumer goods to a degree that many in the West cannot conceive. There will be a sharp and painful break between generations, between teenagers and young adults on the one side, and their parents on the other, as their experiences and orientations—and opportunities—diverge so completely.

The cultural change will be disorienting and threatening for a Russian society caught up in its great transition, and there will inevitably be a reaction against the influences from the outside world, portraying them as dangerous and destructive. How strong this reaction becomes, and whether it takes on a nationalist or a religious character, are some of the most important questions for the future. The response could take the form of a regrounding—a reassertion of values, a greater sense of security, and a renewed sense of identity—that would help the Russian people make their way through the tumultuous transition.

But, if the disappointments are too great and the fears too large, then the new Russian revolution could be captured by extremists, who would mobilize their supporters by attacking the familiar villains favored by both the Communists and the Russian right—beginning with the outside world itself and the "collaborators" within. That reaction has already begun.

"Prime movers" is the term used in scenario development for the actors able to alter the "rules of the game"—able to change the way our scenarios unfold. When we say prime movers, we do not mean individuals so much as broad interest groups and institutions. We are particularly interested in those helping to write the rules and create the institutions that will run tomorrow's Russia.

The future president of Russia in the year 2010, for example, is a person probably already over thirty years old, building a political career somewhere in Russia. We just don't happen to know who he is yet, and neither does he, except that, given Russian society and the way women have fallen out of politics in the new Russia, he is likely to be male. Probably he is a heavy smoker but may be only a moderate drinker or even a teetotaller. And unlike the Russian leaders of a generation ago, who were almost always engineers by education and rose through the ranks of the professional party apparatus, the future Russian president of 2010 could be a private businessman, or a soldier, or a deputy mayor of some medium-sized city, or the leader of some political party that does not even exist yet.

It is a measure of the fluidity of Russian politics these days that no one has any idea through what channels he is rising or what political trumps he is putting together even now, on the way to his future office on Old Square.

6

Players and Prime Movers

The United States has an unusually open political system. Given the right circumstances, almost anyone can climb into the arena of politics, make headlines, change history. The old Soviet Union was the opposite extreme. With very few exceptions, politics was closed to all but a handful of players, all of them state and party institutions. The most important one was the apparatus of the Communist party itself, and far and away the most powerful individual within it was the general secretary of the party.

All that has changed in Russia today, and there is even more change to come. Consequently, as we build scenarios of the Russian future, among the most important questions are "Who are the players that can change the course of history in Russia? Who will be the new players tomorrow?"

The striking thing about Russia today is that, except for Boris Yeltsin, very few truly powerful or dominant personalities have yet emerged who could potentially shift Russia's course by virtue of their personalities or the political resources they command. There is no lack of forceful people. What they mostly lack is a strong national political base. Rather like a kremlin—which means "fort" in Russian—rising up from the flat Russian plain, the Russian presidency, despite its weaknesses, dominates an otherwise relatively featureless political landscape.

POLITICS STILL BASED ON THE STATE

Russian politics today is still mainly an elite game, played mostly by the leaders of state-affiliated corporate groups and competing government organizations. The big difference is that these groups now include regional and local governments, and that in the absence of a single dominant body, all government bodies are in constant and fierce competition with one another.

A Westerner, studying the political landscape in Russia today, will be struck immediately by how great the differences are from the Western political scene, despite the surface similarities to more familiar parliamentary systems. In Russia, the state is still never far from people's minds. Most politicians or managers in Russia today still belong to state organizations or maintain some affiliation with them; after all, only a few short years ago nearly every Russian worked for the state. The large private banks and companies that have emerged in recent years are mostly spinoffs of state bodies and take care to include governmental bodies among their shareholders. Their leaders frequently continue to play dual private-public roles.

Therefore, Russian politics is still focused, much more than Western politics, on the state. People want to gain access to it, get jobs in it, or obtain favors from it. Whether they like it or not, they depend on it. Even private bodies find it difficult to be independent of the state. Most Russian newspapers rely on government subsidies to cover the high costs of paper and distribution. Many private banks are still mainly conduits for government funds. Commodities exchanges broker barter sales among state enterprises, or more lately, trade privatization vouchers, issued by the state. Thus, one of the tactics that Boris Yeltsin has been able to use in dividing opponents is simply to offer them jobs in his government, and the secret to the former parliamentary speaker Ruslan Khasbulatov's influence was that he was a master of the art of allocating patronage to deputies.

Private organizations and groups in Russia are not yet able to shape the economy and the society on their own. They can do so only if they influence the government and move the levers of state policy. Therefore, the government is both a prime mover and a prize.

These broad features of Russian politics are changing as society grows stronger and richer. The private sector is growing like yeast, unregulated, unreported, and untaxed. The reach of the state is gradually shrinking. Large private companies and groups, especially a handful of powerful banks, are emerging and are beginning to test their political muscle. Russian politics will soon become more wide open; more players will climb into the arena. And what will expand the arena faster than anything is private money and open elections.

PRIME MOVERS

Not all the players in Russian politics are prime movers. That is, not all are capable of changing the rules of the game or of moving Russia from one scenario to another. But the following are definitely prime movers under all scenarios.

PRESIDENT YELTSIN

Nearly ten years after his emergence on the national stage as Gorbachev's "broom" to clean up Moscow, Yeltsin remains a unique political figure and a fascinating enigma. Both his friends and his enemies have consistently underestimated him. Yet since 1990 Yeltsin has been the main agent of change in Russian politics, first as the principal catalyst of Gorbachev's downfall and the breakup of the Soviet Union, and since then as Russia's first popularly-elected president.

One major reason why Yeltsin must be considered a prime mover is his unpredictability as a politician. His unexpected actions clearly have the potential to "change the scenario," as they did in the fall of 1987 (when Yeltsin challenged the conservatives in Gorbachev's Politburo) and in the winter of 1989 (when he won a seat in the Supreme Soviet over the bitter opposition of the Communist leadership), and again in the fall of 1993, when Yeltsin unexpectedly dismissed the old parliament and then evicted it by force.

Given his mercurial nature, his will, and his history, Yeltsin may be counted on to uncork a few more surprises in coming years. He has the politician's art of keeping his opponents off balance. The main question now is whether Yeltsin will run again in the 1996 presidential elections. Regardless of his true intentions, Yeltsin can be counted on to keep his opponents—and his supporters—guessing until the last minute.

Yeltsin is equally enigmatic as a president, and he will be a difficult figure for future historians to interpret. His tactics frequently baffle even his closest supporters, and many question whether he has any clear strategic vision. It is not even clear how deeply Yeltsin is committed to the market and democracy, or why. But he has been the chief sponsor of economic and democratic reform in Russia since 1989. While many charge that his natural impulses tend to be authoritarian, yet his policies on the whole have been democratic.

What is certain, however, is that Yeltsin is bent on building strong presidential authority, and the new Russian constitution, adopted in December 1993, gives him exceptionally broad powers. He is backed by a rapidly-growing presidential apparatus, already 1500 strong, through which he is seeking to gain greater control over the "power ministries" (military, police, and state security) and the governors in the provinces. In contrast to 1991–1993, when Yeltsin's power was weak and uncertain, from 1994 on the odds favor the presidential side.

Yet even if his critics declare that Yeltsin has authoritarian leanings, the least one can say is that he is anything but systematic in his pursuit of power. Yeltsin is at his best in a tight corner, but when there is no crisis he seems to grow almost bored with the day-to-day exercise of his office. He is not a "hands-on" president. He appears unwilling or unable to resolve rivalries among his staff. He has no presidential party and until recently has resisted the idea that he needed one. On several key occasions, he has accepted decisions by the judiciary and the legislature that limited his power. In interviews, he frequently speaks of his job as a burden. The main explanation may be poor health: Yeltsin is known to suffer from severe back pains and other health problems.

Yet this reluctant founding father remains the most important single player in Russian politics today. Like Ronald Reagan or Charles de Gaulle of France, Yeltsin has an instinctive feel for the mood of the Russian people which no other Russian politician—with the exception of Vladimir Zhirinovskii—has been able to match.

THE FUTURE PRESIDENT?

The campaign to succeed Yeltsin as president has already begun, and new candidates are emerging practically daily. Some believe that Yeltsin will be forced to call an early presidential election. Others are already positioning themselves for 1996, when Yeltsin's present term legally expires, although challenges of one kind or another could appear before. The elections could also be postponed.

The candidate most prominently mentioned is the current prime minister, Viktor Chernomyrdin. He has many virtues: he is an able manager and an astute tactician. He is a steady, reassuring figure. Because of his credentials and experience, he has a much better chance of pulling the managers of the old Soviet economy onto a reform path than "academics." Nevertheless, he would have several important liabilities in an electoral campaign. He seems to be more of a technocrat, a manager rather than an instinctive politician. He has no party organization behind him, and his natural constituency, the industrial manager class—while still very much in place economically—were practically blown off the political map in the December 1993 elections. But above all, Chernomyrdin will be held accountable for the performance—or rather, the perceived performance—of the Russian economy by election day. This is hardly likely to win him votes—unless there is the perception of a corner turned.

The "Red Browns" have two leading candidates, Aleksandr Rutskoi and Vladimir Zhirinovskii. Zhirinovskii is a true demagogue, an instinctive politician with a genius for the political uses of television. His success in the December 1993 elections marks him as the first "new era" politician in Russia. But his staying power is another matter. His mercurial personality and extreme opinions are his chief asset—along with his rabid hates and bizarre and paranoid assertions—but also his worst liability. He titillates Russians, but he also scares them. He also, at least so far, has no obvious economic ideas—only targets of blame and hatred. In contrast, Aleksandr Rutskoi will appeal to many Russians as a more familiar, steady, and trustworthy figure. A former air force commander who was shot down twice in Afghanistan, Rutskoi exhibits a rough-hewn patriotism and popular manner that many Russians can identify with. He is also animated by an extreme hatred of Yeltsin. Again, he seems to have no economic program to respond to Russia's needs.

If the right-wing vote is split between Rutskoi and Zhirinovskii, and if the communists put up a candidate of their own, a moderate democrat might stand a chance. He would have to be a new and exciting figure who could appeal to the younger urban voter, someone untarnished by any past association with the unpopular Gaidar administration. At the moment, the person who most closely matches this description is Grigorii Yavlinskii. An economist, Yavlinskii was one of the principal authors of the "500 Days" program of radical economic reform in 1990. Passed over by Yeltsin in favor of Gaidar in the fall of 1991, Yavlinskii became a critic of the Gaidar program, but from a pro-market position. In 1993, Yavlinskii co-founded a party that came to be known as the "Apple" Party ("Yabloko," from the first letters of the names of its three founders). Yavlinskii's party ran well in the December 1993 elections, and Yavlinskii's own standing as a potential candidate was enhanced.

These are only four of the possible candidates for president. There will be many more. For instance, the new chairman of the Duma, Ivan Rybkin, though elected under the label of the Agrarian Party, is putting a notable emphasis on cooperation and consensus. He could emerge as a pragmatic centrist not so burdened by the recent past.

Unless some sort of primary election is held to narrow down the field, the next Russian president could be elected by a minority of the voters. Still, the powers of the president under the 1993 constitution—if it remains in force—are so sweeping that the next future Russian president must be considered a prime mover, until he proves otherwise.

LEGISLATURES: THE SOVIETS

The network of legislatures that arose between 1990 and 1993 was the descendent of the "soviets," maintained as rubber-stamp bodies with vestigial power through the decades of the Soviet era.* After they were revived by Gorbachev in 1989–90, each soviet asserted its supremacy over the other branches of government and claimed absolute sovereignty over its own area. These claims to absolute power plunged the country into a "war of laws." Anyone could write laws but no one could implement them. In Moscow, for instance, the city- and borough-level "soviets" and the mayor all issued competing decrees and rules—and with good reason, for they were battling over the disposition of the richest prize in Moscow, real estate. In western Siberia's Tiumen province, Russia's oil and gas country, the provincial government and the

---

* Although the "Soviet Union" disappeared, the "soviets" remained, as the word "soviet" means council. But the new legislatures are to be called "dumas," reviving the pre-revolutionary term.

two "autonomous" districts (*okrugs*) within it have all been busy passing their own laws and decrees and just as busy nullifying those of the other authorities. The *okrugs* have even succeeded in gaining for themselves the same juridical standing as the nominal provincial government; their budgets, augmented by oil and gas income, are larger than those of the province.

At the center, and in most regions around the country, the soviets were at daggers drawn with the executive. This caused the soviets to band together into a loose alliance led by the speaker of the federal parliament, Ruslan Khasbulatov.

Khasbulatov was a unique phenomenon, a minor academic who initially rose as a protégé of Yeltsin and then broke with him, emerging over the last two years as his most dangerous enemy. His specialty was intrigue and the manipulation of patronage. He transformed the Supreme Soviet into a personal power base. The dissolution of parliament in September 1993 threatened to eliminate him as a political figure, and he fought desperately to save the institution on which his power rested.

The shelling of the White House in October 1993, and the electoral campaign that followed, wiped away Khasbulatov's power structure, but returned a body of deputies very similar to the old.

The Parliament

The newly elected parliament consists of two separate houses, which for now sit in different buildings. The upper house (the Federation Council) consists of 178 elected members, two from every constituent region of the Russian Federation. Most of those elected to this house are the political leaders of their regions, or at least leading figures; many of them (the so-called "heads of administration") are Yeltsin appointees. The Chairman of the Federation Council, Vladimir Shumeiko, was Deputy Chairman of the old parliament before he switched sides in 1992 and became First Deputy Premier under Yeltsin. He is regarded as a close Yeltsin ally.

The lower house, the State Duma, contains 444 deputies, consisting of two groups of deputies, elected by two separate methods. Half were elected on party lists, and came into the parliament with at least a loose party label. The other half were elected from single-member constituencies, some running under an explicit party label, but many not. Some of the latter have now formed "fractions" (i.e., parliamentary blocs) of their own. After considerable maneuvering in the early weeks, most of the Duma has settled into four groups of roughly equal size:

- the "democratic reformers" (Russia's Choice, Yabloko, and December 12 Union, with a total of 117 deputies);

- the "regional reformers" (Russian Unity and Concord and New Regional Policy, totalling 97 deputies);

- "communists" of various types (the Communist Party of Russia and the Agrarian Party, with 100 deputies); and

- the nationalists (the Liberal Democratic Party and the Russian Way bloc, with a total of 89 deputies).

In addition, there are 27 deputies from the Women of Russia party, who range in views. If this party can stay together, it will have significant influence as a swing bloc.

Yeltsin is evidently counting on the upper house, the Federation Council, to be his line of defense against the lower house in case things go seriously wrong. Under the new constitution, the President's veto can be overridden only by a two-thirds vote by both houses (Article 107). And although the lower house can impeach the President, only the upper house can remove him from office (Article 102).

Some of the Federation Council's other powers could also prove to be critical. It appoints the judges of the highest Russian courts, including the Constitutional Court (Article 102). It can veto any law passed by the Duma, which must then muster a two-thirds majority to override (Article 105). Above all, constitutional amendments require not only a two-thirds majority of the Duma, but also a three-quarters majority of the Federation Council (Article 108). Clearly, then, if it chooses, the Federation Council can be the President's key ally.

The Federation Council consists largely of regional political leaders. It was their failure to work with one another and with the President—as in 1993's "constitutional convention"—that gave heart to Khasbulatov and Rutskoi and set the stage for the final confrontation between the President and parliament. The running dispute between the provinces and the so-called "autonomous republics" could rear its head again. This would paralyze the Federation Council—thus helping Yeltsin.

But, if the provincial leaders can agree among themselves, Yeltsin might be forced to buy the support of the Federation Council with key concessions to the provinces. In that case, he might find himself in the same weak position as that of the last two years. Moreover, unlike the Duma, which can be dismissed by the President, there is no provision in the constitution for the dismissal of the Federation Council (Article 109).

BIG INDUSTRY

The largest ten thousand state enterprises are more than just the country's main employers. They are also its biggest landlords and its largest providers of food and services. Within this group, the defense industrialists are the best organized and the most active politically. Big industry is not necessarily reactionary. Its leaders support the transition to capitalism if it seems clear that they themselves will become the capitalists. But most of them want ample state protection, orders, credits, and subsidies, and they want the state to preserve their status and advantages in society.

In the first year after the attempted coup of August 1991, it appeared as though the managers of the large industrial enterprises would emerge as a major political force. They organized a large pressure group, the Union of Industrialists and Entrepreneurs. By 1992, it had become the most important force behind the Civic Union, a centrist political coalition that briefly became the best-organized political group in Russia.

President Yeltsin and his advisers initially tried to turn to the Civic Union and the industrialists as a counterweight against the president's increasingly bitter opponents in the parliament. But it soon appeared that the industrialists were deeply divided among themselves, and as a result the Civic Union did not become a united or effective political force. By 1993 the industrialists had faded as major players on the political scene, and Yeltsin had turned for support to the local politicians.

As time goes by, the industrialists are still likely to be prime movers in the evolution of Russian politics, but not as a single group. More probably, at least four industrial groups will emerge, with distinct political interests and programs: the defense industrialists (who are still the most influential element in the Union of Industrialists and Entrepreneurs) and other entrepreneurs, those from the extractive industries (chiefly oil and gas), the managers of the large privatized industries, and the owners of small and medium-sized enterprises.

LOCAL POLITICAL MACHINES

The politics of the regions are a mosaic of highly individual cases. This reflects an important new fact about Russia: Politics is becoming more local and regional, and it is only by looking at those levels that one can really understand it.

There are two kinds of local governments in Russia today. The first is the provinces (or, in Russian, *oblasti*), in which most people live. The second is the twenty-one so-called "autonomous republics and districts." These make up 15 percent of the population of the Russian Federation and have special rights and privileges under the Federal Treaty adopted in 1992. For example, they retain most of their tax receipts and have managed to gain some control over their own natural resources. The *avtonomii,* as they are called in Russian, nominally represent non-Russian ethnic groups, but in fact Russians are a majority in most of them, and most of their elites (if not the actual political leaders) are Russians of much the same type and background as in the provinces. The provinces resented the greater privileges of the *avtonomii.* In 1993, the Russian provinces and cities took to declaring themselves independent republics for the very purpose of gaining privileges similar to those of the *avtonomii.*

The constitution of 1993 resolves this issue, on paper at least, by eliminating practically all of the special advantages of the *avtonomii.* But that is only on paper. In practice, the *avtonomii* are holding on to their gains and the issue is hanging fire. In the winter of 1994, the Federal government concluded a treaty with Tatariia, which confirms that republic's special status. So far, then, the central government is moving cautiously.

Just who is in charge in a Russian province varies very much from place to place. The three major contenders in many provinces are, first, the "head of administration" (*glava administratsii*), typically but not always a Yeltsin appointee. The second is the provincial legislature, which is usually conservative but has in most places been greatly weakened since the fall of 1993. Last, in most provinces there is also a "presidential representative," a new and fairly hazy position, intended as a combination of presidential watchdog and ombudsman. Whereas the heads of administration and the leaders of the soviets are mostly experienced politicians and administrators, the presidential representatives are usually "democrats," in most cases newcomers to politics. In most places, the presidential representatives are weak, and are widely derided as "toothless commissars."

In some places in the last days of the Soviet regime, Communist-apparatus officials managed to change their colors and stay in power. In other places, the party leaders were virtually overthrown in 1990 and 1991 and replaced by newcomers. The difference seemed to be how unpopular the local Communist party apparatus was in each location. By and large, the broad pattern is that democrats made greater headway in cities than in rural areas, while Communist-derived conservatives have survived better in agricultural provinces than in industrial ones. Many of the former Communist functionaries moved into quasi-private businesses in 1990–91, frequently using the funds and connections of the party to establish themselves. Some of these "nomenklatura capitalists" are now returning to local politics.

In most provinces the politicians who control the legislatures have viewed the government and its market-oriented reform program with suspicion, although they welcome private enterprise for themselves. The heads of administration give the government reserved support. When Yeltsin dissolved parliament in September 1993, the heads of administration supported Yeltsin; most of the local soviets opposed him.[1]

Yeltsin responded to the challenge by issuing an decree abolishing the provincial soviets and urging the legislatures of the *avtonomii* to do the same. Many complied—in part because this provided a convenient opportunity for the professional politicians in the local governments to eliminate the remaining amateurs. Most of the new provincial legislatures are smaller and weaker than their predecessors. Power is concentrated in the executive branch, and is based on an uneasy alliance between the local *nomenklatura* elite and Yeltsin's appointed governor. Most of the democrats who came into politics between 1989 and 1991 are now gone. These changes have taken place without much protest from ordinary citizens, who have increasingly turned their backs on politics at all levels. As a result, the local political executives have become, on average, more powerful than they were between 1991 and

1993. Some use their power to support market reforms, others to oppose them.

THE "SWORDS AND SHIELDS": THE MILITARY AND SECURITY POLICE

These groups remain large and relatively strong. The military is the most highly centralized group in Russian society, and therefore potentially the group most capable of political action and intervention. Its strong nationalistic values and corporate pride logically place it in natural opposition to the liberal reformers. But the events of 1991 and 1992 have demoralized and divided the "coercive élites" and made them resentful. The disappearance of the one-party system removes what was traditionally the main barrier to the military's direct participation in politics. But the ranks of military and security officers are deeply split, often along generational lines, and there is no single "military" or "security" point of view.

What was special about the Soviet army and the secret police was that they were the "sword and shield of the revolution"—two élite formations in a state perpetually organized for war. They were the recipients of every privilege and honor the Soviet regime could bestow, and the beneficiaries of an entire economic system built to channel resources on a priority basis to its war and security industries. The military and the police as a group stayed out of politics, but their top chiefs were part of the political leadership itself, members of the board of "USSR, Incorporated," and the voice of the coercive élites was a strong one within the Soviet system.

The collapse of the Soviet Union and events in Russia have been as traumatic for the Russian military and police as a defeat in war. Military officers, in particular, were the last true, if troubled, believers in the core virtues and achievements of the Communist system, and specifically in the doctrine of "Soviet internationalism." Now they have lost territory, resources, equipment, strategic position, status, and privileges—and all without having had a chance to fight (except for the veterans of the Afghan War). Above all, the country and system they were sworn to defend has disappeared, and along with that any clearly defined military or security doctrine or mission.

The Russian government has been unable to give adequate pay or housing to its officers returning from Eastern Europe. Defense Minister

Pavel Grachev is reported to have distributed hard currency in cash when he visits Russian officers in the field. Draft evasion has become the norm, and fewer than 50 percent of draftees report for duty. Sergei Stepashin, former chairman of the parliament's defense committee and now head of the FSK, the successor to the KGB, commented acidly that the Russian army is becoming an "all-volunteer army, consisting of officers only." There is not sufficient fuel to power ships or planes, and vast fleets sit at anchor. Much advanced ground equipment, not to mention nuclear missiles and warheads, was lost to Ukraine. At this moment, the Russian military can no longer field a world-class fighting force.[2]

The policy of Yeltsin and the Russian government toward the military and the security police has been consistently careful and respectful from the first. Yeltsin has reined back attempts to purge the officer corps or to downgrade either institution. Within the limits of his finances he has attempted to cushion the fall in officers' living standards. There are still over 2,200 generals and 690,000 officers for an army of less than 1.5 million, and lately the number of generals has been growing again.

Yeltsin has not prevented senior officers from speaking out on political topics. In 1992–93 Defense Minister Grachev differed sharply from the Ministry of Foreign Affairs on such topics as the Baltics, Armenia, the Kurile Islands, and the Transdniester region of Moldova. In practice, Russia's military commanders have played a more influential role in day-to-day Russian policy toward the former Soviet republics than have Russia's official diplomats. Since the December 1993 elections, the entire Russian political establishment has shifted toward greater nationalism. The Ministry of Foreign Affairs has moved over to the positions of the Ministry of Defense. As Muscovites say, "Smolensk Square now sounds like Arbat Square."

In many respects the Russian military and the security police remain states within a state. The military and the security forces still command large blocks of property in the form of parks, sanatoria, dachas, housing, clubs, bases, schools, and institutes. There have been many charges recently that senior officers have been selling these properties into private hands—or their own. But Yeltsin has so far refused to open an investigation that would embarrass his senior officers. Both the military and the security forces have resisted internal reform, and as time goes on this resistance is likely to grow.

The functions of the former KGB have been diminished but have not disappeared, by any means. In fact, the agency has been given some new jobs. The security forces have been enlisted to fight smuggling and corruption, and to protect Russia's economic security (as Western companies know well, since their own electronics experts tell them their Moscow offices are being closely watched). Undercover informers and "officers on active reserve" (i.e., KGB officers seconded to other agencies, usually secretly) are still on the payrolls, and there have been no witch-hunts, unlike east Germany.

Yeltsin's careful treatment of the military and the security forces paid off in September-October 1993, when the senior military commanders rallied to his support and crushed the parliament and the Red-Brown allies. Yet one should be cautious about reading too much into the high command's support for Yeltsin. It was given after considerable hesitation, and only after civil order in Moscow had broken down. Only a handful of élite units were involved. In the future, the problems of the military and the police will continue, and their loyalty will inevitably remain a central question mark.

That may explain why Yeltsin has recently taken steps, for the first time, to shake up the ex-KGB and put it under closer presidential control. In December 1993, he stripped the KGB of its prisons and its criminal investigators, cutting the official complement of the agency nearly in half. At the same time, he changed its name from the Ministry of Security to the more innocuous-sounding "Federal Counterintelligence Service," or FSK. In March 1994, he appointed the 42-year-old Sergei Stepashin to oversee the new FSK and complete its revamp. This is the first time that Yeltsin has reached outside the ranks of the professional *chekisty* (as KGB officers used to like to call themselves, after the name of Lenin's Cheka, or Extraordinary Commission).[3]

On the military side, Yeltsin and his prime minister have been standing firm against the pleas of the military and the defense industry for higher budget allocations. This has been a surprise to observers who were sure that Yeltsin would have to pay his debts to the military for their support in the fall of 1993.

Nevertheless, in the long run the government has little choice but to continue to give sympathetic attention to the needs and views of the military and police commanders. The country faces a crime wave, extremist political groups are gaining strength, and Russia's borders are uneasy. The Russian government, in years to come, will need more intelligence and coercive power, not less.

POLITICAL PARTIES: LEFT OR RIGHT?

Political parties in Russia are still small and weak. Most Russian parties lack a strong social base and do not yet play the same prominent role as parties in the United States or Western Europe. Some of the functions that parties have traditionally performed in the West, such as transmitting opinions and interests from society into politics, are falling to the new industrial and professional associations instead. The mass media also substitute for parties to some extent, by influencing public opinion and bringing new political figures into the public eye, such as the Russian fascist leader, Vladimir Zhirinovskii, who is a product of television.

Until 1990, the Soviet Union was a one-party dictatorship, that of the Communist Party. In that year Gorbachev took the fateful step of altering the Soviet constitution to end the monopoly of the Communist Party and legalize other parties, but the 1990 elections to the Russian parliament (and local parliaments in the provinces) took place before new parties had a chance to organize or to play any significant role. Under the electoral rules used in 1990 legislative elections, nominating authority was reserved to "workers' collectives" and "public organizations" (such as labor unions or research institutes). Parties could not nominate candidates, and therefore remained weak.

The next three years gave Russian parties little further opportunity to develop. Between 1990 and 1993 there were no legislative elections. Unlike the East European countries, which had held "founding elections" shortly after their communist regimes fell, Russia did not hold a founding election until two years later.

By the beginning of 1993, there were some 50 "proto-parties" in Russia. But most of these groupings were really the personal followings of individual politicians, most of whom had emerged only in the previous three years. Almost none of these "proto-parties" had a clearly formulated platform or program. None had any real national organization. They shifted, split, and recombined, according to the tactical whims of their leaders, who were absorbed in the political game in Moscow and gave little attention to building organizations.

The only partial exception was the Russian Communist Party, which was relegalized in late 1992, after having been banned in the fall of 1991 following the August coup. By 1993 it claimed 500,000 newly registered members. All other parties combined claimed fewer than 300,000, probably a substantial overestimate.

The electoral campaign of the fall of 1993, following the dissolution of parliament, gave Russian politicians, for the first time, a real incentive to organize themselves. An electoral law, promulgated by Yeltsin, created a mixed system of representation: half of the deputies to the lower house of parliament were to be elected from party lists (which encouraged new parties to emerge to try their luck), the other half under a "winner-take-all" single-member system (which encouraged parties to combine into electoral blocs). As further incentives to fusion, parties had to gather a required number of signatures to be officially registered for the campaign, and had to obtain 5 percent of the total vote to be represented in the parliament.

For the first time, parties mattered. They nominated the candidates to the party lists. In the single-member districts, many candidates sought party labels. Thus, the December 1993 election was the "founding election," marking the true birth of party politics in Russia.

Thirteen electoral blocs obtained the required number of popular signatures and were registered to participate in the campaign. Of those, eight succeeded in getting at least 5 percent of the vote and obtaining seats in the lower house of the new parliament. But the election returns astounded all observers and the players themselves: the democratic-reformist wing, which had been favored to win handsomely, garnered barely 60 out of 225 seats. The industrialist center, which had also been expected to do well, was crushed, and as a result is virtually absent from the parliament.

The big shock of the election was the sweeping success of the extremist and reactionary parties. Zhirinovskii's Liberal Democratic Party gained 59 seats. The Communist Party and its ally, the Agrarian Party, won 53 between them. Though the lopsided victory of the "Red-Browns" was diluted somewhat by the better performance of the middle in the single-member races, the democratic reformers did no better there than on the party lists.

The December 12 election was a landmark in other respects as well. Television proved to be a crucial resource, and no one used it better than Vladimir Zhirinovskii, while the government made little use of its potential power to deny the medium to the opposition. On live national television, Zhirinovskii played to Russians' prejudices with a comedian's unerring timing. At a televised public meeting, when quizzed about reports that his father was Jewish, Zhirinovskii quipped, without a moment's hesitation, "Those reports are false. My mother was Russian. My father was a lawyer." Russians chuckled all the way to the polls.

Private money also became an important factor in the December 1993 election for the first time. Politics is still cheap in Russia; a winning campaign cost only about $8,000. But that is a princely sum in today's Russia, and the central budget provided only 5 times that amount for an entire party. Candidates openly solicited private money, and the new Russian capitalists responded generously. The rules on campaign donations are still lax: though they limit private donations to individual candidates to $1200 apiece, there is practically no enforcement mechanism. For the same reason, there is little information available about which sides various private donors chose to support in the campaign. In many cases, Russian businessmen donated to several groups simultaneously, for political insurance, or gave money on the basis of prior friendships. For example, Vladimir Gusinskii, head of the powerful MOST financial group, was formerly an economist working in a think tank headed by Grigorii Yavlinskii, co-founder of the "Yabloko" Party. MOST donated heavily—but not exclusively—to Yabloko.

The two years that elapsed before Russia had its "founding election" had fateful consequences. After two years of chaotic half-reforms, any popular consensus that might have been mustered for rapid marketization had disappeared. The losers had found a voice—or several voices— in politicians like Vladimir Zhirinovskii and Gennadii Zyuganov, the chairman of the Communist Party. For this, Yeltsin must bear much of the blame. He could have held elections in the spring of 1992, and won handsomely. His reasons for not doing so remain a mystery.

What is the future of Russian parties after the December 1993 election? Despite predictions that the deputies to the Duma would abandon their party labels as soon as they were elected, that has not yet happened—mainly because the Duma has adopted an internal rule forbidding members to change groupings. But within each major bloc in the parliament cracks are rapidly appearing, as politicians already begin to position themselves for the next round of legislative elections in late 1995.

The main lesson of the December 1993 campaign is that any politician who hopes to win must develop a grassroots organization and master the art of television politics. But neither task will be easy between elections. Private money has dried up, amid a chorus of complaints from Russian businessmen that their campaign contributions bought them little influence, and that politicians now ignore them. Yeltsin's advisors are urging him to restrict the number of parties, tighten the rules for registration of parties before elections, and monitor their finances more strictly.[4]

In sum, the next stage in the growth of Russian parties will not come until the next round of elections, and it will depend on the electoral rules adopted for the campaign.

In the meantime, Russian observers point to the fact that mainstream Russian politicians are rapidly growing more pragmatic, because they increasingly represent interest groups rather than isolated personalities. This is causing professional politicians to converge toward the center and to talk of accommodation with one another. This could lead to the emergence of several large electoral blocs in coming years, representing various flavors of more or less conservative economic reform.

In contrast, extremist groups continue to organize at the fringes of the political system, but they remain fragmented into a bewildering variety of small groups. The neo-Nazis in Saint Petersburg, for example, go under the names of the Russian Guard, the Russian Party, the Venedov Union, the Popular Social Party, the National Democratic Party, and many others.[5] Vladimir Zhirinovskii is attempting to consolidate his Liberal Democratic Party (LDPR) into a tight national organization, but he too has been hampered by lack of money and by revolts among his top lieutenants. Many of the party's members jumped on Zhirinovskii's coat-tails in the 1993 campaign, and are now ready to jump off again.

Several Russian parties and politicians appear split between these two contrary trends. The Russian Communist party, for example, appears tempted to go both ways at once. Part of its membership looks and acts increasingly like moderate social democrats; others are extremists. The chairman of the Communist Party, Gennadii Zyuganov, tries to play both sides of the street.

At bottom, the weakness and instability of political parties in Russia stem from the fact that there are not yet clearly defined social or economic groups with clear political leanings. When these emerge, they may be more likely to be represented by special-interest lobby groups, local old-boy networks, or media personalities. These trends can be seen in the West as well, where the era of powerful parties may be passing. In Russia, it may never arrive.

The main point about these parties and fractions is that they have little in the way of a popular base, and they are not growing quickly, because public opinion is largely indifferent to them. This is potentially a dangerous situation, because there is little structure to form and channel public participation or to absorb public energies if they begin to spill into the political arena.

In the meantime, so long as the mass public remains largely absent from the political game, the most influential bodies are those that represent élite groups with something at stake. If politics remains largely an élite game, as it still is today, these organizations will ultimately lead to a sort of corporatist political system, in which society is represented through its main "corporate" interests—industries, farms, small business, and so on. Once popular elections are held, however, the significance of political parties will increase sharply, especially if electoral laws allow candidates to run on party lists.

PUBLIC OPINION

Public opinion is still a very weak force in Russian politics. Since a brief peak in 1989 and 1990, interest and participation in politics have dropped off sharply. Most citizens are simply apathetic; fewer than 10 percent express any interest in politics and almost none belong to parties or are otherwise politically active.

Nevertheless, elections and referenda are now real political instruments, and votes are a real political resource for politicians, or at least a threat to be manipulated and controlled. At a time of crisis such as in 1991 or 1993, local public opinion can make the difference, even if the mass of the population is passive. "Street power" may turn out to be crucial in other ways. Therefore, one cannot discount the potential role of public opinion as a "state-changing" variable, and so we present public opinion as a prime mover, however weak and uncertain it may be.

Opinion polling has come to Russia in the last five years, and a host of polling organizations has sprung up, many operating in partnership with well-known Western polling companies. But opinion polls have not become the focus that they are in the West, and opinion polls are not yet a major weapon in the arsenal of Russian politics. Like their colleagues in the West, Russian pollsters have discovered how unpredictable public opinion can be: in the referendum of April 1993, opinion polls gave little hint that Russians would come to the polls in the numbers they did or that they would give President Yeltsin and the marketizing reforms as much support as they did. Pollsters were taken even more by surprise in December 1993. Barred from taking official polls in the final weeks before the election, Russian polling organizations failed to chart the last-minute surge of the communists and nationalists. They predicted that the reformist parties would win a majority of seats in the new parliament, and failed altogether to anticipate the stunning performance of Vladimir Zhirinovskii.

ELITE OPINION AND OPINION-MAKERS

The views of economists, scientists, and journalists have been enormously influential ever since the beginning of reform in the mid-1980s, and even before. These groups have shaped state policy in two ways. Through the media and communication with policymakers, they have exerted indirect influence for some time. But as some of those élite experts become policymakers themselves, they have begun to exert direct influence on policy. Others are being bypassed, their views unsolicited, and their opinions unheeded.

Initially, under Gorbachev, most élite opinion (or at least the most vocal part of it) seemed liberal, democratic, and Western in its orientation. Now intellectual opinion appears to be shifting, as once-liberal intellectuals become disillusioned by current events and by their own loss of status. As a result, élite opinion in Russia today is highly mixed, and so is its influence on politics.

The alienation of many Russian intellectuals from the changes currently taking place in Russian society may ultimately prove to be a serious liability for the future of Russian democracy and the market. Given the revolution in social status taking place in Russia today, and the Russian government's chronic lack of funds to support its educational and research system, the intelligentsia may lose much of its traditional influence on Russian thinking—or influence it in a negative direction.

THE NEW PRIVATE SECTOR

The private sector has grown enormously since the late 1980s, even as the old state economy has shrunk. Most of Russia's small shops, restaurants, and other small businesses were privatized in 1992–93. Then came the turn of medium and large-scale enterprises. By the end of 1994 70% of these were in private hands.

But even more significant than the privatization of state property is the spontaneous rise of new private businesses where practically none existed before. Whole new branches of the economy are arising from nothing, such as computer assembly, cellular telephony, software services, truck farming, advertising, insurance—the list goes on.

What is behind this yeasty growth of the private sector is a rapid transition of the entire Russian economy from manufacturing to services, and from capital goods to consumer goods. In 1994, for the first time, the contribution of services to Russian GNP surpassed that of manufacturing. The consumer sector, long starved under the Soviets, is on its way to becoming the dominant part of the Russian economy, just as it is in the West.

The private sector is fast becoming a prime mover in several senses. It is the major force driving Russia decisively away from the Soviet past. With the Russian state still weak and unable to invest, it is the private sector that is already shaping the Russia of tomorrow.

Politically, the private sector is starting to organize itself and make its voice heard in the government. Private companies are banding together into lobby groups. Private bankers are contributing to political parties and politicians' campaigns. The views of private entrepreneurs are increasingly listened to by state functionaries, at both the national and the regional levels.

Not all of this new power is benign, by any means. The seamy underside of the private sector is the criminal world, from which no enterprise is entirely free. The power of criminals in Russia, itself a by-product of the legal void at the center of Russia's still embryonic capitalism, inhibits real legal reform and thus perpetuates itself. Criminality in Russia is one of the most powerful forces that could prevent "Muddling Down" from becoming "Chudo."

NON-PRIME MOVERS

The Federal Bureaucracy. Although it is regularly denounced in the liberal Russian press as the source of all evils in Russia today, the federal bureaucracy has shrunk considerably in power and prestige, if not necessarily in numbers, since the Soviet era. But it is still a vast jungle, consisting of hundreds of agencies, some well known but most obscure, even to Russians. Through the tens of thousands of regulations it issues each year, the federal bureaucracy can sidetrack or derail the laws and policies adopted by politicians at the top of the political system, and thus it can slow down reform or hold it up for ransom. But the federal bureaucracy is not able, on its own, to change the course of Russia as a whole from one scenario to another.

The same is even more true of the bureaucracies at the provincial and local levels. These are inherited from the old system of the "ispolkoms," as the local executives were known under the Soviets, and they were traditionally underfunded, understaffed, and quite weak. This is one of the main reasons for the general weakness of Russian government at the local level today. The local bureaucracies are most definitely not prime movers.

The Russian Orthodox Church has enjoyed a limited renaissance since the mid-1980s. Churchgoers are no longer harassed. Many churches have been reopened and refurbished. The church is expanding, and beginning to found schools and charities. But the church, like all Russian institutions, is internally divided and troubled. The upper hierarchy is viewed with some suspicion by the faithful for having coexisted with the Soviet regime. The church is increasingly identified with Russian nationalism and with conservative political forces. Lately the church enlisted the support of the former parliament to limit the activities of Protestant evangelists. In the "dissolution crisis" of autumn 1993, Patriarch Aleksii II tried to mediate between the presidential and parliamentary sides. Overall, however, the church has not yet become a major force in Russian politics. It remains heavily dependent on government funding, but the state is too poor to give it strong support.

The Former Soviet Republics and the Russian Minorities. Russia's relations with the fourteen former Soviet republics lying outside the Russian Federation, together with the approximately twenty-five million Russians living in them, will be a major source of issues and problems in decades to come. But with one major exception, the former republics are not large enough, powerful enough, or strategic enough to be prime movers in the future of Russia. That one exception is Ukraine.

The Mafia. As powerful as organized crime has become in Russia in the last few years, it is not a prime mover in the fate of Russia and will likely not become one. Although organized gangs are frequently composed of non-Russians, the ethnic groups from which many of them come (Chechens, Azeris, etc.) do not form large resident minorities within the major cities of Russia. Consequently the problem of organized crime is not tied to sensitive issues of ethnic politics at the Russian core, and gangs lack social support in the major Russian cities.

The present power of organized crime is not a cause, but an effect of larger political trends, and the strength of organized crime in the future will depend on which political path Russia follows. Under a strong Russian government, there would be little in the way of legal barriers to prevent the police and the courts from repressing organized crime quickly. The chief protection of organized crime is the greed of corrupt politicians. Organized crime is a symptom, not a prime mover.

Organized crime is currently a major economic force, and as its illicit taxation of the population continues, criminals and their protectors will grow rich indeed. At that point, one of the most important issues for the future is how the next generation of gangsters will choose to invest their gains and how they will exert control.

Extremist Groups. Communists and neo-Communists on the left, and neo-fascists on the right, are not presently prime movers in Russian politics and Russian life, but they are almost certain to become so in coming years. The likely mixture is unfortunately all too familiar: There will be a large population of uprooted, angry people. There will be easily exploitable grievances, such as resentment of the West and anger over the treatment of Russian minorities in the non-Russian republics. The political middle is likely to be weak and unstable for some time to come. And there will always be ambitious and unscrupulous people ready to try to turn this mixture into political power.

That there will be a rising tide of extremism at both ends of the political spectrum is a certainty. What is uncertain is how the center will stand up to it.

The Media have been transformed since the breakup of the Soviet Union and its elaborate system of censorship. The changes in the print media have been especially striking: new newspapers have sprung up in every Russian city, expressing every shade of political point of view.

Television has been slower to follow, yet in addition to the two national state-owned channels, several private television companies have appeared in Moscow, as well as a bevy of local ones. The most noteworthy new national station is the Independent Television Station (NTS), founded by a former expert on U.S. foreign policy, Igor Malashenko, and backed by three private Russian banks. The vigorous efforts of the legislative branch and the various opposition movements to seize control of television and key newspapers show what a critical political resource they have become. The decisive moment in October 1993 came when the paramilitary groups sought to occupy the Ostankino television tower. However, by themselves, the media, precisely because they are divided and their independence is uncertain, cannot force a change in the scenarios on their own.

Labor Unions and Strike Committees. Labor unions are not currently prime movers on the Russian political scene, although they could become so in the future.

Labor unions were an important part of the Soviet system of rule—but on the side of the regime and the factory managers. The labor unions were the administrators of the welfare system inside the enterprise, and as such were not without influence. But when the Soviet system broke up, the centralized labor union system weakened. In many localities, the traditional labor unions were completely discredited and have been displaced by locally organized "strike committees" (*stachkomy*).

Western Governments and Institutions are not included on the list of prime movers. They certainly have an important role in Russia's future. In the end, however, external actors on their own lack the power to change the fundamentals of Russia's underlying situation. In other words, the Russians will make their own future. But they can be helped or inspired by the outside, or troubled by the outside, or dismayed by the failure of the outside to support reform at critical times and in critical ways. For example, if the Russian monetary system collapsed, the International Monetary Fund (IMF) would surely play a major role in determining how the crisis was resolved. But it would not have caused the crisis.

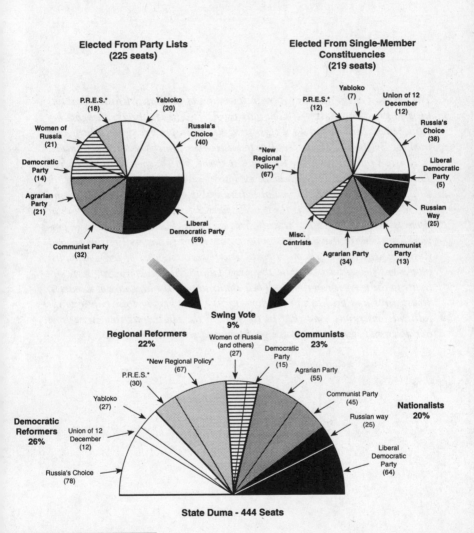

The State Duma 1994

Elected From Party Lists (225 seats)

P.R.E.S.* (18)
Yabloko (20)
Women of Russia (21)
Russia's Choice (40)
Democratic Party (14)
Agrarian Party (21)
Liberal Democratic Party (59)
Communist Party (32)

Elected From Single-Member Constituencies (219 seats)

Yabloko (7)
P.R.E.S.* (12)
Union of 12 December (12)
"New Regional Policy" (67)
Russia's Choice (38)
Liberal Democratic Party (5)
Russian Way (25)
Misc. Centrists
Agrarian Party (34)
Communist Party (13)

Swing Vote 9%

Regional Reformers 22%

Women of Russia (and others) (27)

Communists 23%

"New Regional Policy" (67)
Democratic Party (15)
Agrarian Party (55)
P.R.E.S.* (30)
Communist Party (45)
Yabloko (27)
Nationalists 20%
Russian way (25)
Democratic Reformers 26%
Union of 12 December (12)
Liberal Democratic Party (64)
Russia's Choice (78)

State Duma - 444 Seats

Source: Cambridge Energy Research Associates, FSU Watch

* P.R.E.S.-Party of Russian Unity and Accord

99

The ancient Greeks saw the future in the hands of the Fates. Russian peasants liked to say "Bog dast"—"God will provide." The Bolsheviks thought they knew better: "history" and the class struggle would provide, with a little help from the Bolsheviks. Westerners like to believe they can choose their own future.

Russia's future may be the Russians' to choose, but the choice will not be free. The previous chapters examined the explosive driving forces emerging from the collapse of the one-party Communist dictatorship, the command economy, and the Soviet empire, as well as the prime movers. In the next chapters we look at elements that are, for all practical purposes, given. History will indeed "provide"—not in the way the Bolsheviks expected, but rather by limiting choices. Russia is still in the grip of its past. It will bear the scars of the Communist experiment for decades. Despite the forces pushing Russia forward, there are limits to the ways it can change. These limits are, in the language of scenarios, "constraints and predetermined outcomes." We turn first in this chapter to the political constraints, and then in the next to the constraints that arise from economics and society, and to the predetermined elements, the givens.

7

That the Guard Not Tire

Prior to 1991, Russia's experience of democracy was very brief. In January 1918, the Constituent Assembly, elected by popular suffrage, met at four P.M. in the Tavricheskii Palace in St. Petersburg. The majority of the delegates belonged not to the Bolsheviks, who had seized power in a coup two months before, but to a rival party. Lenin himself arrived at the palace, determined to disperse the Assembly and consolidate the Bolsheviks' grip. For the next several hours, his eyes "distended and aflame," he masterminded the Bolshevik strategy. At ten P.M., after hours of speeches and wrangling and jeers, Lenin left, confident that events were going his way. Later, the rest of the Bolsheviks walked out.

As the delegates continued their debates past midnight and into early-morning hours, others departed as well. At four A.M., the chairman of the assembly was proclaiming the abolition of private property in land. At that moment, a sailor who was commander of the assembly's guards mounted the tribune and touched the chairman on the back.

"The guard is tired," he said. "All those present should leave the Assembly Hall."

When there were protests, the commander forcefully ordered that the hall be vacated immediately. Shortly thereafter, the Constituent Assembly was adjourned. It was scheduled to meet at five in the afternoon. But it never convened again.[1]

The Communist regime reduced all subsequent legislative elections to an empty ritual, and for the next seventy-one years the Constituent Assembly remained a historical oddity, Russia's last popularly elected legislature.

Is this going to be the fate of democracy again in Russia? To many people in the West, military dictatorship or some other authoritarian system sounds like an only too plausible outcome of the present revolution. It will be an enormously difficult task to build democracy in Russia, based on such a past. Yet it is not impossible.

Russia is a unique political case. No other country went so far toward building a truly totalitarian state for such a length of time. No other country had so elaborate a ruling ideology; none went so far in uprooting a market economy and private enterprise; none made so systematic an attempt to smash society and to replace every part of it with agencies of the state; none waged all-out war on its own people, killing or exiling tens of millions and then holding the rest in a tight police grip. None conquered so extensive an empire. Other regimes—Hitler's Germany, Mao's China—have matched the Soviet Union in many aspects, but only the Russian Bolsheviks did it all for so long a time.

Can the Russian people escape from such a tyranny, for good?

On the face of it, the odds against the evolution of democracy in Russia are daunting. Russia has never lived under a democracy. Though it has a new constitution, its institutions are mostly inherited from the Soviet period, and the rule of law is but a gleam in the eye of a handful of Russian liberals. The potential enemies of democracy are many—nationalist-fascists, Communists, and undoubtedly more than a few officers, bureaucrats, and factory workers. Perhaps the greatest enemies of all are the masses of skeptical souls in Russia itself, who do not believe democracy can exist in their country.

Moreover, the present circumstances are unpromising. As a result of the collapse of the Soviet order, Russia inherits a weak political system. It has little authority, its power is divided, and there is no social consensus behind it. It is easier for politicians to use their political trumps to block and attack one another than to act together.

In poll after poll, Russians speak of their longing for order and a leader. The word *demokrat* has become synonymous in the public mind with "irresponsible talker" and "thief" (*demokrad*). And in the midst of all this, the economy continues its ghastly decline, savaging a whole population's savings, security, and hopes. Can this be fertile soil for democracy?

All in all, there are severe political constraints on the organization of a market economy and the building of a constitutional order. Yet the Russians do not have the luxury of waiting a century for the proper "mores and manners" (as Montaigne once put it) to evolve by themselves. If stable institutions do not soon emerge, Russian politics will degrade toward the cruder forms of power, corruption, and coercion, wielded by demagogues and extremists, who will exploit the power of the mob in the streets or disaffected military and police units.

Yet, despite the risks, there is also opportunity. It is precisely the present weakened state and the political paralysis in Moscow that create an opening for the evolution of Russian society and politics toward democracy and the market.

There are four main issues to be confronted: the initial building and testing of democratic institutions; the rule of law; the relations of the military and the police to democracy; and the rise of democratic culture.

CREATING DEMOCRATIC INSTITUTIONS: THE FIRST HURDLE

Russia today is a pre-democracy. There are no settled rules and most of the people are not represented in the government. The game of politics is being waged by a small handful of players, consisting mostly of former members of the Soviet nomenklatura. There is as yet little role for interest groups and parties representing broad social groups. Politics in Russia is still largely a game of élite politics, as described in chapter six—played out against a countrywide battle for power, revenues, and property.

It is perhaps a hopeful sign that most of the political jousting is not primarily ideological. Rather, politicians are battling for material advantage. That may make them more willing to strike bargains with one another. But over time, increasingly ideological motives will come into Russian politics, as popular resentment builds over the inequalities engendered by private enterprise and the market and over the conspicuous consumption of the new rich.

One hopeful development is that after three years of political warfare, Russia's politicians have begun to show some willingness to compromise with one another. It took the shock of the shelling of the White House in October 1993, but Russia now has a constitution, which has calmed down the political game. However, the constitution of December 1993 may well turn out to be more like a treaty or an armistice than a durable set of rules for conducting politics. Russia could well go through more than one constitution between now and 2010.

In the coming half decade, as privatization proceeds, the current alliance of manager and worker will split and militant labor unions could well rise to defend the workers' interests, while the managers develop stronger business associations and lobby groups. Meanwhile, groups that are currently demoralized and divided, and thus largely on the sidelines of politics, may find a common and more assertive voice. Such groups include the military and the police.

Russian politics could become more unstable and competitive, not less, and more class-based and ideological, as players enter the ring who represent the deep-seated emotions and interests of broad social groups. These powerful latecomers to politics will not have been parties to the first round of institution-building, and they will not owe any particular allegiance to those institutions. This second phase will be a powerful test of the institutions built in the preceding years.

There are two main dangers. The first is that massive social movements, representing the have-nots of the new Russian society, will form large national parties. If such parties win elections and form a government, they may use their power to try to redistribute incomes and bring the new private sector to heel. This could put an end to liberal economic reform and to progress toward a free market.

The second danger is that the new haves of the private business class may ally themselves with the current political élite and form a broad coalition with the military and police to keep popular movements under control. This is the point at which Russia will be most vulnerable to taking an authoritarian turn.

In this new phase of political tensions, the institution that may come under the greatest pressure will be the judicial system. How strong will it be by then?

THE RULE OF LAW: BEYOND "LEGAL NIHILISM"

The foundations for a strong judiciary and the rule of law, which are an essential part of democracy in Western countries, remain very weak in Russia. An elaborate legal system actually existed in the Soviet Union. Jurists and police officials in the 1930s combined Leninism, European civil law, and Russian tradition into a legal amalgam that was designed exclusively to serve the state and the political purposes of its leaders. Laws were often mostly window dressing. Actual administrative decision making was based on tens of thousands of so-called "sub-laws" (*podzakonnye akty*), issued by any number of government agencies. Most of these sub-laws were secret. (In this world-behind-the-mirror system, a plaintiff could sue on the basis of such a sub-law if he could prove its existence in court!)

Soviet judges were anything but independent; they knew that in cases of any significance they were to check with the local headquarters of the Communist party apparatus before deciding on a verdict; this practice came to be known as "telephone justice."

The Soviet legal system was thus highly politicized in every sphere, but where the interest of the state was directly engaged, even the semblance of due process went out the window. The existence of such a "zone of state interest," where the sphere of law shrank accordingly, was one of the most important features defining the Soviet system as totalitarian. Today, Russians sarcastically sum up the main principle of Soviet legal practice as "legal nihilism."

Gorbachev began to change the basis of the legal system, with his push for a "state of laws." But it is one thing to proclaim this principle, quite another to apply it. Clearly, it will be a long time before the Russian legal system has what it takes to support a strong society or a democratic state.

To begin with, the laws themselves are inadequate. The technical quality of the laws being written by legislatures at all levels is poor. For much of their legal business Russian jurists are still operating with Soviet-era laws. The result is a legal vacuum. As Veniamin Yakovlev, the chairman of the Higher Arbitration Court (the highest Russian court for economic matters) exclaimed, "We are being asked to solve complex equations in multiple unknowns without so much as a multiplication table to guide us."[2] The central mission of the parliament elected in 1993 is to create the vast array of founding "laws" required by the new state and a market economy.

Implementation is the next hurdle. Russian governmental agencies continue to issue an abundance of rules and regulations. There is no Russian equivalent of the *Federal Register,* where the daily output of such agency actions is published. The notion of a public hearing is still exotic to Russian bureaucrats' ears. The accountability of Russian agencies to the public, or even to other branches of government, is only weakly established, even in theory. The spirit of the system remains resolutely statist.

As for the independence of Russian judges, "telephone justice" is no longer what it was, because the old party line has gone dead. Russian judges have been granted tenure to age sixty-five and have been given the power to nominate and discipline their colleagues. But that does not mean that Russian judges are any more independent in practice; in most Russian provinces, the local governor or the chairman of the local duma is a strong political figure, and smart judges continue to gauge the wind before issuing verdicts. Their perquisites, their housing, their automobiles, all come from the federal government or the province administration.

The Russian legal system is far smaller than that of a free-market civil society. There are about twelve thousand judges, twenty thousand prosecutors, thirty-six thousand "lawyers" (*advokaty*), and five thousand notaries. The litigious United States, where the number of lawyers has doubled in the last twenty-five years and there is now one lawyer for every three hundred people, is not necessarily everyone's model of the right lawyer-to-citizen ratio. But Russia has one lawyer for every four thousand people. These numbers suggest that the legal profession in Russia will have to grow before it can serve a free-market economy and a "government of laws, not of men."

At the same time, because of its Soviet traditions, the Russian judiciary may simply go on doing what it has always done: defending the state and whoever is master of it. This in itself is not fatal to democracy. What really counts is that the state itself, and the major state institutions, including the military and the secret police, must accept being bound by the state's own laws. That is ultimately the central question: Will they?

CIVIL-MILITARY RELATIONS

We have already examined the critical role of the military and police as prime movers. The military is under great stress as it grapples with its post-imperial role and its loss of primacy and status. The military will play a crucial role in the development of democracy, either by supporting the democratic process, or by interrupting it. The Russian military comes at this with a tradition of acceding to higher authority—the state and the party—but no experience at all of coexisting with a civil society and democratic control. In addition, it has yet to define its own purpose in the aftermath of the breakup of the Soviet state.

All this means that civil-military relations will be a critical constraint on the evolution of democracy in Russia. The future of those relations will depend on four things:

- Tension would rise if the military came to believe that there is an imminent threat to national interests and that the civilian leadership is not responding. Tensions would also develop if the military found itself thrust more and more into the demoralizing role of maintaining internal order, rather than defending national borders.
- If the military becomes a small, closed, all-volunteer force, the result could be a social wall and rising hostility between the military and the civilian worlds. A contributing cause of such isolation would be a growing gap in living standards between an impoverished officer corps and an increasingly comfortable and materialistic civilian society. However, the officer corps may not remain poor for long.
- The Soviet military was loosely controlled by the apparatus of the Communist party, but those instruments have disappeared, and their replacements (Security Council, parliamentary committees) are of uncertain strength and views. A move to appoint a civilian defense minister was defeated by military objections. There is no particular evidence that civilians have broken the military monopoly on information. At this point, the outlook for civilian oversight is not very good, although a form of it may exist in the penetration of the military by the FSK, which then reports to the civilian leadership.
- As Russian pride returns, respect for the military will surely rise as well, but much will depend on how the "pride factor" plays out. If tomorrow's Russia is hostile toward the West and resentful of the West's role, hostile toward its neighbors, jingoistic in defense of Russian national minorities outside its borders, then the Russian government may be correspondingly pro-military, officers will be members of the government, and the regime could become militaristic.

Whatever political form it takes, the military-and-police factor will be an inescapable mortgage on the future of Russia, a legacy of the war state from which Russia has just emerged and of the torn society that Russia is likely to be for the coming generation.

NO DEMOCRACY WITHOUT DEMOCRATS

When all is said and done, the prospects for democracy will depend on the quality of the human material, the civic values of the community, the attitudes of individuals. In the long run, there can be no democracy without democrats, without a democratic culture.

Many of the traits Russians show in political dealings with one another are not especially democratic. Leaders usually feel superior to ordinary citizens, and citizens typically relate to leaders as clients to patrons. Since most people are someone else's client or subordinate, the buck tends to be passed up to the top, and top-ranking officials are besieged with requests for favors.

Feelings of mutual trust and tolerance are low, not only among different nationalities but even among neighbors and colleagues. Most everyone is convinced that corruption is the norm, and most everyone demands sterner discipline. The time-honored motto of most Russian politicians seems to be "Do lest you be done unto." An offer to compromise is frequently seen not as a way of resolving a problem but as a sign of weakness. People traditionally form circles of friends in self-defense against the state, to beat the law rather than influence the making of it.

On the whole, apart from a brief surge of interest in the late 1980s, much of the Russian population shows little interest in public issues and expresses great contempt for politicians and politics, while simultaneously surrendering the initiative to them. A classic expression in Russia is *"Nachal'stvu luchshe vidno,"* or roughly translated, "The bosses know better." Because most people's experience in actual local politics is small, their political sophistication and competence and their ability to get things done are low. Most people feel powerless and exploited, but still do not imagine that it is possible to improve matters through their own political initiative.

GROUNDS FOR OPTIMISM?

Not an encouraging picture, on the whole. But it would be astonishing indeed if it were any different, since Russians emerged so recently from a near-totalitarian dictatorship. What chance is there that the quality of the Russian "civic community" will improve? There are four grounds for optimism.

First, the core of the Russian Federation is now largely Russian. This relative ethnic homogeneity should help in providing a foundation for democracy. One frequently hears that Russia is about to break up. A more sophisticated but hardly more comforting view holds that "if Russia is democratic, it will not remain whole. If Russia remains whole, it will not be democratic." But in fact, the situation may not be nearly so dire. Unlike the old Soviet Union, in which Russians made up barely 50 percent of the population, the Russian Federation, as we observed earlier, is now over 80 percent ethnically Russian. Of the so-called twenty-one "autonomous republics" of the Russian Federation, in only six does the titular non-Russian nationality constitute a majority of the population. Most of those are in the north Caucasus—troublesome, but not strategically vital to the survival of Russia or of Russian democracy.

Second, the Russian economy may start growing again before long. Economic growth provides a more fertile soil for democracy than economic decline.

Third, many of the political skills needed for democratic politics do exist among educated citizens. Russian managers and administrators, for example, developed considerable political skills in the Soviet period. Russia has many educated people. Political skills can be learned, competence quickly acquired, self-confidence quickly built up.

The fourth is the burden of history. With the disappearance of the walls around the Soviet Union, Russians can easily look at the rest of the world. As they do so, they can see how their past cheated them out of a better life, and they do not want the new opportunity to be stolen from them.

One must be realistic about what it will take to build a democratic system. There *is* a road to democracy in Russia. It is a long and narrow one, with sharp drops on either side. To say that is simply to recognize the enormous difficulties posed by the threefold collapse that is the central theme of this book. Democracy is a long-term process. Success or failure is measured not in years but in decades. The hope is that this time the "guard" will not grow tired.

8

The Rough Road to the Market

"Everything we built, everything our fathers and grandfathers built, will end up belonging to someone from some unknown place. Where does the money come from?"

—*Ex-reformer*

"We need neither hyperinflation nor a turbulent country."
—*Prime Minister Viktor Chernomyrdin*

"Russia is living through the toughest phase of its transition."
—*Russian Deputy Prime Minister*

People living in the Western world may not readily grasp just how formidable the obstacles are to building a free-market economy. It is man's instinct, Adam Smith once argued in his classic *The Wealth of Nations,* "to truck, barter, and exchange." But these are not the same thing as a modern market economy. A market economy is not simply something one chooses; its organization has to evolve. Getting the pieces in place in Russia will take a long time.

Modern market capitalism is a complex machine that, in the West, grew up over centuries, developing by trial and error, frequently disastrous ones. No one has ever tried to build a market economy from scratch before. Russians themselves are only just beginning to realize how utterly different a market system is from a command economy. The recent experience of the Eastern European ex-socialist countries, and Russia's current economic turmoil, tell us that building a market economy is not, as the Russian expression has it, "simply like walking across a field."

It is particularly in economic life that Russians find themselves feeling that they are with Alice "in the world behind the mirror." For everything seems to have become so inverted and confusing. The danger is that they may take the distorted reflection of the market that they see on the other side of the mirror and turn resentfully and angrily against it.

THE MARKET SYSTEM

Modern market systems come in many forms. In the American system, government is distinct from the private sector. In the classic Latin American model (though now undergoing change owing to privatization and liberalization), the state is directly and heavily involved in the economy. State-owned enterprises account for a substantial part, perhaps even the greater part, of gross national product, and the state intervenes in other sectors. Private enterprise coexists with this large state sector, often as a client. In the Asian model, the invisible hand is substantially supplanted by the "guiding hand" of the government, which seeks to determine strategic directions and investment, manages competition, and sometimes even seeks to guide many of the more mundane, day-to-day decisions. The German model emphasizes the "social market," with the banks playing a central, strategic role in the economy, while the French market has very strong central direction from a coterie of civil servants.

A market system can exist with low inflation or with high inflation. It can deliver high growth rates or stagnation. It can be made up of a legal "white" economy and an illegal, unregulated "black" economy. And, as must be noted, the market is not synonymous with democracy, and indeed can function in an autocratic political system.

In the real world, there is no "perfect" or "ideal" market system, as there is in theory, nor is there any absolutely "correct" recipe. Markets are very much colored by the kinds of societies in which they emerge, by the particular institutions and traditions that provide their context. Yet, in a rough-and-ready fashion, we can point to certain basic features that do define a modern market system, the identification of which helps us to understand how difficult is Russia's road to the market.

At the heart of the market system is a competitive price mechanism. Prices are mainly determined by the bidding of buyers and sellers in the marketplace, reflecting their own perceptions of their interests and the forces of supply and demand. Prices, not the decisions of bureaucrats, signal the relative value of raw materials, labor, goods, and ideas. These various "factors" can move about relatively freely, in response to prices and demand.

A second element is generally agreed-upon "rules of the game" that underpin behavior in the marketplace and bring some predictability to it. They determine the control and very meaning of private property. These may include general values, such as people's acceptance that the market is not a corrupter, but rather a good thing, and that businessmen are not parasites and vampires, but rather contribute to the overall weal through their particular activities. These rules also include norms. For instance, instead of putting murder contracts out on people who don't pay their bills, one goes to court. The rules also get down to specific laws and regulations: for instance, insider trading may be prohibited; royalties are paid to inventors and authors; interest rates are clearly revealed to would-be borrowers.

Third, a market system is embedded in a legal, cultural, and institutional context that supports market activity. Among the most critical elements are protection for contracts and property rights, and a functioning credit system. A central requirement in the years ahead—perhaps the single most critical one for a market system—will be the working out of a meaning for "property," not only for ownership, strictly speaking, but also for access and use.

THE BAZAAR VERSUS THE MARKET

Stacked up against this checklist, Russia is still far from a market economy. The greatest success story so far is the freeing of prices. But while most prices are officially decontrolled, they may still be unofficially controlled through such things as profit margin guidelines, local regulations, trade regulations, and quotas. There is not yet a nationwide market for labor, and that for capital is only beginning. The state is in confusion about what its role in the economy will be. There are no rules of the game, nor any mechanism for enforcing them were they to exist. Market values hardly seem widespread; no doubt a majority of the people still fear them. Old Communists and new extreme rightwing nationalists regard the market as an evil, perpetrated from the outside. Property rights based upon explicit legal protection do not yet exist, nor does the legal basis for contracts.

And there is hardly any tradition or social memory on which to draw. Russia was developing a market system prior to the Bolshevik revolution. In fact, some historians regard the years from the 1880s to the beginning of World War I, when Russia industrialized rapidly, as the country's first "economic miracle."[1] Russia had another, brief, and partial experience with the market under Lenin's New Economic Policy (NEP), but that was terminated by the end of the 1920s.[2] Anybody who participated in the NEP as an adult (and managed to survive the Stalinist terror against the "Nepmen") would be in his or her nineties today—not exactly the age, alas, at which one takes on entrepreneurial risk.

It is, of course, still very early in the new Russian revolution—after all, only two years have passed since the Soviet Union collapsed. In that time, the development of market elements has certainly moved, promoted by privatization as much as anything else. But the working-out of the market system will take a number of years. It will require the creation of an entire body of rules and laws now missing, as well as the development of "market skills," and will be the subject of bitter controversy, nasty accusations, and tough bargaining. The development of the market will encounter crises and cause turmoil along the way, and will, no doubt, need police power to enforce that part of the rules of the game known as the criminal law.[3]

Many Russians think that they are already witnessing, or experiencing, capitalism, and this is what they expect it is all about. And the "Wild East" business scene in Russia today—the real-estate speculation, the protection rackets, the instant fortunes, the overnight minting of uncapitalized banks, the unregulated exports, the payoffs—is certainly a form of capitalism. But it is far from the modern market economy. Still to come are all the elements described above. This disparity is what some Russians have in mind when they say that the Russian economy today is "a bazaar, but not a market."

THE BURDEN OF THE PAST

Russia has made some of the tough choices that will eventually get it to the market, but others it has not. Extricating itself from the past will be, in many ways, the toughest job. As it struggles to do so, the Russian economy will be inefficient for some time to come.

The Soviet command economy had a powerful inner logic and language all its own, which made the Soviet system more than just foreign, but rather like some distant civilization. Its customs seemed altogether strange, but they did make sense once you understood them in context. Two generations of Russians were raised on that logic and language, and the whole economy was built on them. That is why it is so hard to undo the legacy and to build what amounts to a completely new civilization.

Consider the economy's physical attributes—the factories, the railroads, and so forth. The entire Soviet system was organized around heavy industry and defense. Most of the economy's output came from gigantic state monopolies. Each major type of product, whether tractor or reactor, came from only one or two enterprises that served the entire USSR. This helps to explain why the breakup of the USSR was so devastating for the economy. To take just one example, Russia today makes a lot of hay. But it makes no hay balers. The Soviet Union's only producer of hay balers was located in Kyrgyzstan, which is now an independent nation.

The output of these monopolies was shipped over enormous distances to other monopolies. In such a system railroads and pipelines made more sense than trucks, and thus the Soviet Union built the world's most heavily used rail and pipeline systems, but very few roads.

In this bureaucratic, nonmarket system, who needed to communicate with anyone except superiors and subordinates? So every ministry and industry had its own internal telephone system, which did not connect to anyone else's telephone system. Every industrial giant built its own housing and ran its own welfare system. This added to costs, but who looked at costs in a system that only rewarded increases in output? For the same reason, the Soviets kept old factories and machines going forever. Many Russian manufacturing towns are practically industrial museums, with some plants dating back to before the 1917 revolution. Every enterprise tried to be as independent of unreliable suppliers as possible; thus nearly every large factory has its own inefficient foundry and wasteful generating plant.

This inherited stock of plants, railroads, and their infrastructure is quite unsuited to the needs of a market economy. For instance, in the energy sector, the gas distribution system is equipped to serve large factories, not the needs of small businesses and households. The oil refinery system produces fuel oil for large power plants, but not enough gasoline or diesel fuel for the automobile revolution that has already begun. There are not enough roads even to begin serving a market economy. It is as though Russia had only large arteries but no capillaries.

All this is what Russia inherited, and there is very little the Russians can quickly do about it. They will have to live with it for a long time. There is not enough wealth in Russia today to tear down the old factories and replace them, or to build a vast network of roads and telephone lines overnight. What may be different is a wholly new telecommunications system, leaping over the existing one, and the widespread dispersion of computers and information technology.

Owing to the nature of the Soviet economy, the cities have too many industrial workers, by some estimates by as many as 20 million. As Russian heavy industry shrinks down in coming years, as it must, these people will have to be retrained for completely different jobs. But they will have to be rehoused as well, because the new jobs will not be located in the company towns where most of them currently live.

Yet housing is perhaps the scarcest thing in Russia today, as it was throughout the Soviet period. And because housing is in such woefully short supply, very little of it will be torn down. Most people will still be badly housed. The downtown areas of the larger cities will acquire a brighter look as buildings are turned into offices and luxury apartments, and there will be a suburban housing boom around the peripheries of large cities. (It has already begun, especially around Moscow.) But most of urban Russia will still look gray and shabby. The lack of decent housing will be one of the greatest obstacles to the growth of an efficient market, one in which workers can move to follow jobs.

THE SPECIAL PROBLEM OF MILITARY CONVERSION

The most difficult legacy of the Soviet system is an enormous military-industrial empire. This system employed 8 million people directly in the manufacture of weapons and other military equipment, or about 20 percent of the total industrial workforce. By some estimates, the output of the nine military-industrial ministries (sometimes known in Russian as the *deviatka,* from the nine military-industrial ministries responsible for this area) accounted for as much as 50 percent of Russian industrial output. They also turned out considerable civilian goods, including most of the country's televisions, refrigerators, and washing machines. In twenty provinces of Russia, military-industrial enterprises account for up to 60 percent of all economic activity, and in one or two cases up to 80 percent. Many of these enterprises are giants, employing up to 30,000 workers apiece.

This sector is now in a deep depression, because military orders from the Russian government have plunged by 70 percent in the last two years. In some places, complex high-tech facilities are in danger of falling apart, posing extreme danger to their surroundings. One of the most frightening examples is Krasnoiarsk-26, which makes plutonium for nuclear weapons. Two out of three underground reactors have been halted, but one remains in operation, because it supplies electricity as a byproduct to the inhabitants of the complex, who number 100,000. The plant stores hundreds of millions of curies in liquid and solid radioactive wastes. Financing for the facility has been cut drastically, but workers have nowhere to go. Work standards are dropping, workers are showing up drunk, and managers warn that an accident at this plant could be equal to "hundreds of millions of curies, or several Chernobyls."[4]

Military industry has several inherent features that make conversion slow, difficult, and expensive—not just in Russia but everywhere else in the world. Military industries are usually very large. They are extremely specialized. They are frequently located far from markets. They work to specifications and tolerances that are usually more exacting, and in any case quite different, from those required by civilian industry. Their managers are specialists in design and production, not in marketing and sales; they are accustomed to having a single stable customer—the government—not to seeking out or creating markets and shaping their products accordingly.

For all these reasons, converting the military half of Russian industry is going to be a slow and expensive process. It is a true dilemma: keeping the plants open to limit unemployment means remaining saddled with dependent industries that do not change. Closing the plants means dispersing and losing irreplaceable scientific and industrial skills. Even conversion means draconian cuts in employment, as non-market economic enterprises adjust to the imperatives of the market-place.

So far, the Russian government is stuck in the fork of the dilemma, not having the money or the coherence to choose either course. As a result, military industry is "winding down," like the rest of the economy, its plants remaining open but its technological potential wasting away for lack of investment.

THE MAFIA: "GOD INSTRUCTS US TO SHARE"

Some problems can be seen or counted. The more subtle obstacles to the market lie in people's attitudes and their everyday experiences of life. Life in the old Soviet system was not free or glamorous, but for most people it was reasonably safe, predictable, and secure. Life now is none of those things. No one's job is safe. The health-care system has broken down. But for ordinary Russians the worst change, the one that symbolizes everything that is wrong with the "market" as they perceive it, is organized crime.

Organized crime is a cancer spreading through the body of Russia, infecting every organ in society. It is estimated that 3,000 to 4,000 gangs of various sizes are active in Russia today. The "mafias," as the Russians call them, sap the energies of entrepreneurs, rob them of profits that they might reinvest, terrify them, and paralyze journalists and law-enforcement officials. Ordinary people are increasingly scared. The characteristic phrase of the mafias when they appear is: *Bog zaveshchaet delit'sia*—"God instructs us to share." But what is taking its share is not God, but the mafia. Most emerging private businesses are forced to pay protection to stay in business. "No honest businessman can do anything in this city," said a local police official in Yekaterinburg, "unless he pays unofficial taxes to crime groups."[5] By some estimates, such protection payments might amount to 20 percent of a private business's turnover, and can go much higher—a major form of "taxation" indeed. The amount of money that the gangsters are already claiming puts them in the position to corrupt widely the police, judiciary, and other government agencies, especially when measured against government salaries.

In addition, the gangsters are expanding their reach and alliances beyond Russia and the rest of the former Soviet Union into Central and Western Europe. They are also organizing the drug trade in Central Asia and the sale and smuggling of stolen weapons from the Red Army. The crime wave could certainly interfere with or even undermine Russia's move toward a market economy, as it corrupts legitimate enterprise, demoralizes and terrorizes businessmen, and drives many out of the marketplace. It has also become a major issue in the newly-born Russian politics. Opponents of Boris Yeltsin use it against him. Yeltsin himself, in 1994, declared that organized crime is the nation's number one problem and that "non-standard" measures are required to deal with it.[6]

Moreover, crime complicates matters, as it is sometimes hard to tell the businessmen from the criminals. Risk-taking is dismissed as "speculation" by a public that grew up under a Communist system that treated private commercial activity as a pathology, as dangerous as rabies.

Much of the new private business activity in Russia today lies in a gray zone somewhere between legality and illegality—not so much because the business is itself reprehensible, but because the law has not caught up with the new fact of private enterprise. Since no one can say with any certainty what is legal and what is illegal, any deal may require a bribe or at least a friendly official who "looks through his fingers." Friendship remains the basis of the Russian economy, just as it was in the Soviet period.

The legal and moral twilight zone hinders the development of attitudes that would support a market system. People must have a minimum of trust in one another to do business. There must be confidence that the law will protect contracts and property. If people do not trust the system and their future in it, individuals will not save and businesses will not invest. No one will willingly pay taxes if he or she feels that no one else does. Few will take a business risk while expecting that any gains will be arbitrarily taxed or extorted away. Inequalities of income and property will not be tolerated if most everyone is convinced that gains are ill-gotten. In short, if people's beliefs and behavior do not support a market system, it will end up developing only in a very truncated way.

THE "INVISIBLE HAND" AND THE "HIDDEN FOOT"

Western experience tell us what forms a market system might take, but not much about how to get there. But "getting there" is a problem all its own, as Eastern European experience already demonstrates. During the initial transition from a command economy to the market, one must turn an exceedingly subtle trick: simultaneously decentralizing the economy so as to give freedom to local managers and businessmen, while at the same time imposing financial discipline on them. If one "grants" market freedom without discipline, the result is high inflation, speculation, and irresponsible stripping of assets.

The Eastern European attempts to manage the transition to a market economy also demonstrate that no single virtuous path exists that can be pulled out of a textbook. There is not the luxury of decades to first do this, and then that. Sometimes, it seems that everything—from freeing prices to encouraging market values—has to be done at the same time, which, of course, is impossible, especially with overloaded and underfunded new governments, a fledgling financial system, and inexperienced entrepreneurs.

Yet it is clear that one of the essential things to do, as quickly as possible, is to try to create the financial framework. That, among other things, will ultimately promote private savings and investment. Russia is still at the beginning of this phase of creation. Such a framework includes a realistic tax system and a mechanism for collecting tax fairly and efficiently. It requires the government's gaining control of credit and its own spending. And it means weaning enterprises from the national budget and getting the managers to operate independently, not as dependents of the government industrial-welfare system. And that, in turn, goes back to reducing credits and eliminating subsidies.

One more critical element in this package consists of establishing some means of putting bankrupt enterprises out of business. In other words, enterprises must feel not only the invisible hand of the market, but also the "hidden foot" of market discipline. This state of affairs needs to be implemented with political sensitivity and alertness to reactions to widespread bankruptcies. But, in Russia as well as elsewhere, "exemplary bankruptcies" could well be required to get the discipline imposed.

Three moments of transition to a new financial regime are particularly dangerous. The first is when subsidies and cheap credits are cut back, causing inflation rates to fall and the purchasing power of the ruble to strengthen. This will undercut the main sources of profits of the private banking sector—chiefly currency speculation and short-term credits for trade—and cause a wave of bankruptcies among the weaker banks.

The second moment is when the government moves decisively to deal with the "crisis of non-payments," forcing enterprises to pay their bills and forcing into bankruptcy or receivership those which fail to do so. This in turn could cause a wave of layoffs—partly as a tactic by enterprise managers to counter-attack against the government.

The third danger point comes when prices are finally freed in every sector of the economy, especially energy. Many industries that are dependent on still-cheap supplies will be disrupted.

This is a revealing list, because these are precisely the three main policies that the Chernomyrdin government has tried to pursue since late 1993. It has had mixed success, which shows how long a road still lies ahead.

SOCIAL AND CULTURAL CONSTRAINTS

There is many a myth in the West (and in Russia) about Russians. But easy generalizations about timeless Russian "national character" should be treated skeptically. The fact is, Russian society has been transformed since the 1917 revolution and the first half of the twentieth century. The average Russian today lives in a completely different way from the average Russian of two or three generations ago. It does not seem plausible that modern Russians should think the same way as their great-grandparents. After all, do we?

Nevertheless, Russians have been stamped by a century of extraordinary striving and suffering. They have borne burdens, privations, and oppression from which they could not escape. Their recent history has been utterly unlike that of the United States or Western Europe. This fact undoubtedly constrains, or at least strongly shapes, the kind of political and economic system the Russians will be able to build.

THE CHANGING FACE OF RUSSIAN SOCIETY

Russians are a recently urbanized people. At the time of the revolution, Russia was 90 percent rural; today, it is 70 percent urban. Many Russian city-dwellers are still only one generation removed from the village, as the last great wave of rural migration took place in the 1960s and 1970s.

Until recently, few Russians owned much property beyond personal possessions, although it was permissible to build and own a cooperative apartment. Only in the last few years has it become possible to own land, although still with restrictions. Quite a number of Russians have long had dachas, or modest summer cottages, on leased land outside the major cities. Prior to the collapse of communism, many Russians had built up substantial savings, primarily because there was not much on which to spend money. Today, however, few people have savings. The high inflation of the last few years has mostly wiped them out. Falling income means that the average family now spends 45 percent of its income on food; the average pensioner spends 75 percent.

The Russian workforce is more heavily industrial than that of Western countries. Russian workers are grouped in large factories and company towns, which typically also provide them housing, food, and other forms of welfare. Wages are very low. A third of the workforce earns less than the official "poverty line." Despite a costly welfare system, Russian labor costs are still low, even compared to costs in Eastern Europe. Labor mobility, compared with that in the United States, is modest, in large part because housing is very hard to find.

Except for the two or three largest cities, the Russian urban family is unusually dependent on the workplace. It is absolutely critical to grasp this fact in order to understand the kind of challenges ahead. The workplace is not only the employer, but also the landlord and provider of essential food and services, and it frequently acts as the center of such community as there is. Russia has no alternative social safety net.

The population is well educated. Two thirds of all Russians have completed secondary education or had some higher education, and women hold proportionately more university-level degrees than men. Functional literacy is very high, and mathematical and engineering skills are very widespread, although typically quite specialized and narrow. But practical civic and business skills are not yet taught in the schools.

Traditional family structures and roles have been weakened or destroyed as people have moved to the cities. The family is under stress, divorce rates are high, and abortion is the only widely available method of birth control, reflecting what had been the Soviet indifference to people's personal needs. Local community structures are weak. Individuals protect themselves through narrow circles of friends who help them cope with the system. There is little broad solidarity among workers of any type (with some important exceptions, such as coal miners). Indeed, Russian workers tend not to strike against local management, but *with* management against the state.

Most Russian families, urban and rural, have only one child. The Russian birthrate had been declining for years, but lately has been dropping even more sharply. Unless this trend changes, the cities will not be capable of renewing themselves or the countryside of supporting further migration. A low birthrate means that at any one time the percentage of young people is small. Indeed, because of a low birthrate and a decline in life expectancy, the Russian population is now declining. The 25 million Russians now living outside the Russian Federation may represent the only potential source of population growth for Russia in coming years.

The weakening of traditional structures and roles has eroded moral values. Indeed, this problem has turned out to be larger than was commonly recognized, because the Soviet practice of limiting access to the big cities (the *propiska* system) led to a large number of "marginals" living outside them. These marginals form a relatively unknown underclass in Soviet society. In addition, there are now more than two million refugees in Russia, most of them living in the Moscow region and in the north Caucasus. This homeless population is bound to grow further in coming years.

A SOCIETY TURNED UPSIDE DOWN

The emergence of a "civil society" is essential to Russia's future after communism. Yet it will be slow to develop. A civil society is one based on private property and legal protection for individuals and groups; crucially, it has an existence independent of the state. Some of the Eastern European countries had a tradition of civil society, albeit a weak one, before the Communist takeover, which facilitates their transitions. A civil society certainly did not exist under the Soviet Communists, nor did it really exist under the tsars, and the social bases for it are weak today. The absence of such a tradition will be a major constraint for Russia in the years ahead.

Russian society has been turned upside down. In the past few years there has been enormous upheaval in the previous rankings and priorities of Russian society. Along with that, the previous income distribution has changed. High-status professionals (party cadres, military officers, scientists, academics) have lost prestige, while previously low-status or underground professionals (shopkeepers, traders, brokers)—and criminals—enjoy or even flaunt their new wealth.

Every group in society has been affected: The old have lost ground to the young. Women bear the brunt of unemployment and have lost what place they had in the political system, while making no gains in the home. To the young, science and engineering no longer seem worth learning, compared to business. Previously secure positions and incomes have become insecure or nonexistent; positions that carried perquisites and privileges have lost them; career expectations have vanished. Law and order have broken down and established values are in disrepute. To hear Russians tell it, corruption rides in imported cars, while honesty walks the streets.

Many of these changes are in *degree* rather than in kind: The relative status of different professions had been shifting for two decades prior to the breakup of the Soviet Union. Also, Soviet society was always far from egalitarian. Status and wealth that derived from state service or from scientific and cultural achievement were officially approved and largely accepted by the population. What is objectionable to many Russians about today's new inequalities is that they are extreme, highly visible, and (they suspect) ill-gotten, being based solely on money.

Some qualifications are needed: Many Russians, especially young people in the cities, are adapting to these traumatic changes with remarkable speed and flexibility. As in any social upheaval, there are winners and losers. Attention from the West has tended to focus on the losers and the most conspicuous winners. But the gains may be more broadly based than previously thought.

AN INSECURE MIDDLE CLASS

Russia has developed a large, educated, urban middle class. At the same time, this class is poor, owns little or no property, has no savings, and has only shallow traditions and structures. Consequently, its middle-class identity and status are fragile. At its edges, it frays into a large population with no structure or roots.

These features of Russian society have political implications. The principal reaction of the Russian middle class and working class to the present upheaval is likely to be insecurity. They are an aging and declining population. Other than their enterprises, they have few resources. They feel enormously vulnerable and exposed, not only economically but also physically. They are repelled by the disorder and what they see as a sudden explosion of decadence. In short, this is not a revolutionary population, but one preoccupied with its losses and with protecting itself and regaining some security in a world that has abruptly become foreign and threatening to them.

Soviet Russia was a hierarchical, semi-militarized, and highly ordered society, but the order was imposed from above. Its internal structure was always more fragile than it appeared, which helps to explain why law and order have proved so fragile. But people are accustomed to order, and their fear and resentment of the present anarchy are political tinder.

The absence of strong neighborhoods and communities provides little base for political parties or for the other intermediate bodies essential for civil society. There is little class or ethnic identity in most places in Russia (other than a Russian identity that is shared by most Russians in most places, or ethnic identities in the non-Russian enclaves), as well as a lack of strong social "transmission belts" (such as trade unions, parties, and clans).

The lack of a strong socioeconomic base for political parties, combined with the universal presence of television, has set the stage for American-style politics on the national level—that is, politics focused on personalities, images, and populist slogans rather than parties. This development is likely to favor Russian nationalism and other "gut issues." It also means that control of television will be crucial in future politics.

PREDETERMINED OUTCOMES

Gradually, all these constraints will yield to time. But 2010 is just over the horizon. Therefore, there are some features of Russia that one can predict with strong certainty. These features, for all practical purposes, are predetermined under all scenarios. Predetermined elements represent circumstances and outcomes that are inevitable. When a river basin experiences record rainfall upstream, it is predetermined that the waters will swell and crest downriver. It is only a matter of time. Such are the predetermined elements.

Countries unfortunately get the environment they can afford, and in the coming decades, Russia will not be able to afford much. Much of today's stock of buildings, railroads, and other infrastructure will be standing and operating in 2010. Certainly, some factories will have been closed down, replaced, or rebuilt. With a functioning market system, the least efficient plants, which often happen to be the most polluting, will be among those shut down first, especially as the demand for their output declines. But the heavy legacy of the Soviet past will ensure that this will not happen anywhere near as rapidly or thoroughly as might be expected. Many polluting plants will still be in operation, owing to capital constraints and political and social requirements—preeminently, the maintenance of employment. Power plants without scrubbers will go on using coal and polluting, because steam coal from politically sensitive regions must have outlets. There are whole cities, such as Dzerzhinsk, that are "chemical cities," where the only employer is the chemical industry. Despite terrible health problems in those localities, the plants are most unlikely to be shut down.

Yet, even if investment capital is constrained and the turnover of the capital stock retarded, industries will not be able to operate with the same environmental impunity as existed under the Communist system.

Managers will be forced, through either regulations or incentives, to pay attention to the environmental consequences of their production. Thus, the Russian environment will improve somewhat over the next sixteen years. However, the investment required for a substantial improvement toward Western levels will not be available. Meanwhile, the risk of some kind of serious nuclear incident will be significant.

Housing

Housing will remain a major social sore spot and a constraint on labor mobility. Much of the present stock is already substandard and poorly maintained, and two more decades of wear and tear will reduce the housing tracts of the sixties and seventies to slums. There will be new construction for those able to afford it, but much of the population will not be able to pay, for lack of savings or a mortgage system.

Agriculture

There will be no strong agricultural revival in Russia by 2010, even if farming becomes largely private. The countryside has been so systematically emptied of its best people that many areas are incapable of supporting modern agriculture. For the past three generations, people with skills and ability have left. Given the lack of able-bodied farmers, only massive investment in labor-saving machinery could generate a rapid increase in agricultural efficiency and output. Such heavy investment is unlikely to be available. Moreover, much of Russia's soil has been badly damaged by Soviet farming techniques. The rural infrastructure, especially the roads and the irrigation systems, is inadequate by the standards of modern agriculture. Russia lacks the necessary scientific and industrial support system for efficient modern farming.

However, market pricing for food would provide new incentives to improve agriculture. The key would be improvements in preservation, storage, transportation, and processing—all of which are now characterized by great wastage. These might be attractive to private Russian capital and to foreign investment. Consequently, the food picture could look better by 2010, even while overall agricultural productivity remains low.

The Welfare Burden

No matter how its economy fares over the next two decades, Russia will inherit a heavy welfare burden, which the state will have to support. Russian birthrates could increase if the economy begins to grow strongly and young people's living standards improve. But the total size of the population will probably still be declining, and there will be many pensioners for every able-bodied worker. Schools, hospitals, and urban services will have deteriorated as a result of years of underfunding by financially constrained governments. The medical system will be substandard. The retraining of older urban workers into nonindustrial jobs will go slowly. All these needs will require heavy government spending, which may not necessarily be available.

Many of the 25 million Russians now living outside the Federation's borders will emigrate to Russia. Indeed, many are already doing so, especially from Central Asia and the Baltic republics. In view of the lack of housing and social services in Russia, this is already a major social problem and a financial burden for government at all levels.

Money

Money already plays a far larger role in the Russian economy than it did in the command economy. The average level of financial and economic sophistication among the leaders and public is rising fast. By 2010, compared to today, Russia will have acquired a more stable financial, budgetary, fiscal, and monetary system. The country will have capital markets, and consequently will allocate financial resources more efficiently than today.

Crime and Violence

Russia will continue to suffer from high crime and ethnic strife. Law and order—coping with and controlling crime—will be a central preoccupation of government and society. Public attitudes toward crime will be intolerant, and consequently the criminal law system will tend to remain harsh on defendants.

Families and Stress

The overall decline in the population's living standards will continue to put stress on Russian family structure, adding to the large population on the margin of society. The chronic problem of alcoholism will remain a social affliction throughout this period. To keep order, large police and military forces will be required. These problems, too, will require heavy state spending.

State and Society

On balance, the state at all levels is likely to remain stronger than society for the foreseeable future. The social institutions, secure property, and private, dispersed wealth required for a strong society are likely to take more than two decades to build. Many Russian institutions will remain affiliated with the state, directly or indirectly, or will continue to depend on it. The legal system, in particular, is likely to continue to serve the interests of the state more than those of society.

PART III

The Scenarios: Stories of the Future

History is customarily written looking backward, sometimes with the implicit vow not to repeat the mistakes of the past. With scenarios, one is writing histories of the future. The following chapters present four scenarios—archetypes of possible futures of Russia to 2010. Each one is built in the same way. The first part consists of a story, written as we may encounter it in some history book (or history disk) in the year 2020. The second part is an analysis of the elements of the scenario, out of which the story grows. Combining storytelling and analysis gives a good way of trying on possible futures, broadening our thinking and widening our horizon.

In developing our work, we have been guided by two principal ideas. The first is direction. As a result of the collapse of the Communist system, the command economy, and the Soviet empire, Russia has been driven inexorably away from the centrally planned economy and the one-party state. There is no going back to the past as it was. The second idea is connectedness. Scenarios are not simply alternative pictures of the future. They are connected to one another. It matters which one happens first.

These two concepts together lead to the basic idea behind these scenarios. It is this: Russia is being driven down a road that leads, in the long run, to a uniquely Russian blend of the state and the market, which we call Capitalism Russian-Style. But the path by which Russia gets there will shape both the character of Russian capitalism and the political regime under which it functions. In other words, the proportions of state and market by 2010 depend on how events play out along the way.

Our scenarios unfold as follows:

- "Muddling Down"—the unwinding of the Soviet state.
- "Two-Headed Eagle"—a reassertion of power by a central government that is based on an alliance of private finance and industrial managers, with the army and the police.
- "Time of Troubles"—a family of scenarios consisting of varying degrees of

chaos and reaction. It includes both the "Long Good-Bye," a Russia of semi-autonomous regions, and the "Russian Bear," a violent breakdown of civil order, followed by a severe reaction.

• "Chudo," the Russian economic miracle.

There are a number of key differences among these scenarios:

• the strength or weakness of the Russian central government versus local political forces
• the rate at which the state sector in the economy declines and the private economy takes up the slack, and the speed with which market institutions arise and begin to function
• the availability of capital, whether from within or without, to build a new economy, and the way in which it is invested
• the sequence in which new political and social groups arrive on the scene of Russian politics
• the success or failure of those groups in building stable economic and political institutions

9

Muddling Down

By the beginning of 1996, after new legislative elections, it is painfully evident that the new legislature does not differ much from the old. Indeed, some of the deputies are the same people. The law under which the voting is held enables many of them to run on national party lists, so that some of the most famous and the most notorious are returned. The new deputies, like the old, mirror the diversity of politics at the local level. Some are Communist reactionaries; some are nationalists; some are reformers; all are eager for Moscow perks and foreign travel. The new parliamentary leaders are soon back in the same old business, judiciously channeling favors to the new arrivals and building up their own influence. The president, for all the powers the constitution gives him on paper, is unable to lead.

The familiar battles resume. The bitterest one is over subsidies for industries and local governments. The chairman of the Russian Central Bank, reading the political wind, shifts his allegiance back to the newly elected legislature. The Finance Minister, who had been fighting since 1994 for tight spending and a curb on subsidies, is outgunned. He resigns and goes off as an executive director to the World Bank in Washington. Prime Minister Viktor Chernomyrdin, tired of the endless wrangling, retires in 1995. After a bitter battle with the legislature, an executive from the defense industries is named prime minister, but he lacks Chernomyrdin's political acumen and pragmatism. The Russian budget deficit begins to swell again and inflation rises above 20 percent a month, causing the IMF to suspend its support.

Scenario Pathways:
Three Roads to Capitalism, Russian-Style

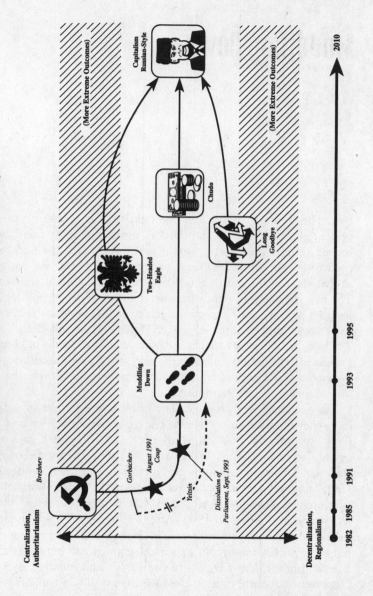

The country is once again in the grip of a payments crisis, in which enterprises do not pay their bills and are in debt to one another. Official GNP continues its downward slide. State enterprises produce without being paid and without paying their own suppliers. Few close down, because there are no strong legal mechanisms to force them to do so, regardless of their losses. But the government continues to extend cheap credit and subsidies, keeping the prices of raw materials artificially low. Thousands of bankrupt enterprises soldier on because no one will lock their doors.

Since the government cannot collect more than about half the taxes due to it, it runs severe deficits, which it covers by printing money and expanding the money supply. Only the government's partial control over hard-currency revenues, plus the undervalued ruble, keep it more or less afloat. But taken together, the economic consequence of political weakness and legal vacuum is high inflation.

The government does not dare to tighten credit, which would force enterprises to cut back or cease production, for it fears the mass unemployment that would swiftly follow. The country lacks any meaningful social safety net—the traditional Soviet state enterprise *is* the social safety net. In addition, tightening credit and cutting subsidies would force the closure of many high-tech industries, which are essential to the revival of the Russian economy in the long run.

Nevertheless, despite the government's efforts, unemployment is starting to rise just the same, putting large numbers of people out on the street for the first time. Here and there, state enterprises are actually closing their doors. The very first official bankruptcy was in 1993, a small cutlery factory near Nizhnii Novgorod.[1] Since then, several dozen enterprises have turned belly-up, more as a result of exhaustion than of legal action, and there are more every day. Meanwhile, privatized enterprises begin to cut their employment rolls and cut back on their social welfare role. Though the government tries to expand the social safety net, both its resources and experience are very limited and it is unable to cope with the flood of new jobless.

By 1996 Yeltsin, discouraged and exhausted, decides to call it quits. Although he had repeatedly said he had no stomach for the constant tensions of the job of president, no one had really believed him. Most people are taken by surprise when Yeltsin really does stand down. The presidential election of 1996 is hotly disputed by six candidates. Capitalizing on the rising unemployment, the fascist and nationalist parties (the so-called Red-Browns), plus the resurgent Russian Communist party and various neo-Communist groups, are the major factor in the campaign. The eventual winner is a moderate reformer who is elected with the support of the reconfigured Russian Communist Party. But the message is clear. The political extremes are continuing to make headway against a paralyzed middle.

BUSINESS BUBBLES

But behind the steady decline of the state economy, the Russian private economy is bubbling vigorously. The trade and services sector is now almost entirely in private hands. Most large and middle-sized state companies have been sold at auction to private owners, mostly their former managers. In practice, nearly every Russian family has at least one foot in the private economy.

Unfortunately, much of the private ownership is still more fictitious than real, especially where the larger enterprises are concerned. Continued state subsidies and a lack of a vigorous bankruptcy policy produce private property without responsibility. There is still no "invisible foot" of financial discipline to go with the invisible hand of the market. Alongside the conventional enterprises, huge private financial structures are emerging, many of them essentially large pyramid schemes, operating virtually without risk of collapse, since no one calls in their debts. Much privatization, in sum, remains pseudo-privatization, protected by the state and state guarantees.

But, to the growing interest of foreign observers, the Russian "business sector" is taking the first steps toward regulating itself. Moscow banks, for example, set up their own citywide settlements system to offset the chronic weaknesses of the Russian Central Bank. Business owners in several cities band together to create their own security forces to fight back against the mafia. The barter system becomes increasingly sophisticated, as brokerage houses mature into commodities exchanges. Privatization continues, thanks to a solid alliance between industrial managers and local politicians at the provincial level.

Business associations, representing the new private sector and headed by influentials like former prime minister Yegor Gaidar become effective lobby groups in the government. Because they have resources and do not hesitate to use them, they manage to work with both the ministries and the legislature, pushing through legislation on such topics as copyright and patent protection and protection of contract and property, and establishing more predictable taxes. Unfortunately, most of these laws and measures are not implemented.

As a result, Russia by 1996 is more than ever a place of contrasts. Financial conglomerates are expanding into insurance, banking, and real estate speculation. In Moscow, particularly, there are signs of new wealth everywhere. Russians, especially younger ones, are much better off than the official numbers indicate. But one has only to go down to Moscow's railroad stations to see the misery of the unemployed, the refugees, and the elderly. The old system of social protection is unraveling, and there is nothing to replace it. Anyone without family, connections, health, or youthful energy is out of luck.

The core problem of Muddling Down is political paralysis at the center. "Stagflation" is the best economic performance this scenario can achieve. In response to people's needs, the government is too weak to do more than improvise day by day. The country's social and physical capital degrades steadily for lack of investment. Most people get by, but they watch with mounting disgust as crime, corruption, and inequality grow all around them. Townspeople fear to go out at night, and a well-known advertisement on television touts steel doors and police locks imported from New York. Muddling Down is a scenario of mediocrity; its leadership can offer up no glory or grandeur, no inspiring purpose, only promises that come and go and are not fulfilled.

THE RED-BROWNS

Muddling Down remains fertile ground for Russian nationalists and neo-fascists, the Red-Browns. After the presidential election of 1996, the political battleground shifts to the local level. The Red-Browns, gradually overcoming the government's attempts to ban them, prove to be effective political organizers in the provinces and autonomous republics. They send speakers and organizers to provinces with sympathetic conservative local governments, such as Volgograd and Mordovia. They preach a message of hatred for the new quasi-market economy and the democratic reformers. They call for national resurrection, defense of Russian minorities outside Russian borders, an end to corruption, and suppression of "speculation," by which they mean private trade and enterprise. They attack Jews, Zionists, America, and the West; promote extreme nationalism; and offer dark conspiracies to explain Russia's current position. They borrow from the litanies of Nazism and fascism as well as Russia's homegrown extreme-right-wing traditions. They get valuable political fuel from the growing number of incidents on the borders of Russia, involving the Russian national minorities in the republics of the former Soviet Union.

The worst trouble spot is Estonia, where for decades the Soviet government had built up defense plants and staffed them with Russians. As a result, Estonians are a minority in their own capital city, Tallinn, and in the northeast part of the country, around Narva. Estonians react in 1993 by passing a stiff citizenship law that disenfranchises most of the Russians in the republic. The first counterreferenda are held in Narva and at Sillamae, a "post office box" defense plant for the production of weapons-grade uranium, staffed entirely by Russians. Ninety-eight percent of the Russians at Sillamae vote for autonomy, followed in nearly equal numbers by the Russian population of Narva.

After 1994, Narva and Sillamae become increasingly independent of Estonia and no longer pay taxes. The Russian Defense Ministry, which increasingly conducts its own foreign policy toward the former Soviet republics, declares that the Russian minority in Estonia is under its special protection. Anti-Russian demonstrations break out in Tallinn, and Russians are harassed on the streets of the capital city. Russian "self-defense" groups, perhaps including some Russian soldiers, are posted near major industrial enterprises, where most Russians work. By 1996, Russian-Estonian relations are at a low ebb, and nationalist groups in Russia are agitating for outright annexation of northeastern Estonia.

The Red-Browns take advantage of every referendum or election to put their own issues and candidates on local ballots. During the presidential elections of 1996, twenty-eight Russian provinces hold separate elections for local heads of administration (informally known as "governors"). In fifteen of these campaigns, candidates affiliated with Red-Brown parties, or sympathetic to them, are elected by wide margins.

THE ELECTIONS OF 1997

In 1997, in an attempt to break the political logjam, the president dissolves Parliament again and calls for legislative elections. Many provinces declare local legislative elections at the same time. The Red-Browns campaign vigorously: This appears to be their big chance.

The legislative campaign of 1997 turns into the most tumultuous event yet in the brief annals of Russian democracy. Campaign meetings frequently turn into anti-government riots or confrontations between Red-Browns and democrats. The Western media watch with dread, certain that the extremists will win sweeping victories.

The results, however, are a surprise: The Red-Browns actually lose ground. By the time the dust settles, they have won substantial numbers of seats in only a handful of local parliaments, and fewer than 10 percent of the seats in the federal legislature.

Analysis of the campaign reveals the shortcomings of the extremists. The government, for all its weaknesses, has the resources to buy media time and give its candidates better exposure than the extremist parties can. The government and local regional leaders have become more ruthless in denying the extremist opposition access to television. The Red-Browns turn out to be badly divided, since they represent the extremes of left and right, and thus have little in common other than their dislike of the government. Many nationalists are not extremists and support the center. Many are also successful businessmen. Thus, in the campaign many nationalists end up "voting their pocketbooks" and supporting the moderate middle. As a result, the Red-Browns find themselves short of campaign funds, compared to the pro-government candidates. In addition, the leadership of the Russian Communist Party has become more middle-of-the-road, and it is no longer clear that the RCP qualifies as an extremist party.

But the most important new factor in the 1997 election is that the newly successful, the young, the privately-employed, are starting to find their political voice. The privatization of land is starting to have an impact, as old-time rural bosses lose power and private farmers make gains. Perhaps Muddling Down is starting to muddle up!

The government's victory in the campaign of 1997 gives the government breathing room, but it is clear that it is no more than a reprieve. The moderate middle must somehow resolve its differences, or the political extremes will continue to gain.

ANALYSIS OF MUDDLING DOWN

Is this the future of Russia—the rise of Russian neo-fascism and neo-communism from the grass roots, growing on the fertile soil of corruption and popular disgust? The answer depends on the ability of the Russian government to weather the coming challenges, the degree of skill and unity of the right-wing and left-wing parties, and the responses of the Russian people.

Muddling Down is the scenario that extends the present. It is the one in which Russia has been located since the failure of the coup of August 1991, the launching of radical economic reform in November 1991, and the breakup of the USSR in December 1991. Despite the replacement of Prime Minister Yegor Gaidar by the more pragmatic Viktor Chernomyrdin, the end of radical economic reform in 1992, and the parliamentary dissolution and October Crisis of 1993, Muddling Down remains the prevailing scenario.

Muddling Down contains seven essential elements:

A weak Russian central government, which has launched a marketizing reform that it is only partly able to implement. The president and his executive branch are not entirely helpless, however, chiefly because their opponents are likewise still disorganized and ambivalent and have no viable alternative program.

A fierce competition for power, revenues, and property among a multitude of players old and new, at all levels, and in every region.

A relatively free atmosphere, due mainly to the vacuum left by the collapse of the previous system rather than to any real constitutional protections or liberal convictions on the part of the players.

A weak and contentious association of former Soviet republics, which can neither live with one another politically nor live without one another economically.

A state economy in decline, sustained by the remaining "informal" features of the previous command system and credits and subsidies from the central government. The private sector is growing strongly, but it is almost wholly lacking in a legal and regulatory structure, and a good part of it is still a parasitic outgrowth of the old economy. The military-industrial sector is suffering from declining orders but is not receiving financial support for conversion.

Weak and ineffective financial restraints on state actors at all levels, from the Russian Central Bank down to state enterprises. There is no market discipline, as there is no effective bankruptcy law to force unprofitable companies out of business. The wildest business deals do not necessarily carry the risk that they should because there is no one with the power to blow the whistle or call in bad debts except the mafia.

A demoralized and disorganized coercive apparatus, whose officers are underpaid, resentful of their lowered status, appalled at the collapse of Soviet prestige and power, sullen over their low living standards, and increasingly afraid of unemployment. Despite their discontent, the military and the police are too divided and dispirited to take effective political action.

MARKETIZATION FROM THE MIDDLE

Muddling Down is a disorderly and unstable environment. Yet in several respects, it is a favorable one for change. For better or for worse, it is the free laboratory of a new society. In its unrestrained atmosphere, new political players—not all extremists—emerge and test new political strategies, using new political resources. New economic classes are being formed and important resources are accumulating in private hands (although some of the new rich are unsavory and some of what is called capitalism consists mostly of speculation). The very lack of a strong regulatory state has opened up space for "rapid marketization from the middle." Russians are becoming used to their freedoms, and are taking advantage of them in growing numbers.

Muddling Down, in short, could be a benign pathway to a Russian version of quasi-democratic capitalism, if it can adapt and survive for a time. Indeed, Muddling Down could lead to a Russian version of an economic miracle. But at the same time it is fertile ground for extremism.

CAN MUDDLING DOWN MUDDLE THROUGH?

Is it possible for the Muddling Down scenario to muddle through for, say, another five years, avoiding the catastrophic crises and collisions that now appear to threaten it on all sides? If it does, what can it achieve, other than buying time?

For Muddling Down to survive for a few years longer, it will have to meet some stiff conditions. The population must not become radicalized by unemployment and disorder. The economy must not collapse altogether. The central government must not become completely paralyzed, or defenseless against its enemies. A cold peace and occasional brush wars along Russia's borders with the former Soviet republics must not degenerate into major conflagrations and bloodshed.

In addition, as a last condition, Muddling Down must remain what it is—no one side can impose its will on the other players, disrupting the rough balance of forces that is the essence of this scenario. This condition is important, because it is precisely the current standoff among the contending political forces that is allowing the rapid transfer of property and capital into private hands. This is the essential precondition for the *Chudo* scenario that follows.

The greatest political danger to the Muddling Down government is unemployment. Nothing could provide as much fuel for political extremism as large masses of people out of work and cut off from the welfare system that the workplace still provides.

At the moment, unemployment is a mounting but not yet life-threatening problem. Official joblessness is still low, although the number conceals substantial underemployment, people on "leave," and arrears in wages. But low unemployment is being purchased at a high price: high budget deficits, overrapid expansion of the money supply, and inflation.

Could the Russian government accept a higher level of unemployment in order to cut back inflation? This is precisely the policy the Chernomyrdin government pursued in 1993–4, but it is an explosive policy unless the trade-off between unemployment and inflation is managed with great delicacy. The reason is that the workplace traditionally plays a much larger role in the lives of most Russians than it does in Western countries. Russian people derive many advantages from their place of work other than wages: housing, a residence permit (in the case of Moscow), some access to internal food networks (some of the larger enterprises own farms), vacation benefits (frequently to factory-owned facilities), a claim on a future pension, and a social identity. Many people's access to a dacha and a small garden is through their place of work, and these have directly and indirectly become, especially in the last few years, a major source of food for up to 75 percent of Russian urban families.

Therefore, what must be avoided is a massive wave of outright unemployment country-wide. However, there is some room here for the government to maneuver. After all, what matters most, from the standpoint of political stability, is whether unemployment can be disguised or otherwise cushioned in its political effects, especially in the largest cities and other politically sensitive places.

First, it is important that people not be released outright from their jobs, and that their enterprises not actually be closed down, even if they are technically bankrupt and not actually producing anything. Rather, it is sufficient if workers remain nominally on the rolls of their enterprises, for in addition they will be sustained by a variety of jobs in the private economy.

Second, outright unemployment must be kept low where it is most damaging politically: in Moscow, St. Petersburg, and the industrial heartland. Military officers and other security personnel, above all, must be subsidized, rehoused, and kept quiet. Joblessness among young males—the most volatile element in any society—needs to be kept low. So long as unemployment is not allowed to reach mass proportions, political extremism will not find fertile ground. In Russia, unemployment is more explosive politically than inflation.

THE GOVERNMENT MUST NOT BE COMPLETELY PARALYZED

To survive for a few years more, the Muddling Down government does not have to achieve miracles; it simply has to be able to keep basic civil order, prevent outright collapse of the official economy, and stop the country from flying apart. So far, it has done so.

In actual fact, the impotence of the Russian federal government should not be exaggerated. It is weak, but it is far from defenseless. Three examples will make the point.

The first is potential control over elections. Winning elections in the new Russia will require money and publicity. The Russian government has sufficient control of television, the prime political medium, to dominate the ether in any campaign. There are no rules on campaign finance to prevent the government from funding its own favorites, and as poor as the government may be, it still commands more resources than the private sector (though the mafia will also become a significant source of campaign finance). In addition, the local state property committees constitute a useful patronage network that can be manipulated by the government to liberate local resources for the government's candidates. In short, in coming years the government's resources in elections will outweigh those of private donors, and will dwarf the resources available to the Red-Brown parties. It is true that the federal government did not make effective use of these resources in the elections of December 1993, but that is partly because it did not recognize the extremist threat until too late, and was poorly organized to counter it.

The second example concerns relations between the federal government and the provinces. What the Russian federal government must avoid is a full-scale tax revolt by the local governments, which would then place the Russian federal government in the same helpless situation in which the Soviet government was in by the summer of 1991. But the federal government is not entirely powerless in this battle. The Far East region, for example, depends on subsidies and allocations from the federal government for half of its supplies of fuel, food, and other essential commodities. In an all-out contest, Moscow can still bring the Far East to a standstill, but both sides know that neither can afford the fight. Indeed, neither side wants to fight; the issue is how to divide the spoils.[2]

Therefore, a vital key to the survival of Muddling Down is that the federal and regional authorities manage to work out compromises over the sharing of power, tax revenues, and resources. The main element of such a compromise would be this: The federal government would concede to all the local provinces a degree of control over tax receipts and export revenues. The federal government would also have to concede to the local governments greater control over the privatization of large enterprises, thus giving official blessing to the growing de facto control by local governments over mines, utilities, oil fields, large factories, etc. Lastly, the federal government must agree to share tax revenues with local governments on a more equitable and predictable basis— unlike the present system, under which the Ministry of Finance and the other federal executive agencies arbitrarily re-route subsidies and revenues to reward friends and punish enemies, or to head off or settle strikes, or to alleviate shortages.

Finally, a third example concerns progress behind the scenes. Away from the headlines, all is not confrontation and paralysis. The Russian Supreme Soviet actually passed a good deal of constructive legislation between the fall of 1991 and its dissolution in the fall of 1993, and government agencies have not been altogether inactive in creating use-ful regulations. A good illustration of this is the handling of hard currency. Slowly, Russia is inching toward full convertibility of the ruble, and one by one, the restrictions on the use of the ruble by foreigners are being removed. Current regulations allow non-resident foreigners to open special ruble accounts in Russian banks to finance the purchase of shares in Russian companies or privatization vouchers; they are also allowed to convert hard currency into rubles for this purpose. For the first time, in other words, foreigners have a clear legal basis to participate in Russia's privatization program.

Another innovation is that non-resident foreigners may now hold ruble accounts to buy and sell products and services with Russians in the domestic market. Although there are some restrictions, this innovation will allow foreigners to take advantage of "ruble bargains" that have hitherto been unavailable. The result will be to assist in the general push of domestic ruble prices up to world levels.

It is the cumulative effect of liberalizing measures such as these, amounting to gradual steps to complete convertibility of the ruble, that is slowly expanding the size of the currency market and stabilizing the ruble against the dollar, despite continued high inflation.

These three examples show how the Muddling Down government, using the meager power at its disposal, must cope, one after another, with the dangers that threaten it. If it is faced with multiple crises all at once, it will go under; but if it is able to deal with them one at a time, it may survive for some time.

CAUTION IN RELATIONS WITH THE OTHER REPUBLICS

The survival of Muddling Down requires that the Russian government manage successfully the problems of the Russian minorities outside its borders, thus avoiding giving cheap fuel to the Red-Browns inside Russia. This will not be easy to do. Russia under Muddling Down speaks with many voices in foreign policy, from the military to the parliament and the president's own Security Council, not to mention the Ministry of Foreign Affairs. Each of these groups has its own policy agenda for the other republics, and as a result there is plenty of potential for misunderstanding and mischief.

Nevertheless, the Muddling Down government needs to look for ways to defuse potentially explosive issues. In Estonia, the eventual compromise solution may be to relocate gradually the defense-related workers of the Estonian northeast back to Russia, while relaxing citizenship requirements for the Russian-speaking population of Tallinn. In Ukraine, one way to contain the separatist tendencies of the eastern Ukrainian provinces is to revive economic ties to Russia, thus alleviating the severe economic depression gripping the region.

These are barely more than stopgap policies, but that is the essence of what Muddling Down is all about. If the worst problems can be contained, the Muddling Down government may avoid the radicalization of the Russian population at home or a remilitarization of Russia.

A TRANSITION

Muddling Down is the scenario under which a new distribution of power and wealth is being worked out—one is tempted to say, "slugged out"—among the former members of the Soviet administrative class, plus a growing number of new players. In Muddling Down, overall economic policy is almost paralyzed, while at the micro-level a new world, or at any rate a new possessing class, is being born.

Muddling Down may therefore be a necessary stage for the development of a market economy in Russia. By itself, Muddling Down can be no more than a transition. On the economic side, because Muddling Down cannot guarantee property rights and stable money, it is unable to promote long-range investment by the private sector, nor is it able to finance investment itself. On the political side, because Muddling Down is still divided at the center, it cannot build effective defenses for the disadvantaged in society. In the long run, it cannot bolster its own legitimacy against the political extremes. It leads somewhere else.

10

Two-Headed Eagle

It is the late summer of 1997. It has been six years since the break-up of the USSR, and Russians are growing tired. The constitution of 1993 has no legitimacy in anyone's eyes and is under constant criticism and challenge. And parliamentary elections in late 1995 have only strengthened the opposition in the legislature and weakened the government's support, deepening the political paralysis at the center. There is still no federal treaty and the federal government continues to wrangle with the regions. In practice, the regional governments are increasingly going their own way, but for many Russians this only brings a sense of despair over the humiliating decline of the Russian nation.

Per capita income and consumption have been on the rise since 1993, and there is actually a boom in housing construction and sales of consumer durables. Industrial production bottomed out in 1995. But the gains are highly uneven. The Chernomyrdin government's attempts to tighten government credits and subsidies in 1994 and 1995 provoked a wave of plant closings and lay-offs, increasing popular discontent all around the country. The payments crisis is still not resolved, and most factories and companies are in debt to one another.

Public opinion polls show that most Russians believe they are worse off, not better. Mikhail Zhvanetskii, Russia's most popular comedian, gets guffaws in Russian theaters, by asking in mock puzzlement, "Much has changed, but nothing has happened. Or is it that much has happened, and nothing has changed?"

147

The polls also show that corruption and crime are the two biggest issues on people's minds. Shoot-outs between rival gangs and executions on contract seem to have become almost daily events, and even government official are not safe from extortions and assaults.

Despite all this, Boris Yeltsin is still president. To the surprise of many who thought he was in ill-health, he ran again in June 1996, campaigning vigorously against a large field of opponents, which included Aleksandr Rutskoi and Vladimir Zhirinovskii. Yeltsin's opponents spent most of their time attacking one another, while the president was helped by liberal use of government patronage, abundant air time, and the grassroots efforts of the new "presidential" party. In the end Russian voters, more out of resignation than affection, gave their votes to the man they knew. They could not have been surprised when Yeltsin returned to his familiar passive but unpredictable style. By 1997 Yeltsin has lost a good deal of his popularity.

Boris Yeltsin's security guards have been warning him for years that he takes too many chances, but like many another leader, Yeltsin draws energy from direct contact with people. On a warm evening, Yeltsin decides to attend a performance of *A Life for the Tsar* at the Bolshoi Theater. He arrives late, during the intermission. As he turns the corner of the building toward the front entrance and passes through a small crowd of theatergoers, a man steps out and shoots him. But a security guard falls against the would-be assassin just as he fires, and the bullet only goes through Yeltsin's shoulder and arm. Yeltsin's wounds are not life-threatening, but for several weeks he is unable to work more than a few hours a day.

The would-be assassin turns out to be a member of a small ethnic group from the north Caucasus. The man, a petty hoodlum who is part of a large gang in Moscow, and one of the most vicious, was a follower of the former leader of one of the north Caucasian republics, who had declared independence from Moscow. After years of the leader's provocative behavior, Yeltsin had finally lost patience and had ordered Russian paratroopers to occupy the republic's capital city. The north Caucasian leader was killed as he tried to escape into the mountains. His followers held Yeltsin responsible for the death.

Yeltsin's close brush renews his standing as a hero. For the Russian élite and public the assassination attempt is the last straw; calls mount at public meetings and in the media for curbs on the mafia, on corruption, and on private businessmen, which are all rolled into one in many people's minds.

This is the political opportunity the prime minister and his allies have been waiting for. They fashion an alliance with top military and police officers to mount an anticorruption campaign. They intend to take advantage of the assassination attempt and the anticorruption campaign to break the opposition to strong central rule and stem the disintegration of Russia.

The "centrists" (as they are soon dubbed) enlist the police, the military, and the media in a massive campaign designed to exploit popular anger against crime and inequality and their perpetrators—mafias of all kinds, private entrepreneurs, and corrupt local officials. The prime minister announces the formation of special "staff headquarters" (*shtaby*) in every provincial capital, charged with directing the fight against crime and corruption. As the least corrupt element remaining in Russia, the security forces of the Federal Counterintelligence Service (in Russian, FSK) are enlisted in the battle. The FSK sets to work with a will.

One lurid revelation of crime and corruption follows another, and special crime squads begin making mass arrests. Public opinion, which politicians once thought was so jaded that it could safely be ignored, shows mounting popular rage directed against them.

As has happened in Russia so many times before, the campaign overheats and gets out of hand. Old enemies, under the cover of the anti-corruption campaign, settle personal accounts with one another through anonymous denunciations. Factory managers secretly smile as the managers of private investment funds, who might have threatened their control over their companies, get arrested. As the police search commercial banks for evidence of crimes, records of debts conveniently disappear. The leaders of the former Soviet labor unions use the campaign to eliminate upstart local unions, the so-called "strike committees," that had sprung up in recent years. And here and there throughout Russia, the luxury homes of the *nouveaux riches* go up in flames, along with innumerable kiosks and private stores.

In many places Russian mobs stage pogroms, beating up local non-Russians, chiefly southerners, and looting their homes. The police look on or actively assist. Chechens, Tatars, Azerbaidjanis, and others, are arrested or expelled from the major cities by the thousands.

The centrist alliance purges the provincial governors, replacing any waverers with proven Moscow loyalists. The climax of the anti-corruption campaign is the election of a new legislature in the spring of 1998. In a key move, prosecutors and military officers are appointed to head local electoral commissions and prevent the remnants of the local political machines from stuffing the ballot boxes.

They needn't have bothered: popular support for the campaign is overwhelming. The centrist alliance wins a convincing victory at the polls. The political landscape is transformed. The center has decisively weakened the power of the regions, while the executive branch has gained a lasting edge over the legislature. A compliant and relatively powerless legislature gathers in Moscow. The alliance is finally free to fashion its policies without interference from the legislature and the regional governments.

Local governments are given a small tax base of their own and a modest share of revenues from resources, but the central government is increasingly able to collect its taxes; pay its soldiers, police, and civil servants; control its borders; and hire and fire local officials. (Repression of the mafia liberates large amounts of money previously "taxed" by extortionists, thus fattening both the profits of businessmen and their tax payments to the government.) The central government also gains more power over the media, although chiefly by selective use of subsidies rather than outright censorship.

The Two-Headed Eagle government moves decisively to quell troublesome separatist movements in the north Caucasus, applying armed force where necessary. The "autonomous" governments of Sakha (Yakutiia), Komi, Tatarstan, and other ethnic republics are brought to heel, though they receive some concessions in exchange, in the form of a share in revenues from resources. Exports of natural resources from these regions are brought back under the control of state monopolies based in Moscow. Presidential plenipotentiaries are appointed to run the "autonomous" republics.

The response of Western governments to these moves is ambivalent. Live reports by CNN and SkyNews showing Russian army troops firing on Tatars in Kazan' provoke public discomfort in the West and calls to suspend aid to Russia. But the German chancellor emphatically declares that order in Russia is an internal matter, and the U.S., though publicly deploring the violence, quietly agrees.

The government moves quietly to quell extremist political groups. They are denied parade permits and are reduced to holding angry meetings in hired halls. On the few occasions when they attempt to defy the ban and mount public demonstrations, they are roughly put down by police.

The Two-Headed Eagle coalition now settles down to business.

ANALYSIS OF THE TWO-HEADED EAGLE

As well as being the symbol of tsarist Russia, the image of a two-headed eagle is intended to convey two meanings, both reflected in this scenario's name: First, it is a non-Communist but relatively conservative government, which faces cautiously both forward (toward a state-managed dual economy) and backward (toward the collectivist and industry-centered values of the past).

Second, the Two-Headed Eagle is the heir to the centralizing, Great Power traditions of the Russian past, and it is the government of a Great Russia that wants to catch its breath, recover its pride, and reassert its interests. It is, first and foremost, a government of consolidation, warmly welcomed by many Russians after a decade of continuous political and economic upheaval.

The key feature of the Two-Headed Eagle scenario is the reconstitution of a stronger central government than now exists under Muddling Down. This is not a scenario of full-scale reaction, but one based on an alliance of moderate-to-conservative groups, who believe that the best way to promote the "market" (as they see it) and economic recovery is through the reestablishment of strong central power and civil order. Their approach is technocratic. They believe that the soundest base for Russia's renaissance is Russian industry, especially defense industry. They are patriots.

Such "technocratic marketeers" are numerous in Russia. But how does the Two-Headed Eagle come to power, when the dominant trends seem to be in the opposite direction, toward the weakening of central government and growing disorder? There is potential public support for a strong hand, because of people's widespread revulsion over crime, corruption, inflation, and the general atmosphere of decadence and disorder, which the Russians call *bespredel*. But what is needed is a catalyst, some shock that gives "centrists" an opportunity to act and to overcome the scattering of power among many players. The attempted assassination of the president provides that catalyst.

But the real causes lie behind the scenes. What has changed in Russia since 1994 is that there are powerful people ready to take advantage of such a catalyst. They are a mixture of old and new elites. The professional apparatus of the president in Moscow has grown to over 4000 people. The military high command and the ex-KGB have recovered some of their strength and nerve. The central Russian bureaucracy has grown, and now employs as many people as the old Soviet one did.

RUSSIA 2010

The new Russian capitalists, whether they are former Soviet managers or newly-minted large businessmen, are heartily sick of being preyed upon by the mafia, and are ready for extreme measures against them. Ironically, the higher reaches of the criminal world—typically ethnic Russians—want protection against newer competitors from the streets, who are more often non-Russian southerners. They also want a more settled environment, in which to launder their gains and "go legit."

The anti-crime campaign simply brings out into the open what had long been taking shape behind the scenes: the fusion of new and old elites into a conservative political order. But the centrist alliance consists of more than opportunistic "haves." It also contains a number of career officers and civil servants, who are increasingly able to live on their officials salaries and perks as the taxation powers of the federal government improve, and are determined to stamp out the grosser forms of official corruption. For a variety of reasons, all these groups look to stronger central government in Moscow, rather than the regions.

Two-Headed Eagle confronts economic reformers and private entrepreneurs with a special dilemma. On the one hand, they welcome the prospect of effective police protection against extortion, and the opportunity to construct a sound financial and monetary structure for the Russian economy. This had been impossible to do under Muddling Down. But on the other hand, reformers and businessmen also recognize that Two-Headed Eagle puts power in the hands of senior technocrats who have little basic understanding of the market and whose instincts are interventionist. The outlook under Two-Headed Eagle is for more and more state regulation and interference, which reformers fear will squelch the growth of the private sector.

In sum, the fear of reformers is that Two-Headed Eagle heralds the *premature reconstitution of a strong state,* before private society and the fledgling market economy are able to defend their interests.

THE POLITICS OF TWO-HEADED EAGLE

The Two-Headed Eagle is based on a coalition of three groups: managers of large industries (with the defense industries at their core); the central bureaucracies in Moscow; and military, police, and state-security officers. In the provinces, the executive branches of local governments back Two-Headed Eagle, and support for the new government is

152

especially strong among many Russians living in the "autonomous" republics, who regret having initially encouraged the ambitions of the local non-Russian populations.

ECONOMIC POLICIES AND PERFORMANCE

The central aim of economic policy under the Two-Headed Eagle scenario is to take advantage of the central government's strengthened powers to pursue a controlled, state-directed transition to a new economy. However, the leaders are themselves unsure about just what they want that new economy to look like. In some respects, the Two-Headed Eagle looks backward. The leaders and their industrial supporters continue to have a close attachment to heavy industry and a strong defense industry. They are mostly engineers rather than economists. They find it natural that the state should subsidize leading industries. Above all, they are afraid of unemployment, and they are determined to prevent a further decline in popular living standards.

The leaders of the Two-Headed Eagle coalition do not have much instinctive feel for the role of law in a modern economy, or much sympathy with the idea of an independent judiciary. They put an end to experimentation with constitutional interpretation by the Constitutional Court. State bureaucrats interpret Two-Headed Eagle as a green light to return to their old ways, ignoring laws and ruling by administrative fiat instead.

At the same time, in other respects Two-Headed Eagle looks forward. The leaders have no wish to return to the Communist command economy. Therefore they continue to support privatization and marketization, but under strict central-government controls, and with the Russian government as the principal stockholder in the most strategic sectors, such as energy. Small shops and other small trade, privatized in 1992–93, are mostly left alone after the initial wave of harassment.

The Two-Headed Eagle coalition does accept that military and heavy-industrial production must decline over the long run, and that the consumer and service sectors must grow. They have become more sophisticated about money than they were ten years before, and they now understand the crucial importance of controlling and managing the money supply and the credit system, and of developing a modern system of banking and taxation.

They also accept the need to reach an accommodation with the Western international financial institutions and to encourage Western investment, although they are determined to remain in charge of any large Western projects. Finally, as privatization of large enterprises proceeds, the industrialists in the coalition acquire a growing stake in secure property rights.

All is not harmony within the ruling Two-Headed Eagle coalition, by any means. The industrialists themselves are divided between the large manufacturing sector, which wants cheap supplies and cheap loans, and the extractive industries (especially oil and gas), which want higher prices for their raw materials. The manufacturing sector itself is split between makers of heavy-industrial goods and weapons, who continue to look to the state as their principal buyer and investor, and the heads of consumer goods industries, who look to the growth of a large consumer sector and to self-financing. Though all want government subsidies, they differ sharply over pricing policy, taxation, and investment priorities.

Above all, the Two-Headed Eagle regime continues to struggle with the fundamental problems of the post-Communist economy: an output assortment that the government no longer needs and cannot afford (weapons, heavy machinery, too much steel, and the like); a monopolistic industrial structure that removes much of the meaning of price liberalization; primitive institutions for dealing with all aspects of money and finance; inadequate legal protections for contracts and property; and—despite some initial improvements in this area—an underground economy that remains large and difficult for the government to tax.

The Two-Headed Eagle leadership, without sharing the radical marketizing zeal of the Gaidar reformers, quietly adopts key elements of their program, agreeing, in particular, with their conviction that taxes must be raised, the money supply controlled, banks reined in, and state monopolies broken up. But they view the problem of moving toward the market as one of "state-building" and "ensuring governance." They tend to respond to problems with strict state controls.

The practical consequence is this: Under the Two-Headed Eagle the institutions of the market economy are gradually built just the same, but top-down (under state direction) rather than bottom-up (on the basis of society's own needs). Still, the coalition is fairly pragmatic, and economic policy under the Two-Headed Eagle is a series of running compromises to protect industrial interests.

The former Soviet space is now clearly divided into "Russian" and "non-Russian" zones; the latter moves toward separate currencies, while the former stays within the ruble zone but accepts monetary and credit policies from Moscow. As a result, the Russian government is able to regain some control over its own currency. Similarly, by now Russia has established border posts along the borders with the Baltic republics, Ukraine, and the Caucasian republics, and is able to bring smuggling under at least partial control.

The Two-Headed Eagle government practices a moderate policy toward the Near Abroad, aimed at restoring economic ties and trade flows, even with republics that have officially left the Commonwealth of Independent States, such as Ukraine, and the Baltic states.

The Russian leadership under Two-Headed Eagle carefully avoids confrontation over the Russian minorities outside its borders. There is a steady flow of highly qualified Russian immigrants into Russia, which aggravates the unemployment problem in the near term and adds to the later crisis of the regime at the end of the 1990s (see below), but which proves to be a valuable resource later on.

The Two-Headed Eagle continues the process of privatization, favoring ownership by existing managers. Freed from the political necessity to play populist politics, the government downplays worker ownership and takes a tough line toward labor unions. The welfare obligations of the enterprises (which amount to a form of taxation on them, absorbing as much as 30 percent of their profits) are gradually transferred to municipal governments, which are given a correspondingly larger tax base.

By slow degrees over the course of two decades, the managerial élite becomes a capitalist class, but one that remains closely tied to the state for protection and direction.

The most important policy undertaken by the Two-Headed Eagle is to begin shutting down the worst lame-duck industries of the Soviet era while pursuing the conversion of defense industries to civilian output. This is a policy that the Russian government advertised loudly under Muddling Down but was never strong enough to implement, and "bankruptcy" had always remained more of a slogan than a policy. The Two-Headed Eagle coalition deals with it by appointing industrial councils, in which the managers themselves thrash out who shall be eliminated.

This policy of industrial "triage" does not require sophisticated economic models: There are so many industrial enterprises with buildings and equipment more than a half century old that choosing candidates for closure is no problem. Their assets are practically worthless. But the main problem is to find alternate employment for their workers. Therefore, progress on this front is necessarily slow.

As a result of such mixed policies, the Two-Headed Eagle never achieves more than relative success in balancing its budget. Budget deficits are brought back down to within 5 percent of GDP; annual inflation hovers under 100 percent; and thanks to an improved trade balance and hard-currency reserves, the ruble stabilizes.

Most important, the Two-Headed Eagle government is able to collect enough revenue to begin increasing investment. Yet this remains a halting process, because of the continued technocratic biases of the leadership, which lead it to think in terms of large projects and "high" technology.

At the same time, the government continues to neglect humbler needs for more roads, food processing and preservation, health care, and air and water quality. The tax base of local governments is not large enough to enable them to invest on their own, and their meager resources are mostly absorbed in paying the salaries of local state employees and subsidizing food prices within their regions. Similarly, the higher tax burden imposed on industrial profits leaves the private sector with little surplus for its own investment. As a result, most investment is done by the government, on the basis of government programs.

Consequently, the evolution of the Russian economy is slow. Yet this policy of gradualism manages to keep people employed, clothed, and fed, and thus to limit the spread of political radicalism.

THE CRISIS OF THE FIRST DECADE OF THE NEXT CENTURY

By the early years of the twenty-first century, the gradual rise of a Russian capitalist managerial class and a middle class with property interests slowly creates a social base and a political constituency for a transition to a more liberal order, which the state-centered government structure cannot easily accommodate. For the first time since the Two-Headed Eagle coalition came to power, there appears a broad-based demand for change from below, for a smaller role for the government in the economy, for a better legal system, and for a more representative political system. Also for the first time, political parties with a large social following begin to appear.

As these tensions mount, two things suddenly become apparent: The government has failed to invest in retraining the labor force for the new service-based economy to come. And there is deep pent-up resentment among the workers, who feel cheated of the promise of ownership taken away from them over the past ten years.

Labor unions, which have been quiet in the previous five years, become more militant and spawn radical, nationalistic workers' parties. Suddenly, the government faces growing social tensions and a serious decay of the consensus on which it has been based since the early 1990s.

If the political system is capable of responding to these pressures and creating a new social consensus around a more liberal and democratic order, it will evolve into a more "civil" version of Capitalism Russian-Style. If not, it may enter a period of political unrest, from which a more authoritarian version of Russian capitalism may emerge. By this time, however, the transition to a new economy is fairly well along, and it is unlikely that Russia would lapse into any of the variants of the Time of Troubles scenario.

11

The Time of Troubles: Chaos and Reaction

"Our land is great and rich,
but there is disorder in it."
   —*The Primary Chronicles*
      (11th century)

"Let us at long last recognize that so far we have a weak state and that
there is no elementary order in the country."
                                      —*Boris Yeltsin, speech to the Duma (1994)*

WHY IS THERE NO CHAOS IN RUSSIA?

Some might think it remarkable that Russia has not yet collapsed into chaos. After all, no modern industrial society, with the special exception of Germany from the 1920s to the 1940s, has gone through such high inflation and depression, the ravaging of its population's living standards, the destruction of its political system, and the collapse of its official ideology, not to mention the breakup of its borders. Moreover, in Germany these disasters were spread out over a quarter century, while Russia is experiencing all of them at once.

   Yet, as travelers to Russia are invariably surprised to observe, life goes on: The trains and buses still run, as does Aeroflot (after its fashion); the lights are lit; people go about their business, and most of them seem reasonably well clothed and well fed; policemen stand in their traffic control boxes; the streets are relatively safe (by current U.S.

Scenario Pathways:
The Russian Bear

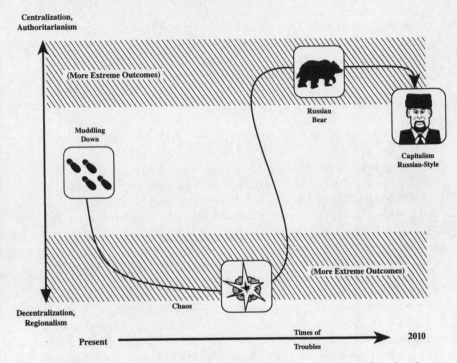

standards, at any rate); and the country, except for some of its border areas, is still at an uneasy peace. Russia today is not in chaos.

What, then, has so far prevented Russia from lapsing into chaos? There are several answers. The political system has unraveled from the top, but local government continues to function, if not competently, at least with some success in keeping order and maintaining services. The state economy, similarly, has not so much collapsed as gradually wound down, but it still supplies food and benefits to its employees. A new economy is growing alongside the old, providing a living, or at least a boost, to many people, especially the young. More than a few, especially in the large cities, are gaining enormously. The energy required to survive day to day, and the opportunities available for the more enterprising, have tended to remove people from politics.

159

Thus, the reasons why chaos has not broken out in Russia have little to do with "Russian stolidity," "stoicism," or other supposed traits of Russian national character. Rather, enough of the old system still survives, and enough of a new one has emerged, to keep most people fed, clothed, housed—and busy.

But this mixture is far from stable. What is certain, as we have seen in earlier chapters, is that Russian society and the economy are under extraordinary stress. Economic output, average standards of living, and personal security are all still declining. If stress keeps on growing, some sort of political breakdown, sooner or later, becomes more and more probable.

HOW MIGHT CHAOS BREAK OUT?

A breakdown in Russia could begin from three distinct sources, political, economic, and social. In practice, all three could occur together. A breakdown is hardly likely to occur simultaneously in all parts of Russia. Some places have already passed the breaking point; others are still relatively unaffected. Russia is increasingly a mosaic of individual cases.

The four-year decline in the Russian economy is not yet a total collapse. But should the large enterprises become incapable of operating—whether because of tightening credit, a failure to be paid, or an inability to obtain supplies—mass unemployment will begin to become a fact. It will not happen equally in all regions, and this is politically crucial. The places most affected will be those that make goods and weapons that the government cannot buy, and produce raw materials that cannot be exported.

The amorphousness of Russian society, analyzed in earlier chapters, carries with it a special danger: The very absence of organized channels means that once a certain level of popular rage and despair has been reached, they could erupt spontaneously into the streets as mob violence. Astonishingly, so far all manner of polls suggest that Russian public opinion has been apathetic. Anger is surely present in abundance, as the December 1993 elections and the success of the Red-Browns demonstrated, but it has not yet taken political form on a massive, uncontrollable scale.

What could cause built-up popular anger to boil into mob violence is a sudden shock, not even necessarily a large one. In past Russian history, defeat and reverses in war have played such a role: The 1905 revolution followed Japan's defeat of Russia; the 1917 revolution was ignited by the ravages of World War I; and, most recently, the collapse of Soviet morale was accelerated by the long inconclusive war in Afghanistan. Since Russia is not at war, no similar jolt appears likely in the near future. But some other development—perhaps involving Russian minorities outside Russia—could possibly act as a catalyst in much the same way.

Another possible catalyst for radical action would be a sudden deterioration in the food supply to the big cities, possibly owing to drought or the disruption of grain imports. Here Moscow and St. Petersburg are especially vulnerable, as they are located at the end of food chains that work poorly. The 1917 revolution was sparked specifically by bread shortages in St. Petersburg.

So far, however, the prospect of a sudden food crisis appears remote, although unquestionably Russians today are spending much of their disposable income on food and are thus highly vulnerable to sudden sharp price increases. Yet physical shortages seem unlikely, mainly because farmers, most of whom are still in collective and state farms (though many of these have been renamed joint-stock corporations and the like), have continued to grow food and send it to market.

Indeed, the one event that would be most likely to produce a food crisis is a sudden and massive privatization of farmland, of the huge state farms into small and uneconomic private holdings. Private farmers, lacking capital and skills and probably facing monopsonistic buyers, might stop producing for the market, thus engendering an agricultural crisis similar to that of 1918–22. The recent example of Lithuania, which has conducted just such a privatization, shows how real this risk is.

FAILURE OF THE FEDERAL GOVERNMENT?

Mass unemployment is the greatest potential cause of chaos. Yet even this can be managed. The absence of deep class identification or solidarity in Russia means that there could be rioting due to mass unemployment or food shortages in one part of Russia without its necessarily spreading to the rest of the country, or even from one neighborhood to another within a single city. Mass strikes among coal workers in the Kuzbas, for example, have not led to walkouts by oil workers in Tiumen. Rioting by white-collar workers in Moscow would not necessarily be imitated by steelworkers in Magnitogorsk. Provided a breakdown in civil order did not engulf Moscow itself, or spread to a number of cities simultaneously, it might be contained without critical political damage. Only if it became an epidemic would it be life-threatening politically.

Incoherent policy and ceaseless political turmoil, resulting from continuing gridlock, would lead toward chaos. In most provinces outside Moscow, the central government has little direct power. But it has a great deal of indirect influence. What keeps most provincial governments within Moscow's orbit so far is that their regions are not capable of self-sufficiency. In most places, their money, their communications, their food supply, and their raw materials are all controlled, however weakly or badly, from Moscow.

In case of trouble, one big question would be: What is politically vital? There are already places such as Chechnia, where the federal government is unable to collect taxes and faces a growing "national" army. But it is not rebellion in remote mountain provinces that will bring chaos to the Russian core. Nor is it, say, the posturing of Siberian politicians. Rather, it is a loss of central control over vital political and economic resources at the Russian core of the country. Above all, Moscow remains the key.

Adding up these diverse elements, what chaos scenarios are plausible during the Time of Troubles? We present two variants—the Long Good-bye and the Russian Bear.

"MILD" CHAOS SCENARIO: THE LONG GOOD-BYE

In December 1993, Boris Yeltsin finally won his fight for a new constitution. But the document is so vague and contradictory on key points that it comes to be challenged on all sides. Many regional leaders question the constitution's legitimacy, arguing that only a minority of eligible voters approved it. After a few years the new constitution begins to resemble the old—a patchwork of amendments, ambiguous on key issues such as the division of powers between center and province. It is eventually rejected by nearly everyone.

Meanwhile, legislative elections in 1995 produce a new legislature that is much the same as the old—disunited and poorly organized, and prone to corruption and manipulation. Voter turnout is low, and there are candidates from over thirty parties, the majority having only a local or regional following. All sides continue to fight over property rights and privatization policy. What laws are passed are vague and are not implemented. In short, politics remains deadlocked in Moscow.

GOING THEIR OWN WAY

The regions are continuing to drift off in their own directions, their ties to Moscow steadily weakening. For lack of investment, new national communications systems have not been completed. In many places it is easier to call abroad than to reach Moscow. Instead of a million new telephones a year as in 1990, the Ministry of Communications now manages to install barely one fifth as many; at that rate, the average Russian will wait fifty years for a new telephone. The national railroad system has not been expanded or effectively maintained; it now takes three weeks to go from Moscow to Vladivostok on the Trans-Siberian, and goods frequently take twice that long. Local and regional media begin to flourish, independently of the central media in Moscow. The Russian military continues to dwindle, and by 1999 some parts of the country have almost no military presence.

Financial trends also contribute to weakening national ties. Moscow is increasingly unable to levy taxes from the more outlying regions. Magadan was the first province, back in 1993, to withhold all taxes to the federal government, and it was soon followed by others. The national banking system remains primitive, but local and regional debt-settlement systems begin to develop rapidly. Most commercial banks remain local or regional. Japanese and Korean banks are granted branch licenses and begin to penetrate the Russian Far East. By 1999, a functional banking system has developed in that region, far in advance of any existing elsewhere in Russia. Trade within or among regions, bypassing Moscow as the center, begins to grow rapidly.

Moscow turns into a more prosperous, cosmopolitan, and, in some people's eyes, decadent city, thanks to foreign currency that continues to pour in, both from export revenues and from foreign investment in offices and services. Moscow becomes more absorbed in its own life and it turns away from the real problems in the rest of the country. This fuels the dislike and contempt that many non-Muscovites feel for the capital. In this environment, three regions begin to develop the basis for economic and political autonomy from Moscow and the rest of the country.

The Northwest: St. Petersburg Becomes a Free Economic Zone

The city government of St. Petersburg gives tax holidays and other advantages to foreign companies. Foreign firms, principally German and Scandinavian, invest in St. Petersburg's industries, taking advantage of cheap and highly skilled labor and proximity to Europe. The city's tax revenues largely escape Moscow's grasp.

Buoyed by all this, St. Petersburg forms a loose "northern confederation" with the cities of Murmansk and Arkhangel'sk. Military industries in these cities, added to the large numbers of officers stationed in nearby Karelia, give the confederation a credible means of self-defense and an advanced industrial base. Oil and gas development in Timan-Pechora and in the Barents Sea provides the region with both near-term and long-term exportable resources.

The Far East Becomes Part of the Pacific Rim

Sakha (the former Yakutiia), Irkutsk, and the Far Eastern maritime provinces turn increasingly to Japan and the Pacific Rim. As early as 1989 the Far Eastern provinces had formed a Far Eastern economic association, and by 1991 there was talk of reviving the short-lived Far Eastern Republic, which had briefly existed from 1920 to 1922 under Japanese protection. The region experiences a wave of strikes, which Moscow proves unable to counteract.

Richly endowed, the region produces 15 percent of Russia's output of natural resources. But its potential is far greater than that: Sakha (Yakutiia) has gold and diamonds; Sakhalin and Irkutsk have oil and gas; and the Maritime Province has military facilities, fishing, and shipbuilding. The region's three principal ports—Vladivostok, Komsomol'sk, and Vostochnoe—handle 30 percent of Russia's foreign trade. They were privatized back in 1993 and have been booming ever since. Vladivostok is also the site of the first stock exchange to trade only in the shares of privatized companies.[1]

One thing the Russian Far East does not have is people—only eight million live there. Moscow is thousands of miles away. As Moscow itself becomes more dependent on the Pacific Rim for capital, it signs a series of agreements giving Japan and Korea more and more de facto control over local resources. Large scale resource development by Japanese companies takes place under a joint Japanese and Russian government umbrella. China, with a hundred million people stretched along the border with the Far East, becomes increasingly involved. Chinese farmers and traders migrate in large numbers into the Russian Far East and begin to account for a substantial part of food production and economic activity. Russians go to work in China. The Russian Far East becomes an arena for competition among Japan, Korea, and China.

Japan and Russia—Beyond the Four Islands

Japan grows increasingly worried by the growing military might of China and its expanding economic dominance in Asia—and by the uncertainty and possible instability that surround political developments in China. In North Korea, Kim Il Sung managed to pass from the scene without using nuclear weapons, and Korean unification has now been completed. Koreans do not make the same mistake that Germans made in raising wages in the former communist area, and the large amount of low cost labor suddenly available gives Korea a new dynamism in the Asian and world economies. Relations with the United States continue to be unsteady, as key groups on both sides take for granted and underestimate the critical importance of good Japanese-U.S. relations to overall global stability.

All of this raises the importance of Russia in Japan's eyes. For their part, both Moscow and the Far East realize that they have not given sufficient attention to Japan. Moscow is eager to get the "Northern Territories" issue resolved, for it recognizes that this obstacle is proving very costly. It is clear that Japan will bristle at any suggestion that it is "buying" back territories—the four southern Kurile islands—that by rights belong to it in any event. Yet Moscow cannot be seen as giving up the Far East to "colonization"—however much the locals may want trade and investment from Japan (and the other Asian neighbors). The Russian president rebuffs extreme nationalist critics by declaring that the seizure of the four islands was "yet another example of Stalin's aggression and crimes, and we should not let the inheritance of Stalin block the Russian people from achieving the better life that will come from normal economic relations."

Settlement is facilitated by the determination of the new Japanese prime minister, Makiko Tanaka, Japan's first woman prime minister. At a summit meeting in Vladivostok, she and the Russian president sign an agreement that provides for a free trade zone and 10-year joint sovereignty, at the end of which the islands fully revert to Japan. At the same time, they establish a Japanese-Russian economic commission to identify joint infrastructure and development projects in the Far East, and joint cooperation to convert Russian defense industries to assembling and supplying goods that are no longer internationally competitive from high-cost Japanese factories. Separately, the Russian prime minister and Japan's MITI and foreign ministers sign a $10 billion package of Japanese credits and investment that will provide the framework for future economic relations.

"For over a hundred years, politics has disrupted relations between our two countries and has made us rivals and adversaries," Prime Minister Tanaka declares. "Now common interests and economic realism will provide the basis for good relations in the twenty-first century."

The rivalry is no longer between Moscow and Japan, but between Moscow and the Russian Far East, and the struggle is over such matters as taxation and investment projects. The Duma in Moscow erupts into an uproar when the governor of Khabarovsk announces that the Far East is as much a part of Asia as it is of Russia. Japanese companies move ahead with business. Both Russia and Japan are all too aware of the vast Chinese population pushing up against the border.

The South Russian Confederation

A handful of southern provinces have exportable agricultural produce and oil (not to mention some tourist potential). High-quality ports such as Novorossiisk and Tuapse give this region export outlets to the Black Sea. There are growing troop concentrations in southern Russia as the Russian military moves returning forces from Europe to that area. Local politicians form regional alliances with Cossacks who add an unruly nationalist tone to this region.

Another significant resource of this region is drugs. Rostov and Krasnodar have emerged as major transit routes for the drug trade from the Caucasus and Central Asia to Western Europe, as well as increasingly important producers of opium poppy (*mak*) and marijuana (*konoplia*) in their own right. This helps to account for the fact that these two provinces lead Russia in the reported incidence of murders and other violent crime.[2]

"UNITARISTS" VERSUS "REGIONALISTS"

By the early years of the twenty-first century, these separatist trends have gained considerable momentum. Other parts of Russia do not have nearly the same potential for self-sufficiency. They look upon the quasi-independence of the three with a jealous eye and begin to lean back toward Moscow themselves. By 2003, this has produced two clear factions in Russian politics: the "unitarists," who support a more centralized Russian government, and the "regionalists," basically the representatives of the south, northwest, and Far East. The "unitarists" become dominant in Moscow, and this finally breaks the long-standing deadlock in Moscow politics.

Meanwhile, other trends have emerged that cause the three autonomous regions to have second thoughts about drifting too far from Russia. In the Far East, the very vigor of the Japanese, Chinese, and Korean penetration begins to cause a nationalist backlash among the local Russians, who fear being swamped by their much stronger neighbors. This causes a "unitarist" faction to grow up in the Far East, and by 2005 representatives of this faction are negotiating with Moscow to strengthen the region's ties with the Russian "mainland" once more.

A similar trend is under way in south Russia. The mixture of ethnic groups, rivalries, and competing claims makes the region highly volatile. Its border areas are aflame with ethnic wars, some of which threaten to destabilize south Russia itself. The members of the South Russian Confederation are a fractious lot: the Kalmyk Republic, Dagestan, Astrakhan', Krasnodar, and Stavropol', together with smaller Muslim areas such as Chechnia and Karbardino-Balkariia. The key resource of the group is oil, based on the oil fields of Chechnia, Ingushetiia, and Dagestan, and control over the key export pipelines from Azerbaijan and Kazakhstan, plus the port facilities at Novorossiisk. But oil proves to be divisive, driving the members of the confederation into conflict with one another. Local wars throughout the 1990s have already made the region an arms bazaar, leading to the buildup of large local concentrations of experienced and well-armed manpower.

In response to these trends, "unitarist" sentiment grows rapidly in the Russian population of south Russia, and by 2005 the dominant politicians in the region are calling for closer ties with Moscow.

St. Petersburg and the northwest were always the weakest of the three regions in their economic potential for independence, and as the military and industrial leaders of the region see the rise of the "unitarist" faction in Moscow, they are naturally attracted to it. But the decisive factor in the northwest is Russian pride and patriotism. The growing reconsolidation of Russia from 2005 brings a strong outpouring of Russian national sentiment, which sweeps the northwest back into the fold.

The key event in this "regathering of the Russian lands" comes in 2008. A new Constitutional Conference, the first since the mid-1990s, convenes in Moscow. The unitarists of the "have-not" provinces form a common front with the unitarist-minded delegates from the three main autonomous regions. The result is a historic compromise in the name of national reconciliation and reunification.

A new constitution is adopted, which preserves the essential economic rights of the regions, yet provides for some revenue-sharing and redistribution of wealth throughout the federation. The new constitution is ratified by large popular majorities in all the provinces. In the presidential elections of 2010, the former mayor of St. Petersburg is elected president of Russia.

ANALYSIS OF THE LONG GOOD-BYE

In this scenario the separatist tendencies of the regions are overcome relatively easily and quickly, and the recentralization of Russia around Moscow produces a mild, even democratic regime. This version of chaos and reaction may seem so moderate that it hardly qualifies as a member of the "Time of Troubles" family of scenarios. But that is the point: At one extreme, regional separatism could be a relatively mild and slow force, overcome without bloodshed and extreme backlash.

There are four elements to the Long Good-bye scenario. The first is that the basis for regional separatism and autonomy in Russia, though it frequently wears an ethnic face and voices nationalistic slogans, is more typically material interest, chiefly involving Russian players. Thus in Sakha (Yakutiia), only 30 percent of the population consists of Yakuts, few of whom live in the cities and towns; most of the leading politicians are Russian. Though these local ambitions are not a force to be underestimated, they are at least not ideological. Any compromise that satisfies the striving of local élites for greater local control of revenues and resources is likely to lead to a reintegration of Russia.

The second point is that few regions in Russia actually have the basis for true autonomy or independence. At a minimum, a region that wishes to be truly independent must have access to the outside world, resources to trade, and some capability to defend itself. By that yardstick, the landlocked republics—for example, Tatarstan, the Volga republics, and Komi—are doomed in the long run to be part of Russia. So are the large blocks of western Siberia and Krasnoiarsk, unless they can form a bloc with the entire Russian Far East (with which, however, the central Siberian provinces have little in common). At the end of this analysis, only three regions appear to be serious candidates, even in theory, for independence: south Russia, the northwest, and the Far East.

The third element of the Long Good-bye is reintegration. At the moment, what gets attention is the divisive forces in Russia. But there are also reintegrating elements, which must not be underestimated. The Russians' sense of national identity is based above all on the Russian language and a sense of shared history, and those are strong forces. Religion is a further glue. Also, all modern Russians have gone through the Soviet era together. Whatever one may think of it, "Soviet culture" made Russia a single entity, and all Russians unconsciously share that culture, even if they consciously reject it. Russians, in a word, understand one another, in the many senses of that phrase, and that too is a powerful unifying force.

Finally, the economic, political, and emotional center of Russia is still Moscow. The only thing that can prevent Moscow from playing its role is political deadlock within it, or the actual physical elimination of the city from politics as a result of civil war.

The Long Good-bye is the most benign of the possible family of scenarios in the Time of Troubles, and one should not underestimate how trouble-ridden even the Long Good-bye could be. For example, with the decline of central power, many of the various Russian provinces could become criminal mini-states (as indeed some are already becoming today), dominated by an unholy alliance of the former nomenklatura and the new mafia. These areas would move wholesale into international crime—trafficking in weapons, radioactive isotopes, drugs, the export of prostitutes, and other lucrative contraband.

However, as profitable as these activities may be, they would enrich powerful minorities rather than the populations of whole regions. Therefore it is possible that popular revulsion against the extremes of crime and corruption could become a rallying force behind the "regathering."

Could the process of disintegration that turned the Soviet Union into fifteen independent republics continue and result in the unraveling of Russia itself? And what might happen then?

THE RUSSIAN BEAR

It is the spring of 1997. The "rotten" summer of 1996 has been followed by a record cold winter. Privatization has disordered the agricultural sector. By the spring, food supplies to the major cities are short.

Many farmers, burdened by taxes and high prices for equipment and fuel, have retreated into subsistence farming. Traders are jacking up prices and accepting only foreign currency. President Yeltsin, having retired, has been succeeded by a former mathematics professor who was elected in a disputed five-man race with only 22 percent of the popular vote. He proves to be a weak president, and popular disillusionment with politics deepens. Angry Muscovites, many of them unemployed women, march in the streets; hotheads begin smashing bread stores. Moscow police, unpaid for months, stand by, clearly sympathetic. Military units called in from recent duty in the North Caucasus refuse to fire on fellow Russians. The crowds grow to hundreds of thousands, and all ordinary activity in Moscow comes to a stop. Red-Brown paramilitary units begin assaults on government buildings defended by loyalist forces. The government goes into hiding, while Moscow falls under the rule of the mob.

The heads of administration of the Russian provinces and the commanders of the military districts meet secretly in Nizhnii Novgorod (formerly Gorky). They quickly devise a plan for the military reoccupation of Moscow. Troops loyal to the government soon regain control of the streets. A crack Alpha brigade surrounds key nerve centers, including the Kremlin, the Ostankino radio and television tower, and the government headquarters on Old Square, as they expel the right-wing groups. Now installed in Moscow, the provincial leaders and military commanders reject the discredited federal government and form a "caretaker council," pending national elections.

It's too late. The turmoil spreads to other cities, and it is soon apparent that elections must be postponed. Moreover, the caretakers, lacking any power of their own or experience of national government, prove utterly unable to resolve the food crisis or to devise even minimally effective economic policies. They are divided internally, between reformers and conservatives and between civilians and officers, and quickly fall to bickering. Government in Moscow is paralyzed once more. Factional fighting breaks out in the regional cities.

While politicians bicker, the Red-Browns fan out throughout the city, propagandizing the military units that have recently occupied it. Many of them are soon won over by the Red-Browns' message of rage and rejection. The occupying forces split between loyalists and rebels. Fighting breaks out again. Moscow fissures into warring neighborhoods, separated by no-man's-lands, as contending groups try to seize stores, inventories, supplies, and strategic points. Red-Browns form local militias and start warring against each other.

The caretaker council, helpless to restore order in the city, withdraws to Nizhnii Novgorod. Moscow is effectively knocked out as the capital of the country. In almost every city in Russia, factions of Red-Browns and loyalists do battle. The president flees to Stockholm.

The Russian defense minister, General Ivan Nikolaev, flies to Rostov and takes over the southern theater command. Nikolaev, a tough former paratroop commander who was twice wounded in Afghanistan, is popular with his troops. Decisive and effective, he is known for his patriotic views and his contempt for politicians. Nikolaev prepares a lightning strike on Moscow and makes short work of reconquering the city from the disorganized and divided Red-Browns.

Nikolaev appeals for support from major military units. The Strategic Rocket Forces declare their allegiance, as do the major paratroop units and mobile ground forces. With no effective military opposition, Nikolaev and his commanders use Moscow as a base for reconquering the rest of the country. With control of communications, railroads, and the like, Nikolaev's supporters soon take control of the rest of Russia, including the rebellious autonomous republics.

The presidential system is now not only discredited, it has been completely bypassed by events. Nikolaev decides to make a radical break with the democracy. He declares himself president for a six-year "recovery" period, but a second term follows. Nikolaev, it seems, intends to be president for life.

THE RUSSIAN BEAR TAKES POWER

The Russian Bear is ruled by the forces that reconquered the country. Thus it is composed mainly of elements of the professional coercive élites—the military, the police, and the secret police—in alliance with most of what remains of the industrial élite and the Moscow bureaucracy. At the head of the new regime stands a small junta of military commanders, led by General Nikolaev, responsible for the key victories in the "regathering." They proclaim themselves the Defenders of the Russian Nation.

The Russian Bear is authoritarian, but it is quite different from Soviet totalitarianism. The regime is not based on the Communist party, even though many former Communists rally to it, nor on Marxist ideology or Marxist internationalism, although it does espouse some socialist principles. Its ideology is vague, founded mainly on militant Russian nationalism and statist conservatism. It celebrates the Red Army and its victories (especially World War II), but without glorifying Stalin or reviving the hammer and sickle.

However, the Russian Bear does rule by terror at first. Basic freedoms are sharply limited, and the independent press is suppressed. When censors start ordering changes in the Russian-language editions of *The New York Times* and the *Financial Times,* their editors instead cease publication. An army general becomes director of Russian television and personally approves the script for the evening news every day. Western popular culture is attacked. The police methodically sweep in and break up a huge rock concert in Gorky Park, arresting over sixteen hundred young people. The regime rules by decree and administrative allocation. The judiciary and the legislature are curbed, and the powers of local governments are greatly reduced. Day after day, the regime spokesmen denounce not only the West and "Western interference" in Russia and the rest of the former Soviet Union, but also the Westernizing course pursued by the "traitors Gorbachev and Yeltsin."

Russian Bear is initially hostile to private capital and to private property in land. Faced with an economy ravaged by ten years of "reform" followed by a brief but violent period of civil strife, the Russian Bear tries to return to administrative methods, including strict wage and price controls and centralized government. With a fury pent up over a decade, it sets out to purge "traitors" and "enemies." It sweeps up crime syndicates, without being very careful whether some of the gang members get shot in the process. It also imprisons some members of the new business class that had emerged since 1985, accusing them of "speculation," "corruption," "profiteering," and working for "foreign" entities opposed to Russian "interests." Most of what remains of Western companies packs up and leaves.

Agriculture, never fully reformed to begin with, returns to state farms and small private plots. Big industry is reorganized into state corporations under central ministries. Small and medium-sized enterprise, including trade and services, are harassed, but continue. Foreign trade is controlled, including the critical export, oil; and foreign investment, at least initially, is scorned.

Despite its militant Russian nationalism and its resentment of the West, the new leadership does not return completely to the defense-first spending priorities of the Soviet regime, mainly because there is no ideological imperative for an arms race, which it cannot afford in any event, and because much of the institutional basis for military spending has decayed. Nevertheless, having reached power thanks to the army, the new leadership is both inclined and obliged to maintain large military forces and to try to support them with modern weapons. It dedicates itself to restoring the dignity of the armed forces, and the media celebrate the military.

For the Russian Bear, the primary threats to the security of the country are the secessionist tendencies within, and it gives top priority to liquidating the "autonomous" regions in Russia itself.

ANTI-WESTERN

The Russian Bear is anti-Western. Unlike that of the Soviet regime, however, its anti-Western posture is not the result of a Marxist belief in world revolution. Rather, Russia is reasserting itself and its interests as a great power. It is reacting against the humiliation of the later 1980s and early 1990s, rejecting the "pollution" of popular Western culture. In other words, while aggressive within the borders of the former Soviet Union, the Russian Bear, although unfriendly, has no global "mission" (or capabilities) and is not necessarily aggressive outside those borders.

Foreign economic policy is another matter entirely. The Russian government suspends all repayment of its foreign debt; it denounces pressure from foreign lenders and threatens to cancel its obligations altogether. The finance ministers and central bank directors of the G-7 nations hurriedly meet in London and announce that, in retaliation, all credits and loans to Russia are suspended. Western businesses, most of whom had closed their offices and pulled out their personnel when civil war broke out, turn their attention to other parts of the world.

But the G-7 is split. The Japanese manage to convey that their long-standing skepticism has now been borne out. The Europeans, worried about the gas trade, caution against breaking all links. Imports into Russia of grain, other foods, and industrial goods shrink dramatically. Russia briefly returns to economic autarky, as in the 1930s. In this environment, naturally, foreign investment is out of the question.

During the earlier phase of chaos, Russian minorities outside Russia came under increased harassment from locally dominant ethnic groups. In Kazakhstan, in particular, long-contained hostility between Russians and Kazakhs had broken into open violence. The new regime in Moscow now mounts a systematic campaign of reprisal and revenge as soon as it has the power to do so. With its large Russian population, Kazakhstan is the first to fall under the eye of the Russian Bear. Russia annexes the key Russian regions of Kazakhstan, along with the hydro-carbon-rich regions of western Kazakhstan for good measure.

Two key potential flashpoints are Ukraine and the Baltic states, both because they contain large Russian populations and because Russian nationalists urge that Russia reassert its "historic sovereignty" over those regions. A series of clashes takes place along the Ukrainian-Russian border. As a result of the confrontations, eastern Ukraine and the Crimea, with large Russian populations, are reincorporated into Russia.

EVOLUTION OF THE RUSSIAN BEAR

Despite its initial aggressiveness, the Russian Bear soon begins to evolve beneath the surface. Without Communist ideology or the Communist party, the leaders have little stomach for a full-scale return to the command economy. They know, as well as anybody does, that it failed the first time around.

On the political front, the initial repression unleashed by the Russian Bear does not last, because (unlike the Bolshevik terror and purges of the 1920s and 1930s) it is not fueled by class hatred and militant ideology, and therefore does not balloon into demonic Stalinist hysteria.

After a gruesome but relatively brief period of intense witch-hunting and reprisals, the level of repression, in Russia at any rate, soon returns to a level similar to that of the Soviet 1970s—that is, the security police concentrate on overt dissidents but leave the rest of the population pretty much alone. In the non-Russian republics—at least, the ones Russia chooses to control directly—repression lasts longer because it is aimed at suppressing local nationalism. On the borders with Central Asia, the Russians have to contend with local guerrilla wars.

The Russian Bear never makes a concerted effort to return to the economic policies and structures of the Soviet period. Once repression has abated, the underground economy returns, the interests of the large industrial managers increasingly diverge from those of the state, and pressures for economic liberalization soon build up from below.

After a few years, the leaders, having no real economic alternative, are ready to listen to market-oriented economic advisers. Over the years, most of the imprisoned private-sector businesspeople are amnestied and released; many of them cautiously return to private enterprise, although none is compensated for confiscated property. But the authorities show no hesitation in periodically using force and police power to harass people they consider black marketeers and speculators, and they are ruthless with suspected gangsters.

Having initially rejected the capitalist path, the leaders of the Russian Bear are led back after a time to some form of it. After much delay, but not more than half a decade, the Russian Bear gradually returns to a path parallel to that of the Two-Headed Eagle, but in a more centralized, nationalistic, and authoritarian form. Some Western countries gradually relax their policies toward Russia and begin to extend export credits again.

ANALYSIS: MOSCOW IS THE KEY

In bringing civil disorder to an end, Moscow is the key, as it was during the Russian civil war, 1918–20. The reasons why Moscow is still significant include:

- The cultural and linguistic unity of Russia and the historic importance of Moscow (along with St. Petersburg) as the center of Russian intellectual, spiritual, and political life.
- The centralization of much of Russia's physical infrastructure around Moscow and the Moscow region—railroads, pipelines, telephones (especially closed governmental and ministerial networks), telecommunications, media, airport facilities, and so on.
- Career ties and extensive personal networks, which converge on Moscow. Local Russian officials have a lifelong habit of looking toward Moscow for decisions and solutions.
- Military, military-industrial, engineering-scientific, and police power, which are also more concentrated in the Moscow area than in any other single region. In particular, the military has traditionally favored a unitary state with Moscow as its heart. Russia's business, financial, foreign-trade, and legal talent, including much of the new private sector, are also concentrated in Moscow.
- Finally, Russia's historic tradition of unitary government, except for brief moments of dire crisis and foreign invasion. Absent are the deeply rooted regional particularisms and loyalties (with the exception, perhaps of St. Petersburg) and the ideological differ-

ences among the regions that would provide the basis for separatism.

The kind of regime that emerges in reaction to chaos depends above all on how severe and violent the disintegration turns out to be, and by what path the country is reunited. The general principle is this: The more extreme the descent into anarchy, the stronger the countervailing reaction, and the more authoritarian the resulting regime. The greater the chaos and the military and political exertion required to "regather the Russian lands," the greater the resulting recentralization is likely to be.

The key judgment in this scenario is that for all their success in disrupting Moscow and the major cities, the "Red-Browns" remain hardly better organized than street mobs. Unlike the Brown shirts of the 1920s and 1930s in Germany, the Red-Browns do not become an alternative army (there are no Versailles restrictions on the size of the regular army) and do not have the tacit support of the officer corps. Few of the Red-Browns are tested in actual warfare and a good part of their troops are middle-aged or elderly. Consequently, the Red-Browns are unable to win in an all-out confrontation with a determined and charismatic military commander.

12

Chudo: The Russian Economic Miracle

"The first stage of the development of securities markets has been
defined by a struggle for control of enterprises. We're now in transition
from the first stage to the second, where enterprises can raise capital
through market structures. In some respects, this development has
occurred more quickly than many people supposed."
— *Deputy Chairman, State Property Commission, 1994*

It is 2002. Russia has been travelling the hard road away from
communism for eleven years. Politically, the worst of the transition
seems to be over. To the surprise of most Russians, the Constitution of
1993 has survived for nearly a decade, providing the new political
institutions the country so desperately needed, and stabilizing Russian
politics somewhat. The president rules alongside a legislature dominated by the regional politicians. Their partnership is uneasy, but there
is no longer the open warfare of 1992–93.

The power of the executive branch in Moscow has grown steadily,
particularly that of the president's apparatus, which is now over 5000
strong. The president has gained relatively secure control over the
military and the secret police. This gives him a freer hand than before
in foreign policy, which he uses to break the Kurile Islands impasse
with Japan, on financial terms very favorable to Russia.

The federal government is also better able than before to govern the
country. It has improved its control over taxes, credit, and money. It
has made some headway against crime—mainly by co-opting the aris-

tocracy of the criminal world into the ranks of the new managers, while ruthlessly stamping out the smaller fry in the streets.

But Russia's hard-won stability appears threatened as the country faces its first transfer of power to a new president. Boris Yeltsin, now over 70 years old and suffering acutely from back pains and headaches that limit his work day to just a few hours, has been a virtual figurehead for years. He was barely persuaded to run again in 1996 and it has long been evident that his political life is over.

A new generation of politicians has been waiting impatiently in the wings. They are no longer the political prima donnas of the early 1990s, but an increasingly professional breed of practical political operators. They speak for interest groups and political parties that, in the space of ten years, have become well organized and politically powerful. The biggest of these represent the banks, investment firms, and insurance companies. Through a complex network of interlocking directorships and stockholdings, the big financial institutions have become the de-facto owners of much of the country's private economy.

The leading political party of the day is the Union for Russian Democracy, a descendant of the moderate reformist parties of the mid-1990s. At a boisterous national conference it nominates as its presidential candidate Aleksandr Karamysyhev, a former physicist and an early —if critical—supporter of democratic reform. Karamyshev had been a Yeltsin advisor and then a provincial governor. He attracted nationwide attention for his active and effective support for marketizing reform and privatization, and for his rare ability to get along with the many different kinds of players now on the Russian scene, whether Moscow technocrats or Volga mafiosi.

In 2000 the Constitution had been amended to restore the post of vice president—a move supported both by Yeltsin's enemies and by those who were afraid he might not live out his second term. As its vice presidential candidate, the Union for Russian Democracy nominates Vladimir Sokolov, general director of the Sputnik Aviation Plant, a factory with a distinguished wartime history and a solid track record as one of the most dynamic of Russia's privatized companies. Sokolov is well known as a pragmatic entrepreneur. He successfully attracted private Russian capital to commercial projects launched by his aviation company. Sokolov's policy was to ask investors no questions about where their funds came from, and as a result his company benefited hugely from new Russian money, amassed, as some entrepreneurs put it, through "primary accumulation."

With Karamyshev and Sokolov teamed up as running mates, a powerful coalition of forces comes together: the democratic reformers, the pragmatists, regional politicians of many different colorations, and the military industrialists. Boris Yeltsin endorses the ticket, putting government support and funding behind the pair. As a result, the Karamyshev-Sokolov coalition appears headed for victory in the presidential election.

THE ECONOMY: TRAPPED IN A BOX

The main issue in the campaign is not politics, but the economy. It seems trapped in a box. There have been solid achievements: Virtually all stores, restaurants, and other trade establishments have passed into private hands, as have a large number of medium and large enterprises. The private sector is increasingly well organized politically. In addition to the powerful financial sector, every branch of the economy has its lobbyists swarming all over Moscow. Property rights are becoming more secure, if only because there are now so many property owners, many of them well connected with local politicians. Capital flight from Russia is starting to be offset by capital return, much of it disguised as Western money.

But the economy is still split in two. The government has not yet succeeded in building the structures required for financial stability. Many banks are shaky, and reporting requirements are lax. Failing industries clamor for support, and the price of maintaining the hard-won political consensus in Moscow is to dole out state subsidies to them all, if not on the grand scale of the early 1990s. Political corruption is still rife, and this prevents the Russian government from controlling imports and exports properly. The private sector is held back. Inflation and foreign debt constantly threaten to run out of control.

Indeed, in the last five years the previous undervaluation of the Russian ruble has faded, with devastating consequences for the Russian balance of payments and external debt. Previously, in the early 1990s, the undervaluation of the ruble (relative to its purchasing power vis-à-vis the dollar) enabled Russians to export anything that was not nailed down. Russian exports of oil, aluminum and other nonferrous metals, fertilizers, and many other commodities, flooded into world markets, causing many commodities prices to plunge.

But as the 1990s wore on, many exports became unprofitable, while now it was imports that streamed into Russian through every port and road. The Russian balance of payments weakened badly, and many Russian industries suffered under the competition of Western products. High ruble costs discouraged Western investors. Yet under the pressure of Russian regional politicians, themselves pushed by their constituents, the Russian government failed to impose import restrictions and tariffs, or to devalue the ruble. The distorted exchange rate has become a major factor in the poor performance of the economy.

And while the old economy is stuck in its ways, it remains politically powerful. Unemployment is increasing rapidly as privatized firms shed layers of excess jobs. Fear of unemployment dominates the government's economic policies, paralyzing serious attempts to break up the large state monopolies or to drive even the most obvious "lame ducks" into bankruptcy.

By 2002, entrapped in these problems, the economy seems about to resume sliding downhill, after stabilizing briefly toward the end of the 1990s. It is increasingly clear that the Russian economy cannot really take off until the grip of the past has been decisively broken. A new economic crisis seems to loom.

As Karamyshev and Sokolov take office, they realize that choices have to be made, but more important, that the country must be galvanized for a fresh effort. Karamyshev resolves to make a major statement that will set the tone for the entire administration.

THE CHUDO SPEECH

Ten years after the beginning of marketization, the Russian public has become cynical about promises, and Russian politicians no longer bother talking about the virtues of the market. More and more Russians have become disenchanted with what they see as the rough side of capitalism. Moscow cynics have revived the nihilistically bitter slogan of the Russian dissident author of the 1970s, Aleksandr Zinoviev: *Chto bylo, budet, a chto budet, uzhe est'*—"What is past is yet to come, and what is yet to come already exists."

Yet the reformist rhetoric of the early 1990s, so long out of fashion, has a certain quaint freshness when revived in the election of 2002. Karamyshev and Sokolov, while on the campaign trail, are themselves surprised by the warm response of Russian audiences to their ringing reaffirmations of faith in the principles of the market and democracy. The Russian people, it seems, having made private property a reality, appears ready for the message that Russian capitalism can be made more "civilized" and more honest.

"We have put the chains of the past behind us," Karamyshev declares. "We cannot allow its chains to hold us back. Illegality and corruption must give way to law and decency in all our affairs. We must perfect the market system. We must build Russia's future with the talents and creativity of the Russian people. In the last ten years, we have achieved many miraculous things. With the resources that God has given us—and the resource of the people themselves—we can strive to achieve an economic miracle for the entire people."

This speech, repeated on the campaign trail (to the point that Karamyshev's aides refer to it as "The Chudo Speech"), is dismissed by Moscow sophisticates as pure corn. The word used by Karamyshev for miracle—*Chudo*—has the connotation as something out of Wonderland. Skeptics around the globe waste no time in dismissing it as a fable, a dream. Russia, after all, has been in a muddle for a decade. Yet the slogan proves to have broad appeal, not only to the new Russian businessmen, the bankers, the beneficiaries of nomenklatura privatization, but also to many Russian young adults, who were still barely more than children at the time of the Gaidar shock therapy. Would it be possible to have an economic miracle in Russia? Why not? Hasn't life since 1991 already been full of astonishing things? And why not go the rest of the way? Indeed, some say *Chudo* already began years ago.

In the end, the "Chudo Speech," and what it represents, opinion polls all agree, turns out to be a major factor in the landslide victory of the Karamyshev-Sokolov ticket. It has not hurt that Karamyshev's home province has turned into a showcase for a relatively civil market economy. In June 2002, Karamyshev and Sokolov move into the Kremlin with a clear mandate for a renewed drive to the market.

FIRST GET THE POLITICS RIGHT

The new administration summons a distinguished panel of state industrialists, private entrepreneurs, and academic economists to analyze the results of economic reform to date. Their conclusions and recommendations are as follows:

- The previous half dozen years have been a period of "primary accumulation of capital" in private hands. It has created a new class of quasi-private industrialists and private financiers and entrepreneurs. It is time to harness them together into a single team.

- These years have revealed that there is no lack of entrepreneurial energy in Russia, and much capital has accumulated in private hands. That's the driving force for an *ekonomicheskoe chudo,* an economic miracle. But for the miracle to take place, politicians at all levels must act to make property rights more secure and to create the expectation of stable money.
- To achieve this, the government must intervene less in the economy, and make the tax regime, export licensing, and other economic policies more stable and predictable.

A task force created by President Karamyshev to study the lessons of other economic miracles around the globe delivers essentially the same message: "There is no single road to *Chudo.* The government alone cannot manufacture a *Chudo.* That depends on the private sector. But it can help get the politics and economics right. Above all, secure property rights and curb inflation. Control crime. And make the rules of the economic game more consistent and predictable."

Building a political consensus behind the *Chudo* slogan turns out not to be a fantasy. The private sector has developed much more rapidly than had been expected by the pessimists in Russia (or the West). There is a widespread desire for stable money, even if that means raising interest rates and cutting subsidies, most of which go to the very largest enterprises anyway. Those largest enterprises are outshouted by the growing chorus of small and medium-sized entrepreneurships, whose influence in the regions is transmitted to Moscow by their deputies in the legislature, newly organized into a faction in the parliament. They argue that subsidies to the largest enterprises (which they irreverently call the Thousand Dinosaurs) should be limited to at most no more than a portion of the wage bill.

To the new class of owners, anxious to trim their own payrolls, unemployment does not seem quite the threatening specter it once did. In any case, those most vulnerable—women, older workers, professionals on municipal payrolls (known in Russian as "budgetniks")—have little political clout.

The government, relying on the growing private sector for support, makes some headway in curtailing credits to the largest industrial enterprises while increasing the powers of property owners. Meanwhile, by promising to share revenue with regional governments, it enlists their support for more efficient tax collection. The budget deficit drops. Inflation falls, and medium-sized companies account for 30 percent of Russian industrial output.

ECONOMIC GROWTH RETURNS

The Russian economy begins to respond to the new environment, and it is private business, not government, that is driving the expansion. While still far from stable, government policies are, for the first time, clearly favorable to private business, and businessmen move aggressively to capture opportunities and meet the demands of consumers. The new government devalues the ruble, bringing its value back into line and pumping new health into Russian exports and the balance of payments.

GDP begins to grow at 5 percent a year, though this is less striking than it might seem, considering how far the economy has fallen since 1988. Russian capital begins to emerge as an engine of growth. The billions of dollars held by Russians outside the country, either earned from exports or parked in Swiss banks by Russian businessmen, start to return to Russia and go into investment. Russian exports stream once more into foreign markets, especially the booming Chinese economy, which soon absorbs one third of all Russian non-energy exports.

Russian exports are aided by continued growth in the European Community. This in turn makes it politically feasible for European governments to resist calls to raise trade barriers. Publicly, they base their opposition on free-trade principles while more quietly also making clear that open markets are necessary to keep Slavic economic refugees from pouring into Western Europe. Taking advantage of a low-cost, educated workforce located near their markets, European companies source production in Russia (and Ukraine). The premier example is Volkswagen. Still suffering from Germany's high wage bill, it invests $2 billion in manufacturing and assembly plants in Russia. At the beginning, these facilities primarily export to Western Europe, but are also designed increasingly to supply the markets of Russia and the rest of the former Soviet Union.

The resolution of the Kurile Islands issue opens the way for extensive investment in the Russian Far East and Siberia by Japan, which is anxious to forestall the Chinese economic offensive. But, progressively, Japanese companies, eyeing the hungry Russian market and concerned that the Europeans will preempt them, also begin to invest in industrial joint ventures in European Russia. The freeing of domestic energy prices in Russia enhances the export potential, and foreign money begins to flow into the Russian oil and gas sector.

Private Russian dollars, added to a flow of ruble savings gathered by the growing array of private banks and insurance companies, spark sustained growth in construction, services, and production of consumer goods. Gazprom, the natural gas company, has already been investing abroad for several years, but now it is joined by the other members of what has become known as the "Thermal Bloc"—the energy companies, including three leading Russian oil majors.

Faster growth soon begins to boost personal income, unleashing decades of pent-up consumer demand. Russian housewives now have the opportunity to buy all the things that the Soviet system denied them—dishwashers, modern washing machines and dryers. Thanks to earlier land reforms, many Russians now hold land for summer gardens, and as disposable income grows they begin to build houses. A housing boom, which had started as early as 1990 to supply the hard-currency market, widens to include a growing middle class that is eager to spend its new rubles. This is further catalyzed by the relative stabilization of the currency, which in turn makes longer-term credit, such as mortgages, possible. Russians begin to flock to suburbs, creating huge weekend traffic jams on the overburdened Russian roads.

THE "DODZHEV LINE"

But this first phase of recovery, though hailed around the world, does not yet amount to an economic "miracle." Is it possible to do better? The answer is not yet clear.

In 2008, Karamyshev and Sokolov are re-elected, and they decide the time has come to lay an even more solid pro-business structure and launch faster growth. The political environment seems favorable: Five years of sustained growth and solid increases in personal income have begun to attract mass support for *Chudo*. In addition, genuinely private industry (as opposed to the "pseudo-privatization" of the mid-1990s) now accounts for two thirds of Russian industrial output, and the influence of the largest state enterprises, long an obstacle to financial reform, has decisively weakened.

Now the Russian prime minister, Iosif Dodzhev, launches the New Economic Program, eventually known to history as the Dodzhev Line. The time is finally right for a currency reform, which at one blow eliminates internal state debt and converts enterprise and farm debt at a steep rate. Subsidies to the Thousand Dinosaurs are sharply cut back, and a tough bankruptcy law is enacted. Inflation falls to a moderate 20 percent annual rate.

The political price is high. Unemployment, which had subsided somewhat in recent years, jumps back to its 1998 high of twelve million. But economic growth responds sharply. By 2009 the Russian economy begins growing at a 9 percent annual rate, fueled by skilled manpower, resourceful private Russian management, high and rising personal incomes, natural resources, and foreign capital. Some commentators note that this is the same kind of growth rate Russia enjoyed in its economic miracle before the First World War. Russian technological innovation becomes a growth engine in its own right, as Russian excellence in electronics, materials science, and applied mathematics, allied with Western partners, begins to produce breakthroughs in world markets. The consumer and service sectors grow strongly, gradually righting the extreme imbalance toward industry created by the Soviet era. *Chudo* proves not to be just a fable or fantasy. Rather, it is Russia's path in the twenty-first century.

Is such a story possible by 2010 or before?

ANALYSIS: THE ELUSIVENESS OF ECONOMIC MIRACLES

The abundance of "economic miracles"—the Japanese and German, the Korean, the Asian, the Mexican, the Italian, the Turkish, and so on —has given rise to a considerable body of analyses. Yet the explanations remain elusive. The miracles are more easily observed and experienced than parsed. Some explanations focus on cultural factors, such as whether the population is literate, has a strong family structure, shows a sense of purpose, or is oriented toward the future. There are explanations that concentrate on savings rates, on technology and technology transfer, and on history and external forces. Other explanations point to government policies, institutions, and the relationship of the government to the marketplace.

In the real world, of course, many of these factors come together. Sorting them out is a subject of continuing debate. Even today, for instance, there is no clear consensus on what got Japan going on the road to becoming an economic superpower. Was the essential factor the destruction of the country's industrial plant in World War II and the opportunity to rebuild everything? Or Japan's prewar economic culture? Or MITI's early postwar policy of "priority production"? Or the Dodge Line and the currency reform of 1949–50? Or was it the sudden boost to production given by the Korean War?

This kind of debate characterizes the discussion of every "economic miracle." "The lecturers in the university are all wrong," one of the architects of Singapore's economic miracle recently observed. "The critical factor was our decision to emphasize science and math courses in the schools, and the mothers' insistence that their children take science and math. It was the mothers that were really responsible."

LESSONS OF ECONOMIC MIRACLES

The German and Japanese economic miracles had their roots in the late 1940s and unfolded in the 1950s. These countries' situations differed sharply from Russia's in that an existing system of private enterprise was firmly established in both nations, and the reconstruction had to reach back over only two decades of dictatorship. Still, they suggest the following lessons:

Two of the most important conditions for achieving the economic takeoff were secure property rights and expectations, and stable money. Strong political action, supported and assisted by the foreign occupiers, was required at the outset to create the right environment. Large pools of educated labor existed on which to draw, as did the capacity to import and implement technology. Private capital, derived from high individual savings rates and retained corporate earnings, proved more important than government capital, foreign aid, and foreign investment, although foreign aid helped to stabilize the economic environment and provide the budget at a critical time. The role of government was important chiefly in shaping the forms of economic activity, without interfering in the actual process. In other words, while the government may have been strong, it allowed the private sector to do its job.

Above all, the German and Japanese miracles did not come overnight. They were long-drawn-out and uncertain, with a number of setbacks and temporary downturns. They were also helped by some outside events, such as the boom in industrial production set off by the Korean War.[1]

The current Chinese economic miracle has had to struggle with a similar legacy of central planning, large state enterprises, and no private property. But the Chinese miracle was initiated and sustained, in its first decade, by local agriculture, altogether different from Russian conditions. Indeed, this miracle began in 1979 with the breakup of agricultural communes. Its second decade was sparked by capital and entrepreneurship supplied by the overseas Chinese, and was concentrated primarily in coastal "free economic zones," characterized by a rebirth of a strong commercial tradition. These vital engines of growth are missing in Russia.[2]

IS A RUSSIAN *CHUDO* REALLY POSSIBLE?

Since the Soviet command economy was unique, it follows that the requirements for a Russian economic miracle will be considerably different from those of previous examples. Just what is it that creates the potential for takeoff, in a country that is now plunged in a seemingly bottomless depression?

First, it is clear that a Russian *chudo* will not come from large additional supplies of raw materials, capital, manpower, and technology, because these are not available—or, at any rate, not cheaply. Indeed, in the current economic chaos, such supplies are declining. (The small inflow of foreign capital is currently outweighed by the outflow of Russian funds.)

Therefore, the basis for a Russian economic miracle comes from two sources: 1) combining existing supplies in more efficient ways (a task made easier by the fact that economic depression has freed much industrial capacity), and 2) producing a new basket of goods, which people actually want and are willing to pay for.

The command economy was so inefficient, and imposed such severe barriers to the rational movement of resources and manpower, that any improvement at all quickly brings benefits. As we have argued, it will be a long time before Russia is able to wring out the inefficiencies caused by outmoded technologies, mislocated industries, scarce housing, poor transportation. But the resource that was the most inefficiently used of all in the Soviet economy was management, entrepreneurial talent, and innovation—the *sine qua non* that cannot be quantified and which economists therefore refer to as the "residual." These can be redeployed more quickly. Already, even today, the reallocation of managerial skills is producing an explosion of activity.

Wealth is as wealth feels. Just changing the output of the economy can make it wealthier: An economy that produces steel and tanks but no consumer goods and services generates little "welfare," but once it begins to reallocate some of the same resources and effort to producing consumer goods and services, it suddenly generates much more consumer happiness. In a real sense, then, such an economy is now wealthier, even though by conventional measures it is "producing" less. By the same token, such an economy can also invest less, but still generate more wealth, provided it invests in consumer goods and services rather than tanks or steel girders for gigantic "show" projects.

In other words, the potential for *Chudo* in Russia comes from the very extremes of inefficiency and distorted output that characterized the former Soviet economy. Even small progress in limiting the grosser inefficiencies, and shifting the mix of output in a more consumer-oriented direction, can produce a sharp expansion of prosperity in short order.

But for the increase in wealth to be sustained and expanded, it must be supported by massive investment. The real test of the plausibility of *Chudo,* then, is whether it creates an environment in which the capital that is now accumulating in private hands can be invested for the long term.

This has been one of the most important factors in past economic miracles: the creation of the right setting for private business. This means, above all, secure property rights, stable money, and a government that shapes but does not intervene. This implies strong but benign political power.

Could Russia achieve such a political setting in the near future? To create the right political setting for a *Chudo* scenario, Russia must steer a course between two dangers:

- Premature reconstitution of a strong state led by centralizing state technocrats whose thinking is still dominated by the shibboleths of the Soviet past. Such a government might be sympathetic to marketization in principle, but like the elephant in the folk tale, it would believe that the best way to nurture the eggs of capitalism would be to sit on them.
- Continued political paralysis and Muddling Down, leading to the scenario of failure previously described, and possibly leading to a breakup of the Russian Federation (the Time of Troubles scenarios). In such a setting it would be much more difficult to ensure monetary stability or property rights.

Here is how the key political conditions for *Chudo* might be met:

- *Property Rights.* It is too much to expect that property rights in Russia will be protected by legal guarantees in the foreseeable future. But property rights will be secured along a spectrum— from political protection dependent on key friendships to some reasonably firm legal guarantees. In the near term, this might involve a political setting in which regional authorities can protect their friends from interference from the central government. This assumes a stable compromise between the center and the regions.

  The danger is that Russian politicians and managers will combine to create *inefficient* property rights—that is, property that is monopolistic, or tied to the state through subsidies and bail-outs. To prevent this, privatization must make the new owners responsible to the market and subject to its discipline.

- *Stable Money.* Unlike the situation in Germany in 1948, when the sources of monetary overhang had already been eliminated and a one-shot currency reform could restore seemingly "miraculous" health overnight, the sources of monetary instability in Russia lie deep in the political system. Politicians compete for allies through budgetary giveaways. The government is too weak to collect more than half of its taxes. Preventing unemployment requires providing cheap credits and subsidies to enterprises and governments.

  Fully stable money cannot be achieved in the first phase of *Chudo,* but some steps can be taken in the right direction. The efficiency of tax collection is already increasing. Credits to the largest enterprises can be negotiated down, allocated by competitive auction, and priced at positive interest rates. The development of a true system of revenue-sharing between the center and the regions will alleviate the need for giveaways to attract political support. Inflation cannot be eliminated, but can be reduced.

- *External Support.* Since one of the possible engines for *Chudo* in its first phase is export income, the West can help by opening the way for increased Russian exports. Similarly, the West can help to lessen the outflow of Russian hard currency by consenting to a phased reduction of Russian debt, both interest and principal.

THE SECOND PHASE

The main danger after the first few years of recovery is that the economy will lose steam if capital is not invested in rebuilding the social and physical infrastructure. During the first phase of *Chudo,* the environment for business investment is still not sufficiently secure or stable to achieve this. Likewise, neither the central nor the regional government has sufficient resources to invest in the country's "social capital" —schools, laboratories, hospitals, etc.

Once again, Russia must steer a narrow course between two dangers. The first is the one just described—inexorable degradation of factories, roads, buildings, and other real assets. The other is excessive dependence on government investment, financed by punitive taxation of the private sector. (At this writing, government investment has been reduced to a small fraction of its previous level, but under a Two-Headed-Eagle government, say, government investment would revive strongly again.) This policy of substituting government investment for private would be the end of *Chudo,* because it would cause capital flight to resume.

Consequently, the only way both to consolidate and accelerate *Chudo* is to embark on a second phase, one of further consolidation of private property rights and stabilization of money. This would include the removal of most restrictions on foreign investment, including public-sector projects such as highways and ports. But for such a consolidation to work, the reformers must have political support. This will be forthcoming if in the previous phase incomes have risen to the point that the majority of people perceive that they are benefiting from *Chudo.* This is crucial, because the only way to achieve the final stabilization of money is to cut back credits and subsidies, to balance the budget, and to increase taxes moderately. These measures will cause a rebound of unemployment.

RUSSIA'S ADVANTAGES

Underlying the idea of a Russian economic miracle is that Russia is an industrial giant, if a misshapen one. Alongside its many liabilities (which have already been discussed in earlier chapters), Russia also has some distinct advantages on which a *Chudo* can be built:

- temporary excess capacity of many raw and semi-processed materials (fertilizers, energy, metals, etc.)
- abundant and low-wage scientific and engineering personnel, trained and literate industrial manpower
- excess capacity in many industrial plants, pipelines, railroads, etc., some of which capital stock is new and relatively efficient
- unexploited managerial energy and talent
- enormous pent-up demand for consumer goods and services, built up over seven decades
- the incalculable benefits of the new "enabling technologies"— such as fax, computers, and telecommunications—that will allow Russians to plug into the world economy
- the linking of Russia's great scientific and technical skills to the marketplace, heretofore something that was impossible.

To all of these must be added the hard work and personal energies of younger generations determined to get beyond the past and to strive for a business culture and standard of living that belong to a modern industrial country.

There is great danger that these various advantages could dissipate. Unless they receive investment, the extractive industries—oil, gas, and mining—and manufacturing facilities, as well as a good deal of the Russian industrial infrastructure (such as oil and gas pipelines) will run down and excess capacity will vanish within a decade or less. Similarly, unless money is put into social capital, health, and the environment, the quality of the workforce itself will decline markedly. These urgent needs will be particularly difficult politically and economically. Despite the current excess of manpower, a strong revival of labor unions, supported by populist politicians, could lead to sharply increased strike activity and higher wages (as in East Germany), nullifying Russia's current potential cheap-labor advantage and undermining labor relations.

Consequently, the first phase of *Chudo,* if not followed through, could prove to be a brief high followed by another slump.

A MIRACLE FOR SOME—BUT NOT FOR OTHERS

Chudo will be unbalanced; there will be growth for some groups, some sectors, and some regions, but not for others.

Three broad regions will emerge:

- Resource-rich areas that can export raw material and semi-processed goods; these will be mainly the Far East and Siberia;
- "Cossack Country"—that is, the south of Russia, the Volga-Urals, the Trans-Siberian corridor, and potentially north Kazakhstan; this cluster is pretty self-sufficient and could become locally integrated;
- "Central Russia," including Moscow and St. Petersburg, where much of the scientific talent and military high technology are concentrated. The big defense-oriented enterprises and military institutes will remain depressed for some time; on the other hand, this is where a lot of the service sector will ultimately develop.

Chudo will vary dramatically by sector:

- *Agriculture.* There will be no agricultural miracle in the sector as a whole. Truck farming and other high-value farming will prosper in proximity to cities, although such land will be under pressure from the spread of suburbs. Victory gardens and private plots will round out the food budgets of most ordinary families, some of whom will move into commercial truck farming. Large farms will be "private in form, collective in substance," and will continue to be held back by conservative management, bad roads, and lack of supporting infrastructure (processing, etc.). The poorer "Non-Black-Earth Zone" will sink into oblivion. The only significant zone of agricultural prosperity will be the best grain-growing acreage of the south, in provinces such as Krasnodar and Stavzopol'. Here, agricultural bosses will use their political connections to split off the most fertile and best-located land for American-style, export-oriented farming.
- *Industry.* Consumer-oriented industry and construction will boom; heavy industry may continue to decline. High-tech industry as a whole will be held back by conservative management, government subsidies, and its mostly military origins. But there will be many individual success stories, especially when Russians ally themselves with Western partners to provide gateways to external markets. Telecommunications will not necessarily be an obstacle, as Russians use the latest satellite and fiber-optic technologies to leap over the lack of infrastructure. One key condition: Ruble wages must remain low and competitive, compared to those of Western and Central Europe.

- *Service.* In the Soviet era this sector was so atrophied as to be virtually nonexistent. The smile, and the attitude that stands behind it, were unknown in Russia. But the service sector is booming now, as people rush to seize new opportunities. Many areas—including information and software services, design and applied research, management, trade, and brokerage, banking and financial services, and the like—contribute to dramatic increases in overall productivity.

Economic prosperity will itself bring some definite health and environmental benefits, but particularly to those with rising incomes, who will be able to afford better diets, better housing, healthful leisure activities, and private medical care. More prosperous regions and municipalities will be able to pay for better air and water treatment. The Russian economy as a whole will move from oil and coal to gas, and the burden of air pollution will lessen as the entire economy becomes more efficient. But the impact will be uneven, benefiting primarily those regions that shift away from heavy industry toward light industry and services.

THE POLITICS OF *CHUDO*

Lastly, what would be the political consequences? Because the benefits of *Chudo* will be uneven, a Russian economic miracle could itself destabilize Russian politics, either reinforcing the basis for democracy or pushing the country toward authoritarianism.

Our *Chudo* scenario is based on three key assumptions:

- A "federal compromise" takes place in the coming half dozen years, laying the basis for a fresh—but still partial—round of marketizing reforms;
- The political environment following this compromise is still dominated by the present players—that is, the mass public remains largely excluded from the arena, and political parties remain weak. As a result, those disadvantaged by the reforms of 2002 are unable to find a strong political voice;
- The initial phase of *Chudo* yields a sufficiently broad improvement in personal income that it strengthens the base of support for the next round of *Chudo*.

In short, the underlying assumption behind the *Chudo* scenario is that Russian political life will remain relatively peaceful, even though both economy and society are changing rapidly and there are growing gaps between the winners and the losers.

How realistic are such assumptions? Prosperity is typically a necessary condition for a stable democracy, but the process of getting to prosperity isn't necessarily stable or peaceful. The experience of other rapidly growing nations over the last generation suggests two main dangers:

- *The losers find their political voice.* Depending on the speed with which mass parties grow and the way electoral laws are written, politicians could forge a mass political base by mobilizing the losers from *Chudo.* Even if this process were peaceful, it could result in runaway wage increases, export controls, high taxes and the like, all of which choke off economic growth. Thus, instead of the "losers" eventually joining the "winners," everyone is pulled back into the "loser" camp.
- *The winners protect themselves.* Faced with a rising tide of political discontent, the new owners of the Russian private sector, many of whom are already closely associated with local political élites, could form alliances with the military, the police, and reactionary parties to protect themselves against popular demands. If people take to the streets, the response of the authorities could be repression. Indeed, it is not impossible that *Chudo* could provide the basis for classic authoritarianism.

And yet, at the very least, *Chudo* helps create the conditions for democracy; for without economic growth and eventual prosperity, democracy is not very plausible.

We have already observed how Russians today anxiously describe themselves, borrowing from the Russian title of *Through the Looking Glass,* as living "in the world behind the mirror." But perhaps a decade or so from now, they will think instead of the Russian title of *Alice in Wonderland—Alisa v strane chudes—Alice in the Land of Miracles.* And they may say, when they think back to their lives under communism, that it is in a land of miracles that they now live.

PART IV

Looking Around
the Corner

13

Capitalism Russian-Style: 2010 and Beyond

"In twenty years, we will be a normal country. In fifty years, we will be a very affluent country. In a hundred years, Europe will join us."
— *Russian economist*

By 2010, Mikhail Gorbachev and Boris Yeltsin are memories as political leaders. A twenty-five-year-old Russian, born in 1985, the year of Gorbachev's accession, takes the collapse of communism and the Soviet Union as the ancient history he learned about in high school textbooks. Russia has changed.

It's the summer of 2010, and the talk of Moscow is a series of spectacular corruption trials, involving the heads of four of Russia's largest public corporations. They are accused of masterminding a vast system of kickbacks to Russia's ruling party, the Democratic National Front. The scandal is an especially juicy one, because it implicates leading members of the first graduating class of the prestigious "NSA," the Russian National School of Administration, founded in 1996 in imitation of the French ENA. The new old boys of NSA rose quickly to the top positions in government and the major state corporations—leading the old "old boys," the industrial managers from the Soviet era, to charge (without a trace of irony) that the new "NSA mafia" is a re-creation of the old Soviet nomenklatura.

In previous years, such a scandal might have been hushed up, but the upcoming trial also represents a test of the independent judiciary. A new generation of well-trained young magistrates, ironically about the same age as the NSA defendants and equally ambitious, are determined to prove that they can call a halt to state corruption, even at the highest levels. The Russian public is eagerly anticipating dramatic revelations at the upcoming trials.

Capitalism Russian-Style is developing quickly by 2010. Some state monopolies have hung on, thanks to the protection of the government. The gas industry is now a semi-private corporation, widely admired for its management skill. It has extended its reach to eastern Siberia and Sakhalin, and will soon supply much of the Japanese and Korean markets as well as Western Europe. It rivals the Saudi ARAMCO as an energy supplier to the world, and has benefited enormously from the global swing to natural gas, an environmentally friendly fuel.

The Russian steel and aluminum producers, organized in large state corporations, continue to receive heavy state subsidies. Most of the defense industry is still state-run, although portions of the aircraft and electronics industries have formed private subsidiaries that have become independent of government control and are competing successfully on international markets. Surprisingly, the Russian coal industry, freed of the obsolete Ukrainian mines of the Donbas, and having weathered a succession of severe strikes in the late 1990s, is now profitable on its own, thanks in part to German investment and technology.

Still, the central government in Russia remains the dominant force in the economy. The Ministry of Finance continues to dominate all financial matters, setting tax and credit policy, regulating Russian banks, and funding state corporations and investment programs. Such a concentration of power under the executive branch of the Russian government has its drawbacks. The financial structure remains the weakest part of the Russian capitalist system.

Contrary to pessimistic forecasts in the mid-1990s, foreign investment began to play a major role in the Russian economy once the Russian government created a "one-stop shopping" system of licensing and approvals directly under the prime minister, and a special administrative court to hear cases involving foreign investors. In telecommunications, Finnish companies have seized a dominant position, having leapfrogged over all technological obstacles by creating a national cellular telephone system. A Danish company has helped Russia build a vast fiber optic system for international communications. Starting from a small joint venture in the Volga Basin, a German oil company and its Russian partners have created a new giant, the fourth-largest oil company in the world.

But all previous foreign investment is about to be eclipsed by a new Russian-Japanese consortium in eastern Siberia, under the aegis of MITI and the Russian Technology Ministry, bringing together dozens of foreign companies for the development of eastern Siberian oil, gas, and minerals. In aviation, American airframe, avionics, and engine manufacturers have created solid partnerships in Russia, bolstered by cooperation from the U.S. government, whose policy of quickly granting airworthiness certification to new civilian airplanes manufactured in Russia opened up the U.S. domestic market. The huge and growing Pacific market soon followed the American lead.

The real surprise, however, is that the Russian government has sought to enlist private capital to invest in basic infrastructure. Western companies have invested with Gazprom and Russian turbine manufacturers in gas-fired generating plants, thus helping to improve Russian air quality and relieve a severe bottleneck in electricity supply. Cutting the ribbon on a newly completed plant, the Russian chairman of "Rosgazenergo" smilingly paraphrases Lenin's famous equation of nearly a century before: "Capitalism," he said, "is Russian power plus foreign investment, plus the electrification of the entire country."

But the showcase project of the new century is a brand-new ten-lane ring road around Moscow, all privately financed and operated as a turnpike by a consortium that is 60 percent Russian and 40 percent German. It is estimated to have saved thousands of lives in its first decade, compared to the deathtrap it replaced, and the Russian government has just begun evaluating bids for similar turnpike highways to link Moscow with St. Petersburg and south Russia.

Two of the richest men in Russia in 2010 are the founders of the Hermes financial and technological empire, Valerii Neverov and Gennadii Danilov. Neverov is a former physicist who became one of Russia's first new billionaires in the 1990s. Starting as an oil trader, Neverov quickly built up an empire of trading and brokerage companies, then moved into banking and insurance. Danilov, a former engineer who rose in the shipbuilding industry, joined Neverov in the early years and became his right-hand man, revealing a rare talent for finance. The two men were among the first to begin buying Russian oil companies and defense plants. By the turn of the century Hermes had become one of the largest producers of oil and oil-field equipment in Russia and the world. Lately Hermes, in partnership with an American investment bank, has begun establishing joint ventures with companies in Houston and Aberdeen.

Neverov and Danilov are representative of a certain type of forward-looking businessman in the new capitalist Russia. They come from small towns in Siberia and have made their fortunes outside Moscow. They are staunch Russian patriots, at home in the world of Russian defense industry and science, and their equipment empire is based on converted military-industrial plants. They understand the need for the new business class to build popular support, and they are active philanthropists. In 1998 Neverov founds the Russian Businessmen's Christian Alliance, which acts as a major source of funds and political support for the Russian Orthodox church.

One of the biggest surprises of Russian capitalism after 2010 is that private money has flowed strongly into the agricultural sector. Much of this comes from the early profits of "nomenklatura capitalism" in the 1990s; these found their way back to the farms because the farms are still a stronghold of the last veterans of the Communist party apparatus. The former apparatchiks were among the first to split off profitable fertile acreage for capitalist farming, especially in the grain belt of the south, thus becoming part of a new generation of Russian *fermery*, private farmers. In the black-earth zone of Russia and in the truck farms around the major cities, heavy investment transforms grain and vegetable producers into modern agribusiness. In addition, Western capital invested in food processing and storage, added to local road construction, enables the farms to cut food waste dramatically; food waste had been the scourge of the Russian agricultural system. By 2005, Russia has eliminated grain imports and is beginning to export food.

ANALYSIS OF CAPITALISM RUSSIAN-STYLE

Whether by 2010 there is one Russia or many, whether its leaders are presidents or generals, one thing is likely to be true: Russia will be on its way to developing its own unique form of capitalism. The main reason? The foundations of the Communist system are truly gone and cannot be re-created. Running the extreme form of total state property created by the Bolsheviks required the apparatus of the Communist party as well as Communist ideology. With both gone, the result is an inevitable trend away from the command economy as it was built by Stalin in the 1930s, toward an economy that contains large doses of private property.

But the form Russian capitalism takes will depend on how it arrives.

"Money," "contract," and "property" are the key words. Just how far Russia has moved toward a civil market economy by 2010 will hinge on whether it has built institutions, lacking today, for the stable and dependable management of money, as well as proper protections for basic business activity, property, and contracts. The growth of capitalism will require a price system that reflects consumer preferences, and markets for capital and labor.

One could argue, of course, that "capitalism" is anything that is not "command economy," and therefore capitalism has already arrived in Russia today. But what Russia has today is still so entangled in the ruins of the command economy that it does not yet qualify as truly capitalist. Russia does not yet have large-scale private property in the full sense of the word, or a monetary system, or real markets. But things are changing fast, and there are reasonable odds that Russia will have laid the foundations for these elements within a generation.

How these elements of capitalism will operate is another matter, and the answer will be determined to a great extent by the path Russia follows in getting there. Capitalism Russian-Style will not necessarily be democratic or liberal. It will certainly not look like capitalism in the United States or the English-speaking countries. Rather, Capitalism Russian-Style will be a unique blend of Russia's past and present. It could bear many similarities to present-day Mexico, Turkey, or even Italy. But as such, it will also have great potential for generating wealth and progress in the following decades, as it mobilizes the talents of the Russian people not for the slogans of a warfare state but for the search for a better life.

RUSSIAN CAPITALISM UNDER VARIOUS SCENARIOS

Less than two years after the beginning of full-scale marketizing reforms in Russia, a great deal of economic activity is already in nominally private hands. That is an extraordinary political achievement. But it is still only the beginning of the long road to a market economy.

Thus, if Muddling Down were to continue indefinitely, the capitalist system that emerged would be misshapen and impoverished. The various levels of government, absorbed in destructive battles against one another, would be unable to play a constructive role in building a legislative, regulatory, and financial framework. Protection for property rights and contracts would be weak. Corruption and mafia influence would be strong. Inflation would be high, and thus there would be little long-term investment. After difficult experiences, many foreign investors would be very cautious about venturing further into such a market. The industrial and technological infrastructure of the country would continue to degrade. Private business would attempt to defend and regulate itself, but without political order and stability these efforts would not go far.

Under Muddling Down, Russian capitalism would remain "wild." Still, personal consumption would increase from the present low point, and consumer services and private trade would multiply. Thus, in broad terms, consumer welfare might actually increase in the near term, and the share of consumption in total Russian output would grow. But in the long term, for lack of long-range social and infrastructural investment, the economy would degrade and its capacity to produce wealth and growth would erode. This erosion would become especially serious if major enterprises really did start to go bankrupt and close their doors. Under current conditions, some large defense plants, with valuable engineering expertise, could well go first. In short, Muddling Down really does muddle down.

Two-Headed Eagle is a scenario of recovery of strong central state power. As such, it avoids some of the problems of Muddling Down, but it creates new ones. On the one hand, the technocrats who run Two-Headed Eagle try to create a sounder financial structure, and are successful within limits. They also move to curb the mafia, and are able to put an end to widespread extortion. Political conditions become more stable, and trade within the former "Soviet economic space" revives somewhat. Foreign investment responds to these more stable conditions and begins to flow into Russia, though limited by the determination of the Russian government to retain control and not to give up equity to Western investors.

But the shortcoming of Two-Headed Eagle, as far as the healthy development of a market system is concerned, is that the state remains dominant over society, relaxing its hold only gradually and partially over the coming two decades. The central government retains control over tax revenues, corporate profits, and export earnings, investing them as it sees fit. It continues to control prices and wages, hampering the emergence of real markets. Above all, it continues to apply "reasons of state" to decisions concerning the use of private property and contracts. Legal protections for private property and contracts remain weak. Capitalism under the Two-Headed Eagle becomes a two-tiered affair, in which the bulk of small-scale consumer production and trade is in private hands, but most industry is in state hands. Whether large-scale state industry is gradually privatized in Russia will be affected by whether privatization remains the dominant fashion in the West, influencing Russia tomorrow as it influences Latin America and Western Europe today, or is replaced by some other model.

Chudo is the best environment for the development of a modern capitalist system in Russia. Under *Chudo* there is just enough political consensus to permit basic protections for private property and contracts, and to develop basic financial and monetary stability—and no more. Indeed, the strong development of a private industrial sector requires that the political system be finely balanced between the central and the local governments, so that the private sector manages to escape from both.

One key assumption underlying *Chudo* is that broad-based economic growth and prosperity breed the right attitudes for private entrepreneurship. Thus *Chudo* is a virtuous circle, in which Russians learn to trust and deal with one another because it is more and more profitable to do so, and society and state discover that it is better to work in partnership than in conflict. Entrepreneurial skills and success would be respected, if envied.

The virtuous circle of *Chudo* could also bring in a new factor, of which Soviet Russia had always deprived itself in the past—the energies and resources of its émigrés. The brain and skill drain from Russia could begin to flow in reverse, bringing back to Russia first-hand experience of Western business practices and attitudes acquired by Russians abroad.

In short, in such an environment, Capitalism Russian-Style could evolve toward the kind of balanced market economy now seen in Western Europe.

Under the Long Good-bye, Russian capitalism would be afflicted with the same ills as in Muddling Down, with a few additional pluses and minuses. The Wild East atmosphere would grow even more frantic, because regional governments would prove even less able to provide secure protection for business than the central government did. The rise of autonomous regions would open them up to penetration by neighboring economic powers, especially in the Far East, where Russia would probably play the role of resource provider. Northwest Russia might develop close economic ties with Scandinavia and Germany, benefiting from substantial foreign investment, which could lay the basis for the long-term modernization of the region. But in all cases, the Russian regions would be relatively weak and unstable political entities, which would hamper the development of a healthy market system.

But an important question about the Long Good-bye is whether it would last for more than a few years. In all the Time of Troubles family of scenarios, there are strong forces pulling Russia back toward more centralized government. We have argued that the more likely outcome of Time of Troubles is the reconstitution of a strong Russian central state. In that case, Russian capitalism would resemble Two-Headed Eagle more than, say, *Chudo*.

The Russian Bear is a step backward in every respect. But like the classic Latin American military dictatorships, the Russian Bear, lacking a mass party, a developed ideology, or a coherent economic program, must seek support among the powerful élite groups of the country. Thus, from the beginning, the Russian Bear is weaker and less stable than it appears.

That is why, after a few years, the Russian Bear begins to make concessions to private interests, and gradually, if tentatively, starts to reopen the country to the outside world. Slowly, Russia returns to the road to capitalism. But the searing experience of military dictatorship is a lasting setback for the prospects of a civil market, since the development of legal protections for property and contracts, and the growth of a strong society, are retarded for some time. Foreign capital is similarly inhibited from reentering Russia for a decade or two, and Russia's return to the world economy is correspondingly delayed.

FIVE BROAD FEATURES

Regardless of the path by which the country reaches Capitalism Russian-Style, five broad features are likely to stand out:

Though it will have areas, perhaps even large areas, of prosperity and advanced technology, capitalist Russia in 2010 will not be wealthy or efficient overall, and its development will continue to be uneven, both by sector and by region. This will be true even under the *Chudo* scenario because Russia has so much catching up to do. The job of adapting and converting industry, restoring basic water and air quality, and replacing worn-out capital stock will absorb much of the wealth produced by the Russian economy for the next generation and probably for another generation beyond that.

Capitalist Russia will continue to have strong elements of an uncivil, disor-

derly, and criminal "shadow economy." In most of the scenarios we have analyzed, political power may prove too weak and divided over the next twenty years to allow the job of passing legislation and building institutions to be done consistently. Even if the necessary laws are on the books, they will be enforced inadequately and inconsistently. As a natural response, much private enterprise will stay underground. Organized crime and corruption will become deeply entrenched.

Capitalist Russia will continue to have a strong state sector, while civil society will be weakly developed. While large-scale private enterprise will develop strongly, it will be closely intertwined with the state and dependent on it. The problem of dependence on the state, in the form of subsidies, cheap credits, and bailouts, will take more than one generation to overcome. As a consequence, even private Russian entrepreneurs will continue to look to the government for support and protection.

Russian society is likely to make considerable progress in organizing itself, forming its opinions and interests, and expressing them to governments. But it will take a long time to overcome the tradition that the Russian state "knows best" what is good for society, and to develop legal defenses for the citizenry against the state. A strong civil society requires a broad consensus that the interests of society, as society defines them, outweigh those of the state. But by 2010 this point will not yet be securely anchored.

Capitalist Russia will continue to be ambivalent toward the West and to go through wide mood swings in its attitudes and policies toward Western investment and participation. Russia was a "latecomer" as an industrial state at the end of the nineteenth century and beginning of the twentieth century. It will be a latecomer again in the first decade of the twenty-first century. Consequently, Russia will continue to look to the West for ideas and solutions, but it may adopt them overhastily, and then reject them when they do not work right away. Russians will continue to feel defensive and suspicious toward the West. This will cause Western investment and participation in Russia to be a constant source of internal conflict. Indeed, it could cause Russia to "oscillate" from one course to another, interrupting its progress.

COULD THE EAST BECOME THE SOUTH?

Russia may not necessarily progress down a smooth path to the market, but instead could swing between extremes of acceptance and rejection

—of the West, of the market, and of democracy—as some Latin American countries have done. In such circumstances, Russia's potentially vast wealth would not be realized, its people would not prosper, its politics would not stabilize.

Such oscillation could arise because Russia is a latecomer, and behaves like one. Russia will continue to be deeply divided over the issues that define the key values of a liberal market society: risk vs. security, freedom vs. equality, society vs. the state, individualism vs. collectivism, order vs. disorder, conformity vs. diversity. While such divisions exist in any society, Russia may be more divided because of its history, its traditions, and its experience.

Yet Russia has important strengths that can help it through the transition. Russia is potentially rich and powerful. Russia is not a classic third-world country. It has the industrial infrastructure, the educated population, the history of achievement, and the distinguished scientific culture to produce wealth without relying on outside help. This means that Russia will eventually escape the dependence mentality that causes third-world nations alternately to embrace and reject the West.

Russia's ambivalence toward the West may obscure deeper links. It is rooted in Western culture. Despite much popular history about supposed Mongol and Byzantine influences (which on close examination turn out to be minor indeed), the actual historical record is quite clear: Beginning in the 1600s, Russia turned its steps toward the West and has never looked back. Even the Bolshevik revolution and the Soviet regime were a parody of Western ideals and institutions, and with their disappearance, a Westernized élite and population look to Western traditions and examples more than ever before.

Russia has built a first-class education and research system and an impressive if uneven technological empire. It has also built Western-style cities, imbued with an urban, secular, middle-class, engineering-oriented culture that puts Russia closer to the nineteenth-century roots of European society than much of the rest of the West today. One reason for this adaptive success is that Russia is more ethnically and culturally homogeneous, at its core, than the West gives it credit for.

Russia today is not ideological. For the moment, at least, Russians appear inclined to develop pragmatic approaches to their problems, to cope with them rather than solve them. This may not last, but for the present, at least, the Russians, in throwing off Marxism-Leninism, seem to have rejected all ideologies. To the extent that there is a "ruling idea" in people's minds, it is mainly a diffuse hostility to the former order and the ideas behind it. Russians today are not so much committed to the market as they are committed against Leninist central direction.

Many of the basic institutions of a market system have already been created in embryo. Banks, exchanges, private firms, private shops, financial information systems, and the like have sprung up like mushrooms in the past five years. They operate "irrationally" as yet because they labor under distorted incentives, but the people within them are gaining experience in their roles, and the new institutions themselves have been developing.

There are growing forces interested in pragmatic success. Many people, especially in the big cities, have already gained a stake in the movement toward a new system, and they will work to preserve this movement, thus advancing their own interests.

If there is oscillation, it could take two possible forms. A more moderate version would avoid the extremes, shifting among various scenarios and approaches while maintaining enough stability over the long sweep of time to allow the fundamental processes of market building to continue. A more radical version would feature wide swings between chaos and reaction that would fail to lead to any sort of stability.

Under all scenarios, Russia is likely to keep up its gradual return to the world economy, and to continue moving away from the extreme version of state control and ownership that constituted the command economy. Russian companies will be quoted on the stock exchanges of the world. Sooner or later, the ruble will become one of the world's recognized currencies. There will come a day when the first Russian entrepreneur takes over a major Western corporation. Increasingly, Russian will be a language heard in the financial districts, the industrial fairs, the business hotels, and the ski slopes and beaches of the world. Whatever its precise form, Russian capitalism will be a force to be reckoned with in the world economy.

What follows is a snapshot, taken along Russia's road to the market. These are not scenarios. The people are real, and their words are their own. Except for the tycoon Neverov, only their names and a few details have been changed for their own protection.

14

Chudo at Work—
The New Russian Entrepreneurs:
"Evident but Unbelievable"

Katya is a producer on a Russian television show called "Evident but Unbelievable." It has been on the air for seventeen years. She had recently returned from filming in South Korea.

"We went to South Korea to explain how the South Korean economic miracle came about," she said. "We discovered that there is no miracle, just hard work. The only miracle is to stimulate people to work hard."

Under communism, people did not have to work hard. Sometimes, they only had to show up at their jobs two or three times a week, and they would still be paid for five. On the other hand, they did not get much either. But now, in the world behind the mirror, despite three quarters of a century of communism, Russians are demonstrating the skills of entrepreneurship—and the willingness to work twelve or more hours a day.

The market has attracted some of the most unlikely recruits. "Three years ago, my father-in-law was defending Stalin, telling me that we were going too far in reforms," said a member of the Yeltsin government. "Now, he's in business, always on the phone, trying to be a middleman."

Russia already has produced new billionaires. The best-known is Valerii Ivanovich Neverov, a forty-two-year-old physicist who makes a cameo appearance in the Capitalism Russian-Style chapter. Neverov is a real figure. He got his start in business in his twenties, when he negotiated research contracts with local Siberian defense plants to support his own research and equip his laboratory. A teetotaler, and known to be a Christian, he headed up the local Komsomol. He began producing equipment on contract for the oil industry and then, around 1987, when Gorbachev authorized small private business, he turned his consulting work into a business. He began trading oil through private channels in 1990, forming a company called Hermes, which also began to buy food and consumer goods for the oil industries. Since 1991, Hermes has grown astronomically into a holding company with sixty subsidiaries in everything from commodity exchanges to banking, insurance, and trade, as well as oil production. Neverov warns against surrendering assets or control to foreign investors.

Few others have gotten anywhere near the scale of a Neverov. The *Chudo* scenario is with younger people, who have the energy and the freedom to take risks and do not carry the baggage or commitments of the past. One day, Volya, a twenty-five-year-old who works in a bank, took a visitor to meet his friend Dmitri, also twenty-five, who runs a travel agency. Dmitri was a student at the Foreign Studies Institute and a Komsomol leader in his army unit. He was on the path that, in the past, would have taken him into the foreign ministry or into a state trading company. But 1989 was the year, as he explained, "that I stopped being a Marxist." The historical revelations destroyed his belief in the old system.

At the time, Dmitri was working as an interpreter for Intourist, the state travel monopoly, taking busloads of tourists around Moscow and perfecting his English and German in the process. He and another guide decided to go into business for themselves. They figured they were as qualified to go into tourism as anybody else in Russia. They bought some computers, hired a couple of staff, and targeted the low end of the market—students who like the outdoors.

"We thought, 'Why not, let's start,' " said Dmitri. "Intourist had been the monopoly company for foreign tourists. They would grab all the money, but they did not provide good service. They don't find out people's needs, or their special dreams. What we're doing is a risk. Business is a risk everywhere, but especially here."

They tried to get a bank loan, but the bank manager dismissed them. "You guys are too young to start a business," he said.

But they had their own money, from a summer spent working in camps in the United States, and then traveling around the U.S., washing dishes, waiting on tables, and doing construction. The savings, in dollars, were enough to get going. "Our costs are not high."

They have had to struggle with endless problems—with "the non-stability of the situation," as Dmitri summarized it. "Inflation is the worst thing. Last month, one hotel manager told us he was tripling his rates. We had one night to move our group to another hotel. We found another hotel, but we had to pay off the manager to get in." The other biggest problem is Aeroflot, which tends to cancel flights for lack of fuel. One of Dmitri's groups was stranded for almost an entire week.

"We've learned a lot about the tourist markets. There are a lot of small companies now in Russia. In the future, there will be fewer and fewer small companies, and more bigger businesses. If you don't find your niche, you don't survive. Right now, no one can beat us at our trips, at our prices.

"One thing that I understand now is that you have to be prepared to do everything if you want to succeed. Can you find a way to do it? I take pleasure from solving those problems. You should work twenty-four hours a day. This is not like a bank or a stock company. Here you can work the whole day, and still work at night, on the phones, until two or three A.M."

The generational conflicts that the market brings are reflected in Dmitri's difficulties with his own father, a professor of space technology whose work is so sensitive that even now he is not allowed to travel abroad. "He still doesn't believe my being in business is serious," said Dmitri. "He thinks I should still go back to graduate studies in the university and then find what he thinks is a real job in a state company."

And what of the future? "We don't have to make all our profit in one day or one year and then disappear," said Dmitri. "I'm not a real capitalist, not yet. I don't feel that what I have is a business, a real company, not yet. Older people, during their whole lives, have heard and thought that capitalists are the enemy. It will take our country a very long time to be a market economy."

"There is a great difference between a market and a bazaar," Volya added. "At the metro stop, you see old ladies selling things. That is a small model of our economy."

Dmitri did not quite agree. "We have something new. But what we need is political reform, political stability. Without that, there is no economic stability."

Other new entrepreneurs have had more experience—by a few years.

This is true of Ivan, who is a decade older than Dmitri. On the day a visitor called in, the water had gone off in the office building where Ivan has his headquarters. The hallways outside his office are dingy, but to enter Ivan's own suite of offices is to enter abruptly into the world of stylish, modern furniture.

Ivan is involved with twenty different companies, either as an owner or director. His companies do everything from insurance to trading, to manufacturing clothes and furniture and china. He's building a restaurant. He also had a winery in Georgia, "but it was destroyed in the war there." He sadly pulled out one of his last bottles, with his own label on it, a souvenir of doing business in the former Soviet Union. He offered a glass of wine, but not from his treasured bottle.

Ivan never knew his father. His mother was a cleaner. He was good at sports, but did poorly at school. He ended as a special-education teacher, working with boys who either did not have fathers or had fathers who were alcoholics. "A lot of the boys went into the army and went to Afghanistan," he recalled. "Some came back dead. Some came back alive, and some of them have since gone into their own businesses.

"When Gorbachev started to encourage private business, the local Komsomol suggested that I do something. So I decided to make weight-lifting equipment."

His workshop was under a school in a space so low he could not stand fully upright. At night, he worked as a taxi driver to support himself. He borrowed some metalworking equipment from a factory, and small tools from people in other factories. He brought no expertise to the product. "I had never weight-lifted myself, but there was a fashion then for bodybuilding. So why not?" He developed his designs by studying pictures in magazines. He started with seven employees. At the end of the first year, he had fifty. "I had lots of orders, but in the first eight months, no one paid."

He stayed in the weight-lifting equipment business for three years. "My biggest problem was Soviet psychology, according to which, if it works well, that's okay. If it doesn't work, too bad—and, also, mine is mine and yours is mine.

"It's difficult to be a boss. I believed in communism, I was educated in it. The feeling of comradeship was very important. But, as a boss, you've lost your chains. You have a feeling of responsibility for those who come to work for you."

Altogether, the groups Ivan either heads or is involved with employ some three thousand people. "The fashion is over for weight-lifting," he said. "The fashion today is to work with finance and money—especially dollars.

"I now work day and night," said Ivan. "I start at seven in the morning and go to eleven at night." He owns his own apartment and five cars, both Russian and Western, but he keeps them locked in garages so that they don't get stolen.

To explain how business works in Russia today, Ivan told this story: "Two people meet. The first one says, 'You want to buy a cartload of sugar?' The second one replies, 'Yes, fine.' They agree on a price." He paused. "Then the first one goes to see if he can buy a cartload of sugar, and the second goes to see if he can find some money.

"Business here is a gamble," he continued. "In Russia, it's very complicated. You make money one day, and it can all go wrong the next. The funny thing is I earned money in Russia, and lost a million dollars in Denmark. I signed a contract, but didn't get any goods, or my money back. I went to Interpol. They told me that the money had gone to Holland and then to Indonesia." He laughed. "Something that goes to the sultan never comes back. I've learned that I think of myself as a businessman, but I don't think I'm a good businessman yet. I'd like to be, but a man who lost all his money in Denmark is not a good businessman."

What of Russia's future? "I believe deeply that Russians are very talented people. I think Khrushchev was right. We will overtake you, we will catch up, but not as socialists."

Chudo—an economic miracle in a decade from now? Could that be possible?

"It's going to be earlier. We're at the stage now where even children learn how to make money. What is the miracle? The miracle is the people themselves. I don't think Russians are lazy and passive. Nobody fed us. All these terrible things were done to us. Now the government doesn't know what to do. But in ten years, so much will have changed. Six years ago, I was a teacher, earning a hundred and fifty rubles a month. Now, in Russian terms, I'm already running a middle-sized business.

"There's a lot of stupidity here. There are a lot of bad laws. With one hand, they give you; with another, they take away. But I'm convinced that communism can't come back.

"You've got to risk. The biggest lesson of business for me is that you have to defend and attack." He opened his coat. He had a very specific meaning in mind. One glimpsed something that looked like a gun. As it is for all Russian businessmen, the mafia is a shadow over everything, and a reality.

Three weeks before, the mafia had come to see Ivan. Six of the gangsters stayed downstairs. Five took the elevator up to his office. They knew that he had received a shipment of goods from the West. It was worth $200,000, and it was on consignment, meaning that he had not yet paid for it. They wanted the goods. A couple of them put their guns on the table to make sure that he took them seriously.

"They're not mine," Ivan said. "I can't give them away."

They didn't care. They wanted the goods.

Ivan asked for time and excused himself and went into another office. He was shaking. He hurriedly called a friend he knew from horseback riding. The friend happened to be an officer from the KGB (as he still calls it, though it's now officially the FSK). A squad of FSK came quickly. On the way up, they arrested the six men downstairs. They met Ivan, who had not yet gone back to his own office, and put a recording device on him.

Ivan returned to the room, where the gangsters waited for him. They wanted to know his answer. They started threatening him and his family. They described the different ways they had killed people. Ivan was very scared. He asked for more time.

The mafia boss stood up to leave. He made it clear that he expected the matter to be resolved soon. Some of his men remained, to keep the pressure on Ivan. Finally, on a prearranged signal, he said to them, "There's no need for you to be here."

At that moment the FSK broke in with their guns drawn. They shouted at the mafia men to keep their hands up and not to touch their weapons. They scooped up the guns on the table. They ordered the gangsters up against the wall, frisked them, removing other guns, and then took them away in handcuffs.

"It looked like an American film," said Ivan. "If there wasn't a KGB, the mafia would be in control.

"I've never dreamed about the future," he said at the end of the visit. "And I don't dream about the future now. There's a Russian proverb—that a drunken sailor can come and knock everything over. I always think that a drunken sailor can overturn everything."

Such is the making of a miracle—if a miracle is to be made.

Only one thing about the future is absolutely sure: It will surely surprise us. Like the weather, the future is chaotic, and its flow is constantly diverted from the most reasoned expectations. That is why scenarios do not try to predict or forecast the future, but rather to suggest plausible alternative futures.

Some surprises arise from true chance events, or the conjunction of events. Others occur because people say, "Impossible—that can't happen!" Still others appear to come from nowhere, but in fact have been waiting offstage in the darkened wings. When they occur, they reveal unexpected instabilities or potentials in what was thought to be a predictable setting. Thus surprises can engender effects all out of proportion to themselves. They are catalysts for major change.

Some surprises are not surprises at all, but rather were crises waiting to happen. They occur with the logic and finality of a keystone locking into place. But, because they can create very difficult situations or because there is no ready answer in advance, one does not think them through in advance. When they do arrive, they astonish—or shock—the world all the same. It is only in retrospect that we say, "Of course. We should have expected it all along."

Whatever their nature, these various kinds of surprises act as triggers of change. These "surprises" can be used to explore particular risks, timing, and specific issues. They "test" the scenarios. And, as we shall see, they provide a very important element of flexibility for our thinking—by helping to identify and demarcate paths from one of the main scenarios to another.

15

Surprises

"We have unfortunately the prospect of being substantially surprised by events."

—Admiral Bobby R. Inman, former deputy director of Central Intelligence, on the future of the former Soviet Union

This chapter presents eight surprises, organized thematically. The first two are nuclear; the next two are economic, followed by a fifth surprise based on stress on Russian society. The final three are military.

ANOTHER CHERNOBYL—WHERE NO ONE WAS LOOKING

For years the West worries about the danger of another serious nuclear accident in the former Soviet bloc. Most of the world's attention focuses on the most dangerous category of Soviet-era reactors, the so-called RBMK graphite-cooled units of the kind that are installed at Chernobyl. Despite years of urging from the West, all fifteen RBMKs in Russia, Ukraine, and Lithuania are still operational in the late 1990s, producing over 40 percent of the nuclear power of the former Soviet Union. In 1996, as a second-best to decommissioning, a consortium of Western government agencies and interested private companies is formed to provide advanced training in safety procedures for the operators of the RBMK reactors.

But because so much international attention has been lavished on the Chernobyl-type reactors, both Russians and people in the West are taken by surprise when the long-feared nuclear accident occurs. For it does not involve an RBMK, but another Russian design, the boiling-water reactor (VVER). In April 1998, near the central Russian city of Voronezh, a second generation 440-megawatt boiling-water reactor, the Novovoronezh Station-3, experiences a partial meltdown.

Subsequent investigation shows that international funding for safety improvements on reactors of this type has gone preferentially to Eastern Europe, where identical reactors have been taken out of service in eastern Germany and others have been upgraded in Slovakia and Bulgaria. Meanwhile, the Russian Ministry for Atomic Energy (Minatom), under pressure from international opinion, gives top priority to the RBMK safety program.

"This is a classic case of Trishka's famous cloak," the Russian minister of environment later says, referring to a famous Russian proverb. "When he hiked it up to cover his shoulders, it left his feet bare; when he pulled it down to cover his feet, his shoulders were naked. There just isn't enough money and priority to go around."

The Novovoronezh facility, in operation since the 1970s, is scheduled for decommissioning in the mid-1990s, but the shutdown of the plant is repeatedly postponed for lack of funding and shortage of alternative sources of electric power. Minatom's maintenance and safety crews, ironically, are drawn off to the RBMK program, and replacement parts are hard to find. Inspectors had warned for years of metal fatigue and other dangerous signs of wear at the Novovoronezh facility, but in vain. It comes to light that parts of the emergency system have been stripped by workers who are selling the expensive alloys on the black market for export.

Since Russian reactors of that generation are built without containment vessels, the thin walls of the Novovoronezh-3 plant are easily breached by an explosion, and radioactive debris spread widely throughout the heavily populated central Russian plain. The Russian government, to its credit, makes no attempt to limit media coverage of the accident, and the Russian public is stunned and outraged by the extent of the damage it witnesses every night on its television screens. The Novovoronezh tragedy is as great as Chernobyl in the scale of the human cost it imposes. It also imposes a huge economic cost on a Russia that cannot afford it.

The political fallout is unexpected. The nightly coverage of the rescue operations produces a media hero, Colonel Boris Illarionov of the Special Radioactive Medical Forces, a branch of the army. Illarionov's cool authority and rugged good looks, and his remarkable efficiency in directing operations, contrast so starkly with the obvious incompetence of local officials and ministry plenipotentiaries from Moscow that they make Illarionov a national figure overnight.

Thus one of the most remarkable political careers in Russian history is launched. A year after directing the Novovoronezh rescue, Illarionov resigns his officer's commission and forms the Russian Environmental Party (known in Russian by the letters ZP, for *"Zashchita Prirody"*). It becomes the first true new mass party in Russia, as Illarionov turns out to be a highly effective political organizer. Two years later, in the legislative elections of the fall of 2001, ZP becomes one of the largest parties in Parliament and Illarionov becomes prime minister of a coalition government.

Because of Illarionov's strong support from the military, and because corruption and local incompetence were so readily apparent in the Novovoronezh tragedy, Illarionov turns the elections into a referendum for strong central government. Using slogans like "Had Enough?" Illarionov promises to use police and military power to conduct a purge of corrupt local officials. Once in office, he wastes no time. Muddling Down ends, and Two-Headed Eagle begins, albeit with a strong green tinge.

Analysis

Nuclear power currently provides 11 percent of Russia's total electricity. The assumption behind this surprise is that Russia will continue to be dependent on nuclear power for the coming two decades. Consequently, there will be no decommissioning of RBMKs or the older generations of VVERs. This carries noteworthy risks. In 1993, the Federal Nuclear and Radiation Oversight Committee reported 20,000 safety violations.[1] A second assumption is that Minatom is consistently underfunded and understaffed under any scenario. As a result, even though Minatom has remained reasonably coherent and effective as an organization, it is vulnerable to corruption within its ranks.

The rise of Colonel Illarionov reflects the new power of television in Russia today, as well as the popular thirst for heroes in a time that has produced few of them. Illarionov's conversion to political leader could serve as the catalyst for Two-Headed Eagle. Some such catalyst is required to offset the present strong trend toward disintegration.

IS PLUTONIUM MISSING?

In the Long Good-bye, political weakness in Moscow begins to cause the regions to go their own ways, dividing Russia into have and have-not zones, depending on their natural advantages.

Despite the unraveling of the central government, the Russian Strategic Rocket Forces (SRF) and the Federal Counterintelligence Service (FSK) are intact, but the increasingly weak federal government is unable to muster the funding to support these once-élite services adequately, and disaffection spreads among the officers.

Nevertheless, they continue to dismantle nuclear warheads as called for by START I. Fortunately, there are no diversions. Thousands of so-called pits containing plutonium are already recovered from dismantled warheads. But storage remains a major problem. A storage facility initially planned for the city of Tomsk is completed, but it does not operate because of bitter resistance by the local government. The pits are stored temporarily at the four sites where dismantling takes place. This is an unsatisfactory and insecure arrangement, and for years experts warn that there could be trouble.

One of these locations is Penza province, a relatively disadvantaged region in central Russia that has a history of troubled politics. The governor of the province, Georgii Kondratiagin, is even detained by the local FSK in 1994 on suspicion of corruption and ties to organized crime, but is released without being charged, and is reelected governor on a sympathy vote in the elections of 1996.

In the fall of 1998 Kondratiagin cultivates the deputy commander of the Penza dismantling facility. On a Sunday, while out hunting, Kondratiagin offers to buy plutonium. The officer, a disgruntled colonel who has been denied promotion, hesitates, but only for a moment, before agreeing. In exchange for a remarkably modest sum—$20,000 deposited in a Swiss bank account—the officer transfers four pits, each containing a little over three kilograms of plutonium, to Kondratiagin's associates. The pits disappear.

Kondratiagin is working with a gang based in Yekaterinburg. Their plan is to sell the plutonium to Iraqi agents. But the Federal Counterintelligence Service, which has infiltrated the gang, learns of the theft within twelve hours, interrogates the colonel, and arrests Kondratiagin and his associates. Under interrogation Kondratiagin denies any knowledge. The FSK officers receive an anonymous phone call. "Release Kondratiagin and call off your people," says a voice. "Or Moscow's water supply will be poisoned with plutonium."

Senior security and military officers hurriedly meet at a secret dacha in the woods outside Moscow. They think the threat may be a bluff, but conclude that they must act swiftly. They make the crucial decision not to inform the civilian minister of defense or other members of the federal government. The FSK interrogates Kondratiagin again. He tells them what they need to know. Within a day all four pits have been recovered at the sites indicated by Kondratiagin—one of them already loaded in a truck ready to drive off.

The news of the attempted diversion and the arrest of the Penza governor breaks in Moscow two days later, spread by a ham operator near Penza who overhears local police radio traffic. It causes a political crisis in the federal government. The prime minister attempts to sack the officers involved, but the civilian defense minister sides with the FSK and SRF, and so does the Moscow public, which welcomes the military's decisiveness.

The FSK and SRF commanders decide they must act expeditiously to prevent any diversions in the future. They recall the strategy of the Chinese nuclear forces thirty years before: The Chinese nuclear weapons were removed to Yenching province during the Cultural Revolution, and outsiders were barred from any access. They begin moving the stored pits from the four dismantling centers to the Tomsk storage facility, overriding the vociferous objections of the Tomsk government and the weak protests of the federal government. They demand the creation of an élite corps of officers to supervise the disposal of plutonium through glassification at the Tomsk facility. These measures are taken quickly, with strong support from both federal and regional governments.

The frightening experience of attempted nuclear blackmail, and the strong action taken by the security forces, coincide with a growing view among the regions that they have more to lose from crime, chaos, and separatism than they have to gain from autonomy. The military takes cognizance of the threat of corruption within the ranks of the most élite forces. The plutonium diversion affair, together with the FSK and SRF's strong response to it, becomes in subsequent years one of the elements in a broad swing of Russian opinion toward the reintegration of the regions into a stronger and more centralized Russian government—the regathering of Russian lands.

Analysis

The setting for the plutonium diversion is the Long Good-bye. One key assumption is that local towns have the power to resist even the top-priority national security policies of the federal government. Another assumption is that several provinces are less well off and may be run by leaders on the lookout for any opportunities for gain. A third assumption is that under the Long Good-bye corruption is beginning to spread even to the ranks of the most élite forces.

In this case a catastrophe is avoided, but the main point of this surprise scenario is to emphasize that the necessary elements for a nuclear diversion are present in Russia, and will remain present for the coming decades unless greater security measures are taken. About 130 tons of military plutonium—half of the world's total stocks—are in the former Soviet Union, and most of it is in Russia. It takes only about five kilograms (eleven pounds) of plutonium to make a crude atomic bomb. As weapons are dismantled, an estimated six tons of plutonium per year will pass through Russia's weak control system. The control system is also hampered by bureaucratic rivalry among the inspectorate, the Nuclear Ministry, and the military.[2]

OIL DEFEATED

People all over the world begin to panic in the second half of the 1990s as average temperatures rise, the weather becomes more violent and unpredictable, and evidence grows of increases in the worldwide concentration of carbon dioxide, CFCs, and other sources of ozone depletion. Experts are divided over the causes, and indeed over the consequences, but the accumulation of bad news alarms a public already very environmentally oriented. In American schools, the Pledge of Allegiance to the flag has been replaced by the "Environmental Pledge": Every day, tens of millions of children promise to protect the environment from humanity and personally to reduce their own impact on the environment. Politicians respond to popular sentiment with a wave of environmental legislation, which has no effect at all on major non-Western sources of pollution such as Chinese coal consumption and the burn-off of tropical forests, but hits the oil market hard. Millennial anxieties do the rest, as millions of people seek to cut down on their use of energy. Worldwide, oil consumption drops sharply from seventy-one million barrels a day to sixty-five million barrels a day within four years—an even more rapid fall than occurred in the early 1980s.

Simultaneously, in a largely coincidental development, the automotive market, the largest outlet for oil products, is revolutionized by the development of an effective, economically competitive, cost-effective car battery that enables vehicles to travel up to two hundred miles without recharging. Ironically, it is developed in the research labs of a Japanese oil company. This ushers in the mass electric car. The technological innovations are driven by environmental regulations mandating the introduction of "zero-emission" vehicles and by overall environmental concerns. Car owners can now pull up to a new kind of service station, which does not sell gas but rather replaces discharged batteries with charged ones. A quick change of the global vehicle fleet is impossible, as there are now some 595 million gasoline-powered and diesel-powered passenger cars in the world, all of which continue to consume oil products. But the electric car captures up to 30 percent of the new-auto market in North America, Western Europe, and Japan, and more than half in the rapidly growing economies of China and Southeast Asia.

Between 1998 and 2005 these two events combine to cause a further collapse in world demand for oil, sending prices falling once again—this time to below twelve dollars a barrel for the rest of the first decade of the new century.

Russia, as a high-cost oil producer just beginning to take proper account of its costs, is one of the worst hit. Its oil industry had begun to recover since output bottomed out at five million barrels a day in 1995, and its exports had reached three million barrels a day in 1998 at twenty-five dollars a barrel, thanks to a combination of rising production and falling domestic demand. But in 2005, with prices at twelve dollars a barrel, Russia exports barely half a million barrels a day. Its oil revenues drop from $27 billion in 1998 to $2.1 billion in 2005. The Russian economic miracle, which still depends heavily on oil revenues for capital, is stopped cold, and Russia's economy slumps for the rest of the decade.

Gas revenues, to be sure, remain substantial. Demand for natural gas in Western Europe soars, and the price of natural gas in the European market along with it. But Russia is caught short with no immediately available surplus capacity, and above all, no pipeline capacity to spare. Russia rushes to build new pipelines to Western Europe. Thanks to emergency energy funding from Europe, by 2005 new gas begins to flow.

Gas revenues are insufficient because a great deal of private Russian capital has been invested in oil fields in the expectation of high export earnings. Several of the largest Russian holding companies go bankrupt, taking down with them a gigantic house of cards of stacked holding companies, insurance companies, banks, and brokerages.

The Russian business panic of 2006, coinciding with the severe trough in export revenues before gas revenues begin to rise, exposes the weaknesses and corruption of Russian capitalism. A violent wave of populist resentment sweeps out the pro-business government and brings to power the leaders of the new populist parties. Russian politics swings violently back in the direction of state intervention and discrimination against the private sector, as the market system is discredited. The Red-Browns become a powerful force in Russian politics. Young people rediscover the Marxist texts. Many Western investments in Russia go sour, and the investors have little recourse. Western banks find themselves in very difficult negotiations over Russian debt. New international finance for the Russian economy is not available. *Chudo* is over. Muddling Down is back—an angry, vicious, and bitter Muddling Down.

Analysis

This scenario shows the vulnerability of Russia to technological surprises elsewhere in the world. It would be truly surprising indeed if some technological advance did not overturn some key current expectations. This scenario is based on the assumption that Russia will remain heavily dependent on oil revenues for the foreseeable future, and that gas revenues cannot really replace them. This would be true under all scenarios. In 1993, Russia earned $11.6 billion from oil and $7.3 billion from natural gas.[3] It is assumed that the Russian private sector will invest in real assets inside the country. Clearly, this is most likely under *Chudo*. Such investments would make the Russian private sector highly sensitive to world oil prices, as oil and gas together generate half the country's hard currency. A final assumption is that the Russian financial empires being built today are fragile.

CHINA'S NEW MARCH TO CAPITALISM

As the very last veterans of the Maoist revolution fade from the scene, Chinese politics begins to realign in a pattern familiar from the nineteenth century. The central government in Beijing weakens, while the rich coastal cities continue their economic boom. In the past, Chinese politics was repeatedly disrupted by internal wars and outside invasions, and each time the result denied the coastal cities the political power to which their economic prosperity might have entitled them. Not so this time. The principal coastal cities and southern provinces form an alliance with the intellectuals and technocrats of the capital, and set up democratic institutions. Local military commanders form regional alliances with local politicians, and look to local capitals rather than to their nominal commanders in Beijing. The definition of a unified China—so central to Chinese politics for so long—is undergoing change.

In this favorable political environment, economic growth continues strongly. Economic prosperity is broad-based and provides firm support for the growth of democracy.

China continues to be the fastest-growing economic power in Asia and is a magnet for investment from the entire Pacific Rim. Russia watches with awe and mounting concern as Kazakhstan and other Central Asian states turn their gaze eastward, along with the non-Russian populations of border areas such as Buriatiia, Khakassiia, and Tuva. Even more critically, trade between China and the Russian Far East and Siberia, which has been growing strongly for a generation already, turns the eastern Russian provinces into virtual dependencies of China. Chinese farmers, traders, and businessmen migrate into eastern Russia by the hundreds of thousands, supported by abundant Japanese and Korean capital. Equal numbers of Russians travel to nearby Chinese cities to find employment, much of it menial.

The influx of Chinese is highly profitable to the local Russian élite, the descendants of the "nomenklatura capitalists" of the 1990s, but is resented by the local Russian population, which profits little. Moscow is increasingly alarmed that the entire region is about to slip from its grasp. It also worries about the size and growing technical sophistication of the Chinese military. Moscow's agents provide covert support to local opposition politicians, who mount anti-Chinese demonstrations in an attempt to provoke reprisals and thus to weaken the pro-Chinese leadership of the Far Eastern provinces. Their efforts are only too successful. As incidents multiply in which Chinese farmers, traders, and businessmen are harassed and sometimes killed, Chinese mobs seek revenge by attacking Russians in Chinese cities.

Analysis

Just how this surprise unfolds depends very much on the kind of government existing in Russia at the time. Under Muddling Down, the "agents from Moscow" will be disavowed by the federal government, and it will not be clear just whom they are working for. Under the Long Good-bye, local authorities may have acquired enough power to quell the anti-Chinese demonstrations and restore a surface peace. Under a Two-Headed Eagle, the Moscow government would be hospitable on the whole to investment by the East Asian powers, but might encourage local unrest in the Far Eastern provinces of Russia as means of discrediting local Russian elites and bringing the region back under central control. Only a Russian Bear regime would actually move troops to the Far East.

What is likely under all scenarios, however, is that the rise of the Far East will be a new experience for Russians, and one that may shift their gaze from its traditional focus on the west and the south. Whether the adaptation is peaceful or not, Russia will have to change its attitudes toward Asia and Asians. It will not be an easy adjustment.

AIDS OUT OF CONTROL

In retrospect it should have been obvious that Russia and the former Soviet Union were potentially prime territory for AIDS. In the early 1990s there were already large transient populations, consisting of refugees, migrant workers, and soldiers. Prostitution was common and on the rise, homosexuality was coming into the open, and there was widespread promiscuity. Condoms and other prophylactics were not widely available, and in any event were derided as "galoshes." Hypodermic needles were in short supply, and were often reused, even in hospitals. Popular awareness of AIDS was nil, and the government denied that there was a threat. The public health systems of the former Soviet republics had collapsed, and there was no funding or equipment for blood testing. In short, these were among the conditions that prevailed in Asia before the AIDS epidemic began to spread there.

The first stage of the Russian AIDS epidemic begins silently, as AIDS epidemics always do, in the early 1990s. HIV spreads more and more widely, especially in the high-risk groups and in regions such as western Siberia with large transient populations, but also around Moscow among commuting unskilled workers (*limitchiki*), and in refugee settlements and military barracks. But during the first several years most HIV-infected people develop no symptoms.

It is not until about 1997 that large numbers of the HIV-infected begin to develop the actual symptoms of AIDS. After several months of official denials, the Russian government finally admits the existence of an alarming problem, and asks international health organizations for help in setting up "sero-surveys," that is, large-scale blood testing to determine the extent of the problem. Widespread surveys conducted over the following year reveal to a shocked Russian public that the problem is far worse than expected. There are no less than 300,000 HIV-positives in the Russian Federation, and without any control system in place, the authorities are helpless to halt the spread of the virus.

By 2003 the second stage of the epidemic reaches its height, as Russia reports sixty thousand new cases of AIDS each year, and sero-surveys show that the number of HIV-positives has passed the half-million mark. By 2006 a hundred thousand Russians have died of AIDS.

A Stalinist government in its prime would have taken draconian measures to isolate the HIV-positives in camps, as indeed the Cuban government did in the early 1990s. But the Russian government is too weak and too poor to undertake much of a response at all, and AIDS continues to spread unchecked.

As the disease advances, it begins to have a devastating effect on Russia's politics and economy. Russia's neighbors, panic-stricken, begin closing their borders. Trade within the former Soviet space, which revived after 1995, collapses again. Russian Red-Brown extremists spread rumors that AIDS has been loosed on the Russian population by Western governments. In Siberia pogroms break out, directed against prostitutes, homosexuals, foreigners, and refugees. Non-Russian minorities are attacked in several Russian cities, while Russians are persecuted in Tatarstan and other non-Russian areas. The Russian health system, completely unprepared for a large-scale influx of patients, is overwhelmed, and hospitals begin to resemble war zones.

After 2005, this "third stage" of outrage and despair begins to abate, and the Russian government, with the help of international organizations, begins to organize programs to counter the threat, attempting to limit the spread of the virus through education and prophylaxis. The largest syringe-manufacturing plant in the world is built in Russia. By 2010, all the effort begins to pay off, as the number of new infections peaks. But in that year, it is estimated that there are over a million HIV-positives in Russia, and 300,000 victims have died, with many more to follow.

Analysis

Even before the collapse of the Soviet Union, Russia and the rest of the republics were facing a severe health crisis. The indicators pointed to a decline in health, physical well-being, and longevity. One of the main reasons was the widespread environmental degradation and the lack of official concern for the health consequences of pollution. Under the Soviets, a health system had been developed that delivered widely available but low-quality care. But in the 1980s and 1990s, it has fallen apart. Things the West takes for granted, such as disposable syringes, are not readily available throughout Russia. The weakening of medical services and the shortage of both funds and supplies, combined with the greater ease of travel, make Russia vulnerable to epidemics. The growing incidence of preventable infectious diseases, such as diphtheria and cholera, suggests a population under stress, malnourished, and increasingly vulnerable to illness, as well as a health system that is breaking down.[4]

AIDS would put great pressure on the political system. As the number of infected people and the disarray of the government both grow, fear and agitation about the disease and of contamination by "outside" sources spread throughout the country. It is unlikely that AIDS alone could shift Russia's course from one scenario to another, but the disease could be a catalyst in combination with other causes. If a few years go by, however, and international aid is forthcoming, the political effects of an AIDS epidemic should begin to ease. But, whether it is AIDS or some other epidemic, the point is that Russia is very vulnerable. Its society is disrupted and its health-care system is under enormous strain. Massive health problems could have large political consequences.

IRAN INVADES AZERBAIJAN

It is 2007. Azerbaijan, Turkmenistan, and Kazakhstan are growing into world-class oil and gas producers, and oil revenues are pouring into the region. Oil money, as elsewhere in the Middle East, heightens inequalities between haves and have-nots. Social and political resentments have already, for several years, spread "political Islam" throughout the region.

Azerbaijan is in a special category, because it is the only state with a Shiite population to emerge out of the former Soviet Union. Oil money is making Baku a rich and glittering town, a magnet for Azeris from Iran, who emigrate in large numbers from their overpopulated country.

After a decade of sullen cease-fire, Azerbaijan once again challenges Armenia's control of the disputed Karabakh region. This time victories come easily, thanks to abundant oil money and mercenaries from Iranian Azerbaijan. Success brings heady talk of a Great Azerbaijan. Growing traffic between Baku and Tabriz inflames Azeri resentment of Persian domination in an increasingly overpopulated, poor, and violent Iran. Riots break out in Tabriz and other Iranian Azeri cities.

The Tehran government lashes out, putting down rioters in a deliberately bloody repression. But government troops encounter unexpectedly strong opposition from well-armed and experienced Azeri irregulars, veterans of the Karabakh conflict. Tehran decides to liquidate the problem at its source, and invades Baku.

Iran has been counting on Russian weakness. Up until now, Russia, despite several close calls, has avoided getting bogged down in any of the other new states on its southern border. But this time Russia perceives a threat to the petroleum wealth of the entire region, which is exported via the Russian pipeline network. Also, some Russians have viewed the rapid oil development of the rich offshore Caspian Sea reserves with jealousy and resentment. Nationalists charge that the breakup of the Soviet Union was partly engineered by Western oil companies eager to get their hands on those reserves. In January 2010, Russian troops move south from Groznyi and occupy Baku. There is a brief exchange of missiles carrying conventional warheads. Russia threatens to use its "strategic forces." Iran backs away. Russian troops are in command of Baku. But the Russians' problems are only beginning.

Analysis

Russian foreign-policy analysts have already begun defining the south as a major potential source of threats to Russian security, and they look to Iran and "political Islam" as the main possible sources of danger. But in this reenactment of the Great Game, there must be a prize to be won. It is oil in the case of Azerbaijan, natural gas in the case of Turkmenistan.

A key assumption in this "surprise" is that the Azeri-Armenian dispute over Nagorno-Karabakh will not be resolved in this decade, and that it will flare up again in subsequent decades. A further assumption is that Russia does not intend to reoccupy Azerbaijan physically. If Azeri oil is exported through Russia, and if Russian companies acquire a stake in the Caspian fields, Russia will manage to extract revenues without incurring the liability of actual occupation.

But Iranian motives are more complex, because of Tehran's fear of Azeri separatism within Iran. The Iranians recall how, after World War II, Stalin tried to incorporate northern Iran into Soviet Azerbaijan. In addition, Iran, suffering chronic budget problems and unable to reconcile its economic and political interests, would see Azerbaijan's two million barrels per day of additional oil exports as a very valuable economic prize. The idea here is that, if Iran disrupts the balance of power in the region, Russia will respond militarily. Turkey, the other important regional player, would tacitly welcome this intervention against its rival. But anti-Russian sentiment in Azerbaijan is sufficiently strong that a Russian occupation of Baku could lead to widespread resistance, unlike the Russian occupation of 1990.

Whether Russia would attempt to remain in Azerbaijan, or simply expel the Iranians, would depend on the kind of regime in Moscow at that time. The Russian Bear might well be tempted to stay, and would easily find the ideological justifications to do so. But a reclamation of Azerbaijan by Moscow would alarm the other former Soviet states, causing them to seek new alliances against Russia, and would also trigger a serious problem in relations with the West. The Two-Headed Eagle would probably withdraw, though not necessarily speedily. A *Chudo* government might also be pushed toward intervention on the grounds that Iranian occupation of Azerbaijan is a threat to Russian national interests. Russia in a more chaotic form of the Time of Troubles would not be able to respond effectively to an Iranian intervention. But if, as a result of the occupation, Russia found itself bogged down by a continuing guerrilla war in Azerbaijan, the reaction could be the Russian Bear, or a more far-reaching crisis and a chaotic form of the Time of Troubles.

THE MILITARY STRIKES FROM THE SOUTH

For ten years the Cassandras of a military coup in Moscow wait in vain. The Russian Defense Ministry and the Ministry of Security, well treated by the Russian government, prove to be highly loyal institutions. But in 2003 a military takeover finally happens, in a way no one expects.

Beginning in 1993 the Defense Ministry begins redeploying troops returning from Eastern Europe to south Russia. Rostov becomes a new regional command center, with lesser headquarters in cities throughout the south. It is the Long Good-bye; as the central government in Moscow continues to weaken, the southern provinces of Stavropol' and Krasnodar emerge as quasi-autonomous in their own right. They soon become the core of a south Russian regional federation that includes Rostov and the republic of Kalmykiia.

The politics of south Russia revolve around a trio of players: the local military commanders, the conservative politicians, and the Cossacks. The Cossacks are an unruly element from the start, and become more so as they attract allies among the soldiers in the growing garrisons of the south. The government unwisely gives support to the Cossack leaders, thus turning them into a real political force.

The Cossacks have long laid claim to the western provinces of Kazakhstan, and that is where the trouble begins. In 1998 local Cossacks begin agitating for the absorption of the two westernmost provinces of Kazakhstan, which the Russians call Gurev and Ural'sk, into the South Russian Federation. The two Kazakh provinces are a special prize, because they contain the huge oil fields of Tenghiz and the gas fields of Karachaganak.

The local Russian populations of the two Kazakh provinces begin agitating for incorporation into Russia. President Nursultan Nazarbayev of Kazakhstan, perceiving a dire threat to his country's unity, appeals to his close allies in Moscow for help. Moscow obliges by chiding the Cossacks and reaffirming Russia's commitment to upholding present borders. This move infuriates the Cossacks and local military commanders in southern Russia. They react quickly. Within ten days, armored columns cross into Kazakhstan. Within ten more days, facing little serious resistance, the south Russians occupy the two Kazakh provinces.

As the crisis spreads more deeply into Kazakhstan, the Russian government attempts to defuse it by ordering the south Russians back to their bases. The south Russian commanders refuse. Riots break out in Tselinograd and other cities of Russian-populated northern Kazakhstan, and the chaos threatens to spill over into southern Siberia. Recognizing a threat to Russia's stability as well as Kazakhstan's, the Russian defense minister calls on units based in the Volga and the Urals to move against the rebel south Russian forces.

The cause of the Kazakh Russians is popular in the Russian army, and Moscow's order backfires badly, because it reveals to the southern commanders just how weak Moscow's authority is. The end comes when local Kazakh military commanders attempt to put down the Russian civilians who seized power in Tselinograd, expelling the local Kazakh leadership. Seeing Russians brutalized by Kazakh soldiers, and the Moscow government standing by, the southern commanders resolve to move on Moscow. As they do so, they discover that other army units are with them, and there is no resistance to their advance. One week later, barely two months after the first penetration of south Russian troops into Kazakhstan, the Moscow government is in the hands of the military rebels.

Analysis

This "surprise" demonstrates yet another way that, within the family of Time of Troubles scenarios, Russia could move from the Long Good-bye to the Russian Bear. The main assumption here is that even under conditions of greater disintegration than those of a Muddling Down—that is, in the Long Good-bye—the Russian federal government would still retain the ability to channel resources to the military. Senior military commanders basically favor a strong federal government, and thus remain loyal to Moscow. However, the same is not true of local commanders, who feel a sense of grievance against their military superiors in Moscow.

The next assumption is that Moscow will attempt to retain its alliance with President Nazarbayev, but that some forces in the Russian regions will tug the other way. In this way, regional autonomy can have consequences for Russia's relations with its neighboring republics. The regions will pursue their own "foreign policies" toward their neighbors, and Moscow will be unable to rein them in.

The third major ingredient in this scenario is the presence of the Russian population of Kazakhstan as a catalyst for conflict. The failure of the Moscow government to defend that population is interpreted by south Russian military commanders as a betrayal, and sets in motion a chain of events that leads to the defection of the officer corps outside Moscow. In this case, the road from Kazakhstan to Moscow is open to the Russian Bear.

THE FIRST RUSSO-UKRAINIAN WAR?

There have been so many points of tension between Russians and Ukrainians since the breakup of the Soviet Union in 1991 that it is surprising that there is no actual outbreak of hostilities until 1998. Relations between the two states go from crisis to crisis, but each one is peacefully resolved, always at the eleventh hour. The basic reason is simple: so long as there are relatively strong presidents in both Kiev and Moscow, differences ultimately come down to a bargaining session between former Soviet apparatchiks who speak the same language and understand one another very well.

The situation changes entirely after the mid-1990s, when the economic collapse of Ukraine, which is far more serious than even that of Russia, leads to the fall of the Ukrainian government. For the previous five years, Ukrainian politics were all but frozen, as the Ukrainian president stole the thunder of the Ukrainian nationalist party, Rukh, by becoming more nationalist than they. But the economic collapse finally does him in after five years on the tightrope.

The subsequent elections polarize Ukrainian politics as never before, as a revived Rukh rolls up large majorities in western and central Ukraine, while local leaders, without a major party following, win seats from Russian-speaking districts and from Kiev. The resulting parliament is badly divided, and the Ukrainian government, already paralyzed, proves incapable of any organized policies at all. Unfortunately, the backroom negotiations that had repeatedly defused crises between Russia and Ukraine are no longer possible, as nationalists from Parliament soon determine the appointment of Ukrainian delegations in any delicate discussion with Russia. Simmering conflicts begin to escalate, culminating in a bruising series of confrontations over the Crimea—where the population is 70 percent Russian—and over Russian gas exports in the winter of 1997–98.

But it is ultimately the coal miners of the largely Russian-speaking Don Basin who confront Moscow and Kiev with a crisis that cannot be resolved. Working conditions in the mines, already intolerable in the 1980s, are deadly by the 1990s. Miners labor knee-deep in water, in narrow, steeply pitched shafts over a mile deep, risking their lives for a pittance that cannot even feed their families. The Ukrainian government is no longer able to pay the miners subsidies or support. A series of strikes over the years produces no result.

In the hot summer of 1998 a general strike leads to an insurrection. Ukrainian miners become convinced that if they secede from Ukraine their problems will be solved, and Moscow does not discourage them.

During the following months the wave of secessions spreads throughout the Russian-speaking provinces of eastern and southern Ukraine. The Ukrainian government is too weak to oppose the movement initially, but with the withdrawal of the Russian-speaking provinces, there is little obstacle to the rise of ultra-nationalist politicians from western Ukraine. A new and virulently nationalist government comes to power in Kiev, committed to an aggressively anti-Russian line. Ukraine's very existence as a nation, it declares, is threatened. The two republics are now practically on a war footing, there are a number of incidents, and the slightest spark, it seems certain, will bring open warfare.

ANALYSIS

Military conflict between Ukraine and Russia is one of those surprises that should not be a surprise at all. All the ingredients are already there for chronic and serious tension, and possibly for an explosion. Many unresolved issues between the two countries strike at the very identity of each—large Russian minorities in Ukraine, tension between the eastern and western halves of Ukraine over relations with Russia, large military forces on both sides, serious military issues, Sevastopol' and Crimea, and the traumas of transition in both countries. All these potential conflicts are compounded by the special bitterness that arises from strife between "brothers."

Whether these tensions lead to war depends very much on which scenario comes to pass in each country. Right now, Muddling Down in Russia coincides with Two-Headed Eagle in Ukraine. But if Ukrainian politics lapses into a Ukrainian version of Muddling Down or the Long Good-bye, potential for trouble between the two republics rises sharply. The paradox of the situation is that the recent political freeze in Kiev, which has kept the peace today, has also prevented Ukraine from evolving toward true autonomy from Moscow.

Indeed, Ukraine and the rest of the "Near Abroad" are the single most important matter in the foreign relations of the new Russia.

Events in this great expanse can have a profound impact on the evolution of the Russian scenarios. And, as we shall see in the next chapter, nothing is more difficult and more complicated than Ukraine itself, in whose capital of Kiev both Russian Christianity and the Russian state itself were born a thousand years ago.

PART V

What It Means
for the World

The events of the next decade and a half will establish the new framework for Russia's foreign relations. Today, Russia is preoccupied not with its international influence and power, but rather with its internal reconstruction, both political and economic; and domestic developments are determining Russia's future foreign policy. But one may be sure that Russia will return to a more active role in its relations not only with its near neighbors but also beyond.

In the next three chapters, building on the perspectives of the scenarios, we examine Russia's place in the world from three angles—foreign policy, foreign investment, and the West's relations with Russia.

16

The Return of a Great Power*

That which stops growing begins to rot.
> —*minister to Catherine the Great*

Russia is a kingdom almost unknown in Europe during the last
centuries, and gradually aggrandized at the expense of her neighbors.
. . . This vast empire . . . embraces all variety of climate, and
comprehends every species of resource. . . . Solitary resistance is vain
against an empire which can produce soldiers like grains of sand.
> —*Gustavus III of Sweden*

Russia is the international legatee of the Soviet Union, heir to the
Soviet Union's seat on the U.N. Security Council, to most of its military forces, to its foreign-policy institutions and the Stalinist wedding
cake that houses the Ministry of Foreign Affairs—and to its debts. But
Russia's position and interests in the world are radically different from
those of its predecessor, and its foreign-policy concerns have been dramatically transformed.

Even after separating from the fourteen other republics that are now
independent states, Russia is still the largest nation in the world, com-
prising eleven time zones. It is no longer a global player, although it is
seeking to resurrect its international role. While Russia's geostrategic
position and its military power ensure that, one way or the other, it
will inevitably be a major actor in the affairs of Europe and Asia, its
range of action will be circumscribed. Nor does it have the will for

* **This chapter is authored by Angela Stent, with Thane**
  Gustafson and Daniel Yergin.

involvement around the world. For Russia clearly did not inherit the Soviet Union's ideology and global mission; indeed, it rejects both. It also does not have what were the global capabilities of the Soviet Union.

In terms of the rest of the world, what would have been inconceivable a decade ago is today a fundamental fact. Russia's most important and complex foreign relations are now with countries that did not exist then: the *blizhnee zarubezhe,* or Near Abroad, states that were until recently part of the Soviet Union itself. The Near Abroad embodies the issues that will define the new Russian state and its neighbors. Beyond the successor states of the Near Abroad, Russia's relations with the United States, Germany, Japan, and China will continue to be important, but in ways very different from the past. Economic weakness and reconstruction and a quest for a new identity, rather than ideology, will govern Russia's involvement with the outside world.

A POST-IMPERIAL RUSSIA?

Russia's triple transition—from totalitarianism to democracy, from a centrally planned to a market economy, and from imperial to post-imperial state—is a daunting challenge in all of its dimensions. But the dimension in which perception will most lag behind reality is the third—the area of foreign policy. Many Russians who reject communism nevertheless do not willingly accept the breakup of the Soviet Union. They regard it as a loss, a tragedy, and, more malevolently, as a deliberate plot to dismantle a government and a nation.

Will Russia reconcile itself to becoming, for the first time in centuries, a national, as opposed to an imperial state? What kind of foreign policy will it pursue? What will the new Russian revolution mean for the rest of the world? The answers to all these questions depend on developments within Russia and the other successor states and on the evolution of both Europe and Asia in the post-Communist era. Under the different scenarios, the character and focus of Russia's foreign policy vary greatly. In Muddling Down, Russia would not be a major player internationally, as it will be so deeply engaged in its transitions. In Two-Headed Eagle, Russia's focus would also tend to be internal, though the nation would reassert its interests, as it perceives them, in the Near Abroad by restoring economic links and resisting Islamic fundamentalism. It would be active in Europe and Asia. The Russian Bear would focus on reintegrating, one way or another, the other former republics, using the economic and military means at its disposal. Relations with individual successor states would become more confrontational as Moscow's willingness to compromise diminished, and it would aggressively "defend" Russians living in the other states. Belligerent, antiforeign nationalism would be the hallmark. The likelihood of significant military conflict is greatest under this scenario.

In both the Long Good-bye and *Chudo,* economic interests would be much more dominant. Under the Long Good-bye, Russian foreign policy becomes regionalized. In some areas, armed conflicts either continue or develop. In others, links grow with neighbors. The control of nuclear weapons could be a significant concern.

In *Chudo,* Russia would become more active internationally, because it would have the resources and self-confidence to do so. But it would act as a national rather than an imperial power and it would define its interests and security in terms of economics and the protection of existing borders, not in the acquisition of new territories to act as buffer zones. It could use its new-found influence to cooperate with the West in the establishment of a new European security system. Russia would be more assertive in pursuing its own interests and might emerge as a new rival to the Western powers; however, this rivalry would no longer be based on military factors, but rather on economic interests. Russia would bargain hard on trade issues, which would be a growing source of acrimony with an enlarged European Community. In *Chudo,* relations with the successor states might well improve, provided that they, too, were experiencing some form of economic upturn. Indeed, *Chudo* in Russia would be a magnet for the surrounding states, stimulating their economies, and drawing them back into some degree of reintegration with the Russian economy.

For over four hundred years, imperialism and military might drove the expansion of the Russian empire and then the Soviet Union. But with the collapse of communism and the disintegration of the Soviet Union, the world's second superpower abruptly vanished, leaving the United States the uncontested, if also uncertain, global leader. Russia, as it resurrects itself as successor to the Soviet Union, is trying to redefine its international position and establish its role as a multiregional player, rather than a superpower. But centuries of empire leave a far-reaching psychological legacy, an orientation that cannot be discarded overnight. And this orientation can be rekindled by the politics of resentment and humiliation, by the conviction that Russia was deceived into surrendering its rightful place in the world.

THE DRIVE FOR EMPIRE

In the years ahead, Russia will be struggling to cope with an imperial inheritance that long predates the 1917 revolution. The two successive empires—Russian and Soviet—were war machines. Already by the eighteenth century, both Russian leaders and their antagonists believed that it was Russia's insatiable quest for territory and its ability to produce as many soldiers as needed that were the key to its influence.

The high point of Russian influence in the pre-revolutionary period was between the Seven Years' War (1756–63) and the Crimean War (1853–56). Russia was a major player in all of the European questions that divided the powers because it had become, since the reign of Peter the Great, a large multinational state that was continuing to annex neighboring territories. This inexorable expansion created the largest land empire in the world, which made Russia impervious to conquest, as Napoleon discovered to his dismay.

Geography and natural endowments were, therefore, among the primary sources of Russian power. So were the size of its army and the quantity of its weaponry. The political system supported its imperial policies. Autocracy and empire went hand in hand. Catherine the Great told her courtiers that, even though she herself was a disciple of Voltaire and other Enlightenment thinkers, she regarded a strong, centralized and autocratic state as necessary to keep together and protect the vast Russian empire and govern its sometimes unruly people. The multinational character of the empire was for a long time a source of imperial strength. Until the latter part of the nineteenth century, Russia was surprisingly successful in integrating the élites of the territories it conquered and annexed—whether Germans, Balts, Ukrainians, Tatars, Poles, or Turkic peoples—into its ruling classes. Imperial expansion was from time to time tempered by defeats and retreats that had destabilizing domestic political repercussions.

Ideology—in this case, promotion of Orthodoxy, Russia's claim to protect all Slavs, and resistance to Islamic expansion—was also a factor in imperial expansion. The idea of empire was developed only after Russia actually acquired her empire. Indeed, Russia began to conquer adjacent territories long before the idea of Russian nationhood had congealed. This legacy is still felt today—the Russians began to question who they were after they were already living in a multinational state. And they are still not sure what it means to be a Russian.

The overriding question for today that emerges from the pre-Communist period is, Will the new Russia be able to feel secure as a nation-state without occupying or controlling its immediate neighbors to the south and west? How will it define its national identity and interests?

THE FACES OF SOVIET FOREIGN POLICY

Throughout the Soviet period, foreign policy had two distinct faces—one Communist, revolutionary, and ideological, the other Russian. Before World War II, the revolutionary face was the Communist International, dedicated to world revolution. It did not achieve a single lasting Communist revolution, but it did facilitate Hitler's rise to power by ordering the loyal German Communist party to oppose the Weimar Republic and the Social Democrats in their fight against the Nazis.

The other face of Soviet foreign policy was the more traditional diplomatic. Here, the USSR's main attraction was as a potential ally for either Germany or France and Britain as the European political situation unraveled in the 1930s. The USSR did not then have the capability to pursue an imperial foreign policy.

All this changed dramatically after 1945. By the 1960s there were two superpowers leading global blocs, and the Soviet Union had amassed international power and influence greater than ever before in its history. Moreover, it was no longer the object of other countries' ambitions but, rather, an initiator of policies. By the Brezhnev era, Communist ideology was used to justify a continuation of tsarist imperial policies, but now on a scale that reached far beyond Europe.

What made the Soviet Union a superpower? As in the days of the tsars, the single most important factor was sheer military might—in this case, both nuclear and conventional. In the Brezhnev era, the growth of military spending was justified by the dubious doctrine of "equal" security, whereby the Soviet Union had to protect itself from a possible war against all of its potential enemies—America, Western Europe, China, Japan—at the same time. Yet such spending was out of all proportion to any reasonable definition of threat, and ultimately weakened the state.

From Moscow's point of view, Eastern Europe was a security belt, a glacis to insulate the USSR against invasion, and something to be preserved at all costs. When Alexander Dubček tried, in 1968, to argue to the Soviet leadership that Czechoslovakia's "Prague Spring" was no threat to the Soviet bloc, Leonid Brezhnev bluntly set him straight on the meaning of geopolitics, Soviet-style. "Since the end of the last war

Czechoslovakia has been a part of the Soviet security zone," the Soviet ruler said. "The Soviet Union has no intention of giving it up."[1]* Yet, by the mid-1970s, Eastern Europe's contribution to Soviet superpower status was itself becoming a more questionable proposition. The growing cost of maintaining the empire and the weak legitimacy of the satellite governments meant that the USSR had to pour more and more resources into Eastern Europe in order to sustain its position there.

Another major source of Soviet power was its role in the third world. The Soviet Union exercised significant influence in a few third-world client states, and it also cultivated a number of other countries through aid and weapons transfers. These clients proved to be an expensive luxury. They absorbed weapons and money, but they were at best uncertain recruits to communism. Much of this activity was driven by rivalry with the United States and China. Nevertheless, the Soviets did succeed in the 1960s and 1970s in projecting their power on a global basis.

IMPERIAL OVERSTRETCH

The invasion of Afghanistan at the end of 1979 and the inability to prevail there over the following decade demonstrated the dangers and risks of imperial overstretch. The humiliating defeat Russia finally suffered convinced many Russians that the Soviet Union should give up its attempts to control unstable and ungrateful third-world regimes.

Despite its boasts about output targets achieved and plans overfulfilled, the Soviet Union after the 1960s was not a superpower in an economic sense. The once potent appeal of Marxism-Leninism also faded away, perhaps nowhere more than in countries that were forced to live under it and that saw it as a tool of Soviet domination. Eastern Europeans used to joke that the Soviet Union was the only country in the world entirely surrounded by hostile Communist countries.

With Gorbachev came a redefinition of Soviet international interests and a recognition that the Soviet Union could no longer call itself a superpower unless it put its economic house in order. The result was a striking reorientation of Soviet foreign policy. Gorbachev and his for-

* The Hungarian party leader János Kádár had sought unsuccessfully to warn Dubček on the eve of the 1968 Soviet invasion of Czechoslovakia: "Do you really not know the kind of people you're dealing with?"

eign minister, Eduard Shevardnadze, started to downplay the rivalry with the United States and the West. Instead, they opted for a policy of "mutual security," whereby the Soviet Union anticipated cooperation, not confrontation, with capitalism. Yet, despite all the professions of "new" political thinking in foreign policy, Gorbachev initially believed that the USSR could and should remain a superpower, or at least a major global power, albeit with commitments based on a more realistic assessment of its capabilities. After all, was the Soviet Union not the "homeland of socialism"?

Yet Gorbachev was forced to reevaluate this opinion, too, as Eastern Europe broke loose. The Soviet Union had the military capability but not the will to hold on to its Eastern European empire. As discussed earlier, use of force in Eastern Europe would have jeopardized economic links with the West and arms control, both of which the Soviet Union was counting on for its own economic rehabilitation. The fall of the Berlin Wall and the disappearance of the Marxist-Leninist regimes in Eastern Europe meant the end of empire and removed perhaps the single most important pillar in the Soviet Union's superpower status. At the same time, the USSR's retrenchment in the third world—also a result of declining economic capabilities—further reduced its global influence. With its ideology under assault, its economy in crisis, and its empire gone, the major source of the USSR's international power was its military arsenal.

Gorbachev was admired in the West as a peacemaker. Some, living under other repressive Communist regimes, saw him as embodying their hopes for a leader in a more humane socialist society. But, during his tenure, the global power of the Soviet Union—its ability to influence other countries to change their policies—was greatly diminished. Many Russians today blame Gorbachev for the destruction of Russia's might and prestige in the world.

A GREAT POWER AGAIN

Russia faces a fundamental challenge in the coming years. It is to find a new identity in an era when the rebirth of nationalism and ethnicity is the central and frequently destabilizing factor in all the former Communist countries. Russia dominated its neighbors for hundreds of years; its sense of national identity and national interests arose in conjunction with its imperial destiny, and was inseparable from it. Russia is a very significant military power and will remain so for the foreseeable future. It retains a vast nuclear arsenal and a large conventional force, although its prowess is being weakened by wear and tear on its equipment, increasing levels of draft evasion, and confusion over doctrine and role.

But Russia has yet to fully accept that it has lost its empire—indeed, many do not yet recognize the loss—and it will take years to fully digest this fact. It will take more than diminished means to change Russia's self-perception as an imperial state. After all, one could argue that some in France retain an imperial consciousness, even though France gave up its empire in 1958. But for Russia, unlike France, the former empire lies just beyond its borders, remains economically part of it, and contains 25 million of its own people.

THE NEW FRONTIER AND THE NEAR ABROAD

To make matters still more difficult, Russia has not only lost its external and internal empire, it must now deal on an equal footing with former subject states whose own history of independence and statehood is somewhat ambiguous. Russia will only become a post-imperial state if the forces that propelled it to empire are no longer operative in the next century and it can coexist with its immediate neighbors.

Indeed, the principal focus for Russian foreign policy will be relations with a part of the world that did not exist as a concept a few years ago. This is the Near Abroad, as the Russians like to call the successor states, although the successor states themselves consider that this term implies that they are different from other foreign countries. It is hard to imagine that there could have been preparations for this new reality, given how incomprehensible the very idea of breakup was to the Russians. The new states range from Ukraine, with 52 million people—the size of France—to Estonia, with a population of 1.6 million, smaller than a good-sized Russian city.

The overriding questions between Russia and the other former republics concern legitimacy and sovereignty, issues made all the more complicated by the countries' continuing close economic integration. Many of these states are inhabiting territories marked by borders that do not have pre-1917 legitimacy. The fourteen new nation-states vary widely in their present capacity to be legitimate "states" and in their national consciousness. Some were full-fledged states or kingdoms at various times in the past. Others had never existed as organized independent states, but were created by Lenin's and Stalin's pens, and rose to national consciousness only in the Soviet era.

The new entities are trying to become viable nation-states, and that status is best defined in opposition to Russia and Russian domination. The sense of grievance and injustice is strong. Russians dominated these states; Russian populations were moved into their territories; and Russian means of control included terror, secret police, prison camps, and arbitrary executions. Such historical memories will come more to the fore as nation-building proceeds. And now the tables are turned in relations between Russians and the local populations.

THE "RUSSIAN DIASPORA": TINDER FOR CONFLICT

From Russia's point of view, the most pressing issue in the future involves the treatment of the Russian minority—25 million in all—who live outside the Russian Federation, including the troops who remain in a number of states, most notably the Baltics. Also very important are the unresolved questions involving economic relations and the disposition of disputed territories, populations, and property.

Russians in the successor states do not know whether their allegiance is to the state in which they live or to the Russian Federation. They find themselves potentially or, in fact, real second-class citizens. In Ukraine, for instance, Russians have been granted full citizenship. In Estonia, by contrast, they have been disenfranchised. Many Russians are calling for dual citizenship—hardly a prescription for a peaceful transition. Conflicts over the position of the Russians in the Near Abroad will be fought along the familiar lines of ethnic conflict—citizenship rights, language rights, political and economic power, social position. For the Russians within the Russian Federation, it is still hard to believe that these other republics are now foreign countries. The shock comes down to everyday practicalities. For instance, a woman in Moscow formerly needed only a train ticket to visit her aged parents in Riga, Latvia. Now she also must get a visa, putting up with long bureaucratic delays in the process.

There is no shortage of highly inflammatory rhetoric from both Russian and non-Russian extremists. Vladimir Zhirinovskii may be one of the most extreme, but he is only one among plenty of Russian politicians who give dark warnings about the persecution of Russians and their need to defend themselves, and call for a reassertion of Moscow's influence throughout the region. Despite the dire predictions, however, there have been relatively few outbreaks of outright violence between Russians and non-Russians—with the notable exception of Transdniester and Tajikistan. Russians perceive themselves to be threatened, but in many areas coexist tolerably well with the local population. The potential for conflict is great, but the current reality is more promising than the rhetoric.

UKRAINE VERSUS RUSSIA: THE BIGGEST RISK

As depicted in the "surprises," of all the new relationships involving the successor states, those between Russia and Ukraine are the most complex, with the greatest potential for serious conflict. Ukraine, which as an independent nation did not exist as late as 1991, has not only the third-largest nuclear arsenal in the world, but also the largest conventional army in Europe, except for Russia's. The management of that arsenal is of global concern. Ukraine in January 1994 signed an agreement with the United States in which it promised to transfer its nuclear weapons to Russia. However, the parliament has balked at implementing this agreement. There are a number of other highly contentious issues between the two nations, including both the status of the 11.5 million Russians (22 percent of the population) who live in Ukraine (and have much intermarried with Ukrainians) and the disposition of the Black Sea fleet, whose home port remains along the Black Sea, but now in an independent Ukraine. An immediate and critical source of tension will be the fate of the Crimea, which Nikita Khrushchev transferred from Russia to Ukraine in 1954. The population of the Crimea is mostly Russian, ensuring tension, and its cities include Yalta (where Roosevelt, Churchill, and Stalin met in 1945) and Sevastopol'. Their inclusion in Ukraine denies ordinary Russians the pleasure of bicycle holidays and sanatoria in the sun around Yalta and strips Russia of the warm-water port—Sevastopol'—that it defended against Britain and Turkey in the Crimean War. After the battle of Sevastopol' in 1854, the London *Times* described the city as "the very heart of Russian power in the East," and right up to the present day it has been a strategic asset. Crimea's semi-autonomous government currently calls for reintegration with Russia and distancing itself from Ukraine —an effort that will be stoutly resisted by Kiev.

Russia and Ukraine were so tightly tied together economically that the management of economic relations will be difficult. Russia, for instance, supplies 80 percent of Ukrainian energy, but sees little reason, in the new circumstances, to continue to provide that energy at anything but world prices. For its part, however, Ukraine does not have the resources to pay either hard currency or world prices. Yet, at the same time, most of Russia's gas shipments to Europe, which generate over $7 billion a year, pass through Ukraine.

The issues of sovereignty and nationality cut most deeply. Many Ukrainians insist that Russians have consistently dominated them and denied their country its nationhood. Yet there is not a clear consensus even on that point. Ukraine, lagging far behind Russia in the transition to a market economy, is also a divided country. The western Ukraine, primarily Uniate, sees itself as clearly distinct from Russia and looks toward Europe. Matters are much less clear for the eastern Ukraine, which is primarily Orthodox and was much more integrated with Russia; it remains both economically and psychologically oriented toward Russia. "This separation has cut our very hearts in two," one of the leaders of eastern Ukraine said recently, expressing sentiments that would get him in great trouble in the western part of his country. "Not only have links between factories been severed, but families find themselves cut in two by what used to be a symbolic border."[2] Meanwhile, Ukraine's deplorable economic situation strengthens sentiment among eastern Ukrainians and the Russians in the Crimea for, at least, economic reintegration with Russia.

Emblematic of the confusion over identity between Ukrainians and Russians was the linguistic dilemma of a recent high-level Ukrainian delegation. On the plane from Kiev to Moscow, they chatted energetically among themselves in Russian. Once they got off the plane in Moscow they ostentatiously switched to Ukrainian.

For their part, Russians have difficulty seeing Ukrainians, at least those from the east, as a distinct people and instead argue that the two groups belong together. Many Russians cannot accept that Kiev is a foreign city. After all, as already noted, the Russian state and Russian Christianity were both born in Kiev in the tenth century. Under the tsars, Russians spoke of themselves as the "Big Russians" and Ukrainians as the "Little Russians"—not exactly the sort of hierarchy that pleases Ukrainians.

Ukraine, unlike Russia, has for the last two years been suspended between its Communist past and reform. Its economy has been immobilized and is in much worse shape than that of Russia itself. Ukraine's policies toward Russia, and Russia's ability to influence them, will be much affected by Ukraine's dire economic situation. For instance, in

September 1993, Ukrainian nationalists attacked President Leonid Kravchuk for trying to cede Ukrainian nuclear arms and Ukraine's share of the Black Sea fleet to Russia in exchange for debt cancellation. Kravchuk left no doubt economics were behind it all. "If we were a bit richer and had one billion dollars in our account," he snapped, "then the opposition might have been entitled to say something."[3] A signpost for future relations between the two countries is the character of instability within Ukraine as it makes its transition and struggles to find its identity and a national consensus. Since the election of President Leonid Kuchma in July 1994 Ukraine has committed itself to pursuing economic reform, to improving ties with Russia, and to transferring its nuclear weapons to Russia. Its prospects appear brighter than at any time since independence.

BELARUS AND THE BALTIC STATES

Belarus, which used to be Belorussia, or White Russia, remains very closely linked to Russia and so far has barely become a separate state. It is argued by some that the language of Belarus is much more a Russian dialect than a separate tongue. Nevertheless, national consciousness there is bound to rise over the next decade. In terms of its economic fundamentals, Belarus might have been one of the newly independent republics with the best chance at a successful transition. However, owing to the way the winds blew from the Chernobyl nuclear accident, it suffered, and continues to suffer, particularly heavily. Belarus has gone the farthest in terms of reintegrating its economy with that of Russia.

Relations remain tense with the Baltic states—Estonia, Latvia, and, to a lesser extent, Lithuania—which were brutally incorporated into the Soviet Union in 1940 by Stalin, as part of the Nazi-Soviet Non-Aggression Pact. For both economic and security reasons—and to replace local populations that were deported—the Soviet government encouraged large-scale Russian immigration into these states as it built up defense plants and other heavy industry. Today, the population of Estonia is 30 percent Russian; of Latvia, 34 percent; of Lithuania, much lower at 9 percent. Estonia's citizenship laws have barred most Russians from voting—excepting those who can prove they had relatives resident there before 1940—and there is a large, restive Russian population at Narva. Moreover, non-Estonians cannot own property or partake fully in privatization programs. Today, Russians are almost totally absent from Estonian political life, but are disproportionately active in the economy. The potential for social instability is therefore considerable.

The Russians accuse Estonia and Latvia of discriminating against ethnic Russians, charges much publicized in Russia. "If the call went out," one senior Russian official recently said, "fifty thousand Russians would sign up overnight to go to the aid of the Russians in Estonia." After much mutual invective, Russia has withdrawn its troops from the Baltic States. But the relationship between Russians and the Baltic populations remains tense. Economic ties are also contentious because of the integration of the economies and, in particular, the Baltic republics' dependence on Russian energy.

THE CAUCASUS

Geography divides the Caucasus into two broad regions that pose very different issues for Russian policy. The zone north of the Caucasus Mountains lies—uneasily—within the Russian Federation. It is an asteroid belt of small mountain peoples, such as the Chechens and the Ingush, riven by innumerable ancient hatreds and grievances, both toward one another and toward the great power to the north. The main strategic problem this region poses for Russia is a domestic one: If the small republics of the north Caucasus break away from Russia, that could catalyze separatist tendencies throughout Russia. The north Caucasus will be a running sore for years to come, while the central government in Moscow remains weak, but in the long run the region is likely to remain Russian.

The region on the far side of the Caucasus Mountains, the Transcaucasus, is a different matter. The three nations of the Transcaucasus— Armenia, Azerbaijan, and Georgia—have broken away from Russia definitively. But the region is torn by a many-sided bloody civil war in Georgia, in which Georgians are fighting other minorities within their republic (such as the Abkhaz), but also one another. There is an equally fierce battle between Armenia and Azerbaijan for possession of the disputed territory of Nagorno-Karabakh.

Russia's diplomatic interests are strongly engaged: Azerbaijan is rich in oil and gas, which could yield handsome transit revenues if exported through Russia. Both of the wars in the region pit Christians against Muslims. And Turkey and Iran are extending their own influence into the Transcaucasus. In coming years, Russia is bound to remain actively involved in the region, which it regards very definitely as part of its sphere of interest. But most Russians seem reconciled to the independence of the three Caucasian republics.[4] Russia has begun playing a more active "peacekeeping" role in the Near Abroad. However, as a result of the bloody Georgian civil war, Georgian President Eduard Shevardnadze asked President Yeltsin to send Russian troops to support his side.

The Russian army, or at least individual units within it, is already active in some of the conflicts, such as those in Moldova, Abkhazia, Tajikistan, and Armenia-Azerbaijan. However, it is unclear how much control the central Russian government can exercise over its soldiers in the field. It is quite possible, for instance, that, over the next few years, renegade Russian units could become more active in conflicts outside the borders of the Russian Federation, thus increasing tension between Russia and its neighbors. Moreover, Russian official military doctrine stipulates that Russia has a "legitimate role" to play in conflicts in the Near Abroad.

CENTRAL ASIA

The five Central Asian states—Kazakhstan, Uzbekistan, Turkmenistan, Kyrgyzstan, and Tajikistan—had constituted the major cluster of pro-union forces under Gorbachev and were the Soviet republics least eager to seek independence from Russia. They remain heavily dependent on Russia today. Russia is so far the key to the stability of Central Asia and recognizes that the region remains closely tied to it in every way.

The situation in Central Asia since the collapse of the Soviet Union has been varied and quite tense. From the Russian point of view, the best relations are with Kazakhstan, 38 percent of whose population is Russian. Since Islam plays a less important role there than in other Central Asian states, Russian leaders are less fearful that Kazakhstan will ally itself with a power hostile to Russia. Moreover, because of its proximity, overwhelming economic influence, and ethnically rooted interest, Russia will continue to play a major role in Kazakhstan and relations will remain cooperative, barring the advent of an extreme nationalist leader in either country.

Relations with other Central Asian states are more problematic, because of increasing ethnic tensions and civil wars there and because of the rise of political Islam in some, and its use by opportunistic political leaders. So far, the only Central Asian republic that has actually exploded is Tajikistan. Over a hundred thousand have been killed, and most of the Russian population has fled. Russian troops are now in Tajikistan in a peacekeeping role. The other republics have remained more or less stable, as local leaders have built their power on clan alliances behind the façade of previous Soviet institutions. But Kazakhstan is potentially fragile, divided as it is between a large Kazakh south and a mostly Russian north.

The major Russian concerns in Central Asia are the growth of political Islam that might spill over to the Islamic parts of the Russian Federation and encourage separatism there, and the activities of other powers in the region. Moscow is greatly concerned about Iran's rising profile and about the spread of weapons and ideas from Afghan Islamic extremists to Tajikistan and other new states. Taken together, then, Russia's concerns in Central Asia are very different from those connected to the European successor states.

CONDEMNED TO COEXIST

In none of the newly independent states have there yet been attacks against Russians or Russia (with the one exception of Tajikistan and Transdniester, the small Russian-populated enclave that borders on Moldova) of a kind that could provoke intervention. Still, relations with the Near Abroad will not only preoccupy Russia but also present all too many opportunities for conflict. But, despite these problems, Russia and its immediate neighbors are ultimately condemned to coexist and cooperate if they want to survive and prosper as free-market nations. The former republics are also trying to forge their own international links—Ukraine and Belarus with Central Europe, the Baltic States with Scandinavia, Central Asia with Turkey and the Middle East. Russia, too, seeks to form new partnerships abroad. All of this will take time.

Eventually, some states could decide that Russia is not necessarily their main threat. Just as the former republics are not a homogeneous group of states and have different relations with Russia, they do not uniformly view Russia as their major enemy. Indeed, some Central Asian states see Russia as a natural ally against domestic and external threats. Thus, the international alignments of the post-Soviet states in the next century will be complex and uneven, and some may seek greater economic and political integration with Russia.

THE FAR ABROAD: THE "EURASIANISTS" AGAINST THE "ATLANTICISTS"

For centuries, Russians have debated among themselves whether they are part of Europe and should share in European culture or whether they are something quite different, rooted in their Slavic identity and the *zemlya* (land), and should therefore go their own distinctive way to avoid being corrupted by Western influences. The two sides in this argument, which dominated Russian intellectual life in the nineteenth century, became known as the Westernizers and the Slavophiles. That debate has been reborn in Russia today and will likely last for decades. The Atlanticists, heirs to the Westernizers, argue that Russia should become a democratic, capitalist country, with a foreign policy based on cooperation with the West.

Arrayed against them are the Eurasianists, descendants of the Slavophiles, who declare that Russia is unique and should not simply seek to be "just another European country." They call instead for policies more consistent with Russia's special geographical situation. The Eurasianists also believe that Russia should proclaim the entire geographical space of the former Soviet Union a sphere of vital interest from which the West should be excluded. Indeed, they have called for a Russian "Monroe Doctrine" for the former Soviet Union. The Atlanticists are, by contrast, post-imperial, believing that national security cannot be achieved if it makes other states feel insecure. They stress cooperation with the West.[5] Since the December 1993 elections, the Atlanticist view has become decidedly muted. Even Foreign Minister Kozyrev, formerly one of its most vocal proponents, has insisted that cooperation with the West cannot mean subordination to the West. The May 1994 document written by a Yeltsin advisory committee outlining the main premises of Russian foreign policy reasserts Russia's right to have a sphere of influence in the former Soviet states and insists that the West must accept this right. President Yeltsin reiterated this proposition in his speech to the United Nations in September 1994. This reassertion of Russia's sphere of influence is now the mainstream Russian view.

It is still too early for a consensus to emerge in Russia on what Russian national interests should be and whether Russia should proceed cooperatively with the West or carve out a new international role. And any consensus will be decisively affected by the character of Russia's evolution. In the *Chudo* scenario, the Atlanticist view would be

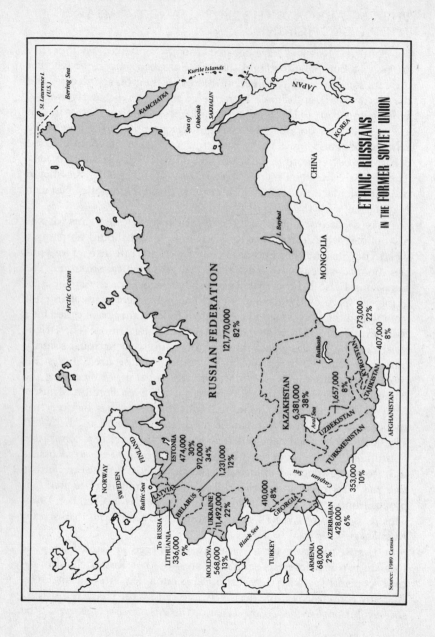

ETHNIC RUSSIANS
IN THE FORMER SOVIET UNION

RUSSIAN FEDERATION
121,770,000
82%

KAZAKHSTAN
6,381,000
38%

KYRGYZSTAN
973,000
22%

TAJIKISTAN
407,000
8%

UZBEKISTAN
1,657,000
8%

TURKMENISTAN
353,000
10%

ESTONIA
474,000
30%

LATVIA
912,000
34%

BELARUS
1,231,000
12%

UKRAINE
11,492,000
22%

LITHUANIA
336,000
9%

To RUSSIA

MOLDOVA
568,000
13%

GEORGIA
410,000
8%

AZERBAIJAN
428,000
6%

ARMENIA
68,000
2%

Arctic Ocean

Bering Sea

St. Laurence I.
(U.S.)

KAMCHATKA

Kurile Islands

Sea of
Okhotsk

SAKHALIN

JAPAN

KOREA

CHINA

MONGOLIA

L. Baykal

L. Balkash

Aral Sea

Caspian
Sea

Sea

Black Sea

TURKEY

AFGHANISTAN

FINLAND

NORWAY

SWEDEN

Baltic Sea

Source: 1989 Census

254

dominant. The Eurasianists would provide the intellectual or ideological underpinnings for the Russian Bear.

From the Russian point of view, the main focus in relations with the West will remain economic. Policy toward the West will be dualistic. Russia seeks Western financial and technical assistance and investment. Yet, it does not want the West to treat it as a supplicant. As former Russian Ambassador to the United States and current Chairman of the Foreign Affairs Committee of the Russian State Duma Vladimir Lukin said in April 1994, "Russia cannot be an American satellite—simply because it is not in the natural order of things."[6] Rather, it wants to be treated as a down-on-its-luck Great Power that needs a helping hand but does not want to be humiliated. Foreign Minister Andrei Kozyrev, heavily criticized within Russia for being "slavishly" pro-Western, embodies this dualism. He has been willing to meet the U.S. conditions for aid, but he also insists on Russia's right to help determine U.N. policy in Bosnia and the terms for Ukraine's renunciation of nuclear weapons. Early in 1994, Russia played an instrumental role in enforcing a U.N. ultimatum against the Bosnian Serbs. However, Russia's traditional alignment with the Serbs has caused tensions with the West. For coming years, however, even Russian Atlanticists are bound to defend Russia's interests more vigorously than they have since Gorbachev's reforms began. As Lukin said, "Russia, by virtue of its size and resources, remains a Great Power with many legitimate interests in adjacent regions."

THE UNITED STATES: BEYOND COMPETITION

Relations between the United States and Russia will be very much on a new footing. Human rights and "the prison of nations," as the Russian empire was called, were a concern of American policy even a century ago, during tsarist days. The original struggle between the United States and the Soviet Union was ideological. Woodrow Wilson issued his Fourteen Points, enshrining self-determination as the lodestone of international relations, in response to Lenin's appeals during World War I to the Western Allies' publics and colonial populations. After World War II, the West was no longer concerned only with ideology and subversion. Rather, it was also concerned with power. The defense of Europe and Asia in the face of Soviet expansionism became the very core of American foreign policy; the Soviet-American rivalry was embodied in the arms race and the balance of terror.

For the future, it seems, much has disappeared—the ideological competition, the global rivalry, the arms race. The human-rights concerns will remain. But the basis now exists for a much more constructive relationship between the United States and a Russia that, as some Russians put it, has become a more "normal" state. National-security concerns are not engaged in the way they were during the Cold War. Nevertheless, Russia's perceived "double humiliation" at the hands of America—being given too little assistance and being treated as a junior partner—played a significant role in strengthening the anti-Yeltsin forces in the December 1993 elections.

In relations with the United States, the major issues will revolve around economic aid, investment, technical assistance, and nuclear weapons. The United States will continue to engage Moscow on the question of Russia's nuclear forces and implementation of the START treaties, and also on broader questions of nuclear and conventional-weapon proliferation as well as the theft and illegal sale of nuclear materials. Russia will not give up its nuclear arsenal, though Gorbachev once explicitly envisaged that, but it will certainly seek to become the only nuclear state in the former Soviet space.

The other issue on which Russia and the United States will be engaged is regional disputes in Central and Eastern Europe and the Balkans—and in the former Soviet Union. Russia will insist that it has the central role and responsibility in handling all issues related to Ukraine and the other successor states. Indeed, publicly at least, it will, over time, become more critical of Western—and in particular U.S.—involvement in the crucial issues involving the Near Abroad. Attacks on "American meddling in matters of Russian security and national interest" will emanate from Russia, and will not by any means be limited to extreme nationalists hostile to the West. In the Russian Bear, these would be central to the rationale of the regime. They would also be strong in Two-Headed Eagle. As these key issues emerge, crisis management could again become an important part of the overall U.S.-Russian relationship. If Russia recovers economically and politically, then it is likely to be a competitor and rival with the United States, although this rivalry will be of a great power, rather than an ideological, nature.

GERMANY AND RUSSIA: RIVALS OR PARTNERS?

Russia's issues with Western Europe will be similar to those with the United States, except for the nuclear issue, in which America will take the lead. In addition to providing economic assistance, the Europeans will be heavily involved in environmental issues, since they are more directly affected by them than is the United States. Such issues include the management and fate of nuclear reactors throughout the former Soviet Union.

At the center of Russia's relationship with Europe is Germany, which will continue to be Russia's major Western partner both economically and in terms of political contacts. Russia's relation to Germany has always been complex and tangled. On the one hand, there is a long tradition of enmity. "As Voltaire said of God," declared the nineteenth-century Russian anarchist Mikhail Bakunin, "if there were no Germans we would have to invent them, as nothing so unites the Slavs as a rooted hatred of the Germans." On the other hand, the Russians have long admired Germany's technical and scientific prowess. As the Russian proverb puts it, "If there is a machine, there must be a German nearby." Both Peter the Great and Catherine the Great brought Germans to Russia, to settle in what became known as the "German Quarter" in many towns and to till the soil. Germans from the Baltic states came to play a leading role in Russian life. By the late nineteenth century, at a time when Germans formed just one percent of the population in the Russian empire, a third of high government officials were of German origin. Fifty-seven percent of officials in the Ministry of Foreign Affairs were Germans, mostly from the Baltic states. (Count Vladimir Lambsdorf, the Russian foreign minister who negotiated the 1893 Franco-Russian Entente treaty, was a relative of Count Otto Von Lambsdorff, West Germany's economics minister and head of its Free Democratic party in the 1980s.)[7]

For its part, Germany is the frontline state with arguably the greatest stake in the Russian transition. Germany and Russia will be the dominant powers in Europe for the first part of the next century. In the context of the European Community, a reunited Germany will be the foremost economic power in Europe, although it is currently debating its new political identity and is less comfortable exercising an overt political or military role in Europe. However, by the beginning of the next century, this debate over national identity will probably have crystallized more clearly than today.

Germany and Russia have historically been both rivals and partners in Europe. They have fought on opposite sides in two world wars, but also have concluded alliances against other European powers in the nineteenth and twentieth centuries. Germany helped modernize and train the Red Army in the 1920s and early 1930s. Patterns of rivalry and cooperation may well reassert themselves once Russia regains its ability to project influence abroad, but they will not have a detrimental effect on the rest of Europe if neither nation aspires to be an imperial power.

Between Russia and Germany lie the newly born Central and East European countries, including Ukraine, all of which have historically been dominated by either Germany or Russia and remain wary of both nations. Germany, already the predominant economic power in this area, will continue to expand its influence in Central and Eastern Europe. It has long historical ties there and is the only West European country with a major stake in the region. It is particularly concerned about stability in these transitional countries because it fears waves of refugees clamoring at its gates if things go wrong.

Russia currently has modest ties with the former "satellites" of Central and Eastern Europe, and these countries are busily trying to build up their economic connections with the West. Moreover, they will continue to be suspicious of Russia for a long time to come, as is inevitable after four decades of Soviet domination. Since all of the ex-Communist states are competitors for limited Western aid, there will also be constraints on their cooperation with each other as each seeks to maximize the benefits from economic ties with the European Community and the United States. Any Russian involvement in conflicts in the Near Abroad will alarm them.

Yet the former satellites are located just on the other side of the Near Abroad, and their relations with Russia, particularly those of Poland, could well revive in the years ahead, especially with the reconstruction of economic links.

Now that Soviet troops have completely withdrawn from German territory, the Federal Republic might decide that Russia is too unstable politically and economically to warrant continued partnership. It might focus on Ukraine and the states west of it to build a cordon sanitaire against an unpredictable Russia. But history and current realities suggest otherwise. Russia is too significant, too attractive economically for investment and as a market, and too important as an energy supplier. And a Russia caught up in a Time of Troubles has too much potential to destabilize Europe; it will not be left to its own devices.

Moreover, there are two million ethnic Germans in Russia and Kazakhstan, the descendants of the German farmers whom Catherine the Great imported in the eighteenth century. They have been cut off from modern Germany; some still speak an archaic eighteenth-century dialect. While some emigrated to Germany before the collapse of the Soviet Union, most remained, but would like to emigrate. Germany, however, is not interested in absorbing any more refugees and is instead helping to reconstruct the cities where the ethnic Germans now live, in order to get them to stay in Russia.

Thus, it is more likely that, once Germany has completed the political and economic process of unification, it will emerge playing a major role in restructuring a European security system, which will include a major role for Russia. If Russia is not included as a player in European regional politics, its capacity to disrupt would be considerable. But a new system will only be effective if the countries between Germany and Russia are also given a role that emancipates them from centuries-old domination by the two European giants. If the United States were to withdraw from Europe, it would be very difficult to accomplish this because an American presence can balance the two European powers and reassure the smaller European states.

THE ASIAN ARENA

Russia's foreign-policy interests in Asia will play out within a triangle involving three strong players—China, Japan, and Russia. A possible fourth, a reunified Korea, could turn it into a rectangle. In addition, the United States remains a major player in the region.

Of all relations with the industrial countries, those with Japan start from the lowest base; but, though hardly recognized today, they could proceed very far. There is a long legacy of mutual suspicion and animosity, going back to the competition for influence in Korea that ignited the Russo-Japanese War in 1904; the Japanese occupation of Siberia after World War I (ended by a silk embargo); and the Second World War. Stalin, intent on territorial aggrandizement, only declared war on Japan after the first atomic bomb was dropped; and the Japanese remain bitter about how the Soviets sent at least 600,000 captured Japanese troops to be slave laborers in Siberia and the Russian Far East. Many did not survive. The seemingly intractable issue of the "Northern Territories"—the southern Kurile Islands, taken by the Soviet Union after World War II—is central to and emblematic of this animosity. With a population of 30,000, these tiny islands would seem of small strategic significance and certainly subject to compromise when put against the vast potential of the relationship between the two countries—and even more so when measured against the territory that Moscow has already let slip from its grasp. Nevertheless, neither side to date has shown any great inclination to bridge the issue. Moreover, the Japanese are highly skeptical of Russian economic prospects and wary of Russia's overall political prospects and international objectives. Russia, for its part, is particularly resentful of the Japanese stance. Among all Western nations, Japan's relations with Russia have been the worst since the breakup of the Soviet Union, and each is convinced that the other is seriously slighting it. The Japanese believe that the Russians do not take them as seriously nor treat them with the respect that they accord Europeans.

This view has not only historic but also recent roots. Until the 1980s, the Soviet Union did underestimate Japan. "The Soviets judged the world by military power," observed a senior Japanese official, "and when they looked at the map of military power, Japan was very small. But in the 1980s, when they drew a world map in terms of GNP, they found a very large country right next to them."

Gorbachev, in particular, came to see the new calculus of power and Japan's significance in it. He also recognized the powerful irony of Japan's becoming an economic superpower—despite its lack of resources and territory—while Russia's military spending was driving its economy towards collapse. Once, when asked who had won the Cold War, he had a quick answer.

"Japan," he said.

But there was little of substance that he could do. For his foreign policy focus was on America and Europe. Yeltsin, too, seems to recognize the significance of Japan. But, so far at leat, he has been inevitably preoccupied with the domestic situation and the Near Abroad. Moreover, the outcome of the December 1993, elections and the reassertion of Russian nationalism has, at least temporarily, reduced his flexibility on the most immediate issue, the Northern Territories.

Yet historical animosities could be overcome, and a powerful logic could bring Russia and Japan closer together. The Kurile Islands are much too small to stand indefinitely in the way of relations between the two countries. Some formula, which attributes the islands' capture to Stalinist aggression, could eventually permit their transfer to Japan. It would be buttressed with an economic package that would satisfy both Moscow and the Russian Far East. At the same time, joint U.S.-Japanese cooperation (a "G-2" instead of "G-7" approach) could strengthen Japanese confidence in going ahead. Indeed, the United States could be useful as a stabilizing force, helpful to both Russia and Japan in putting their relations on a more constructive footing. What draws Russia and Japan together is their evident complementarity: Japan has capital, technology, and an awesome need both for markets and for natural resources, particularly natural gas. Russia has the resources and a vast, underpopulated region in Siberia and the Russian Far East that requires investment and infrastructure and that, because of its underdevelopment, Russia is coming to regard as "strategically vulnerable." Economic connections could grow to a very large scale, and would be state-sponsored on both sides. This would be a feature of the Long Good-bye, but even more prominently, of *Chudo.*

They could be brought together by something else as well: China. The Chinese economy is developing much faster than the Russian. This explosive growth and the political uncertainties regarding China's development could create anxiety for both Russia and Japan. So does the size of the Chinese military, especially as China wrestles with its own political transition. After all, there are only eight million people living in the vast expanse of the Russian Far East, most of them in a thin string along the border with China, while there are 100 million Chinese in the region just south of that border, and they are already beginning to spill across. Japan, too, could become increasingly uncertain about the immense Chinese colossus bounding ahead economically: What would that mean for Japan's own position in Asia? Under such circumstances, Japan might seek much stronger relations with Russia in order, among other things, to ensure that it is not precluded from economic participation in Russia's Far East.

China and Russia had intermittently hostile relations in the nineteenth century, as Russia joined other nations in carving up China. In the 1920s, Stalin's foreign policy nearly destroyed the Chinese Communist movement, before helping it to victory in the 1940s. This mixed heritage helps to explain the unsteadiness of Sino-Soviet relations, which passed from ostentatious friendship in the early 1950s to coldness and tension within a decade. The most acute phase of Sino-Soviet hostility began in 1960. Gorbachev did much to improve Sino-Soviet ties by essentially meeting Chinese demands for normalization

261

and making major concessions on contentious bilateral and regional issues. But Beijing was highly critical of his political reforms. His May 1989 visit to China, where he was hailed by the Tienanmen students as a hero, came days before the crackdown and symbolized for the aging Chinese leadership the perils of political reform that threatened their tenure. China was dismayed by the fall of communism in the USSR, although also somewhat relieved by the breakup of the Soviet Union, which, in their minds, lessened the danger of aggression from the north. Today, Chinese leaders seek to keep the Russian political "model" at bay. Meanwhile, however, economic relations between the "new" Russia and the "new" China are developing rapidly. China's economic dynamism and its rapidly growing market could be one of the most important stimulants for Russia's economic recovery, as we indicated in the *Chudo* scenario.

THE MIDDLE EAST: "SERIOUS INTERESTS"

In general, Russia will retreat from global involvement with the third world. For the most part, there is no obvious gain, and the costs are high. The one obvious exception is the Middle East, where the USSR was deeply involved for decades. As one official put it, "We have to have serious interests there." Russia is concerned about the impact of political Islam on its own Islamic population. Conflicts between Christians and Muslims have now spread to Russia's environs—the Caucasus and former Yugoslavia—thus exacerbating these fears. Russia retains links with its traditional clients although these relations are not as active as they once were. Moreover, the Middle East is an important source of hard-currency earnings, through weapons sales; and, as the same official added, "it is where oil prices are set." Russia has recently signaled a renewed assertiveness in the Middle East, an area in which it had been relatively inactive since the breakup of the Soviet Union.

The region takes on new urgency with the "expansion" of the Middle East to include former republics of the Soviet Union—Islamic Azerbaijan and Central Asia. Instability in the expanded region is virtually inevitable, and Russia is already being drawn in by concerns about its own security. Iran's active campaign to expand its influence throughout the Islamic parts of the former Soviet Union, combined with the endemic instability in the region, increases the likelihood of some kind of Russian-Iranian collision, as suggested in our surprises. Iran's activism is the number-one focus of attention, although Moscow is also concerned about Turkey's influence in both the Caucasus and Central Asia. Moreover, Russia is worried that it will pay the price for Soviet intervention in Afghanistan, as mujahedeen based in Afghanistan, equipped with weapons that were spread far and wide during the Afghan war, try to carry that war into Central Asia.[8]

THE WEST AT ODDS?

As long as Russia's leadership remains committed to reform, the West will remain active in trying to stabilize the situation and support Russia. There may be disagreements over how much aid to give and how stringent the conditions should be, but the G-7 countries will be in agreement on the basic principles involved.

However, if the Two-Headed Eagle, the Long Good-bye, or the Russian Bear develops, then the West itself might be seriously divided over what to do. From the U.S. perspective, the major issue is the continuing nuclear threat emanating from the region. Otherwise, the U.S. is less interested than Western Europe because it is geographically distant and not directly affected by streams of refugees, major environmental disasters, and economic developments. Thus, if more conservative forces came to power, or if the country itself broke apart, the United States might step back and leave the Russians to work out their own problems. This might also happen if Russia is drawn militarily into a conflict involving a Central Asian successor state and another power—for instance, Iran.

The Europeans would not have the luxury of doing this. After all, their interests are more immediate and greater. If the region of the newly independent states is unstable or violent, the potential for refugees flooding the European Community and for further environmental catastrophes will grow and will threaten the stability of an enlarged European Community (including Poland, Hungary, and the Czech Republic). Of all the European countries, Germany has the most at stake and the biggest responsibilities. Whatever happens in this area, Germany and other European countries would remain involved because they would be the most directly affected. They could not cut off all aid and withdraw into isolation, because no one in Europe can be isolated from anyone else anymore, unless the Berlin Wall is rebuilt. However distasteful the government in Moscow may be, relations would have to be maintained.

Nevertheless, NATO's adoption of the Partnership for Peace program in January 1994 points toward the alliance's offering closer ties and possibly eventual membership to the former communist countries. Russia has joined the partnership, but is unlikely to be offered full NATO membership. Central European countries have joined in the hope of obtaining full membership. NATO will attempt to put off resolving these questions for some time, but a Russia that moves away from reform might well tip the balance in favor of a new division of Europe whose boundary might be the Polish-Ukrainian border.

If some of the scenarios, such as the Russian Bear, come to pass, they might lead to a serious rift between America and its allies. There will be no new Cold War, because there would be no new enemy to bind America and Europe together, and no new global threat. But the United States might well use the deteriorating situation in Russia, and between Russia and its neighbors—and its own difficulties with its allies—as the rationale to withdraw from Europe, leaving the Europeans to cope with their own problems. Twentieth-century precedents do not make one hopeful that Europe could deal with these overwhelming difficulties without American involvement. In particular, a Germany and United States seriously at odds over policy toward Russia would be, over time, a major threat to global stability. Coordination and cooperation among the major Western countries are a prerequisite for helping Russia succeed in its triple transition into the twenty-first century.

17

Who Pays for the Plowshares? Foreign Investors and the New Capitalists

"If I were a young man and had a hundred thousand dollars to my name and no more, I'd invest it in Russia and try to run it into ten million. And if I had started with ten million, I'd still invest only a hundred thousand, and try to run it into another ten million!"

—*Robert Strauss, last U.S. ambassador to the Soviet Union and first U.S. ambassador to Russia*

They stopped Napoleon. They stopped Hitler. And now Russia's decrepit roads could also stop capitalism dead in its tracks. So warned a recent report from the Supreme Soviet about the urgent need to expand and improve the Russian road system. Russia has only one fiftieth as much road, per capita, as Western Europe. Only 24,000 miles of Russia's roads—less than 10 percent of the total—are highways. Traffic is growing rapidly, as Russians switch from rail to road. But not only is the network not being expanded, no one is currently paying even to repair the deteriorating roads and bridges now in place.[1]

Those roads, unrepaired and overworked, are themselves enough of an obstacle to economic progress. But they are also a symbol of an entire economy that needs a massive amount of investment if it is not to come to a stop on the transition to capitalism. Some of that money will come from foreigners. A lot more of it will have to come from Russians themselves, including the new capitalists. How it comes, and whether it comes in a timely fashion, will be the economic drama in the years ahead.

PROVIDING FOR THE SEED CORN

Certainly no one ever said that beating swords into plowshares comes cheap. The new Russian revolution, if it is to succeed, will require money, lots of money. The needs are many: Russia must modernize much of its industry, rebuild an infrastructure so that it is suited to the needs of a consumer-oriented economy, convert its defense industries into something else, and clean up the severe environmental problems left by communism. It must invest in the "engines" of growth and export income: energy, manufacturing, chemistry, electronics, telecommunications, and the like. Yet, at the same time, it also needs to put money into the more humble things, such as roads and ports.

But the simple fact is that, two years after the collapse of the Soviet Union, Russia is not investing anywhere near the level necessary, and will have great trouble doing so. The levels of investment are far below what they were under the Soviet system. In one year alone, from 1991 to 1992, investment in Russia dropped by half. In some key parts of the economy, such as the manufacture of machinery, the slide was closer to two thirds.[2] To be sure, the consequences of the decline are not as severe as the magnitudes might suggest, because some of the reduction means that investment is not wastefully going into the "dinosaurs," enterprises and activities whose time has past. Still, the drop is very significant; and without investment, production cannot be stabilized or restored because Russian factories, mines, oil fields, railway cars, and tractors are all wearing out. By failing to invest, Russia is failing to provide for its own seed corn.

The money can come from outside Russia, of course. But to what degree can foreign investment, if applied to the right parts of the Russian economy, help "prime the pump" and supply the missing catalysts that will help Russian growth to accelerate? Can foreign investors, for their part, find the opportunities and returns and business climate sufficient to absorb the risks, frustrations, and dangers of doing business in the midst of the Russian revolution? And there is a third major question about foreign investment: Do the Russians really want it?

The prospects for gearing up the investment internally are not good. As the economy declines and the standard of living goes down, tremendous political and social pressure mounts on the federal and local governments to devote what little wealth is produced to current needs—above all food. Factory managers, who have been responsible for up to two thirds of the nation's total investment in past years, are forced to raise wages and benefits to maintain peace with their workers. In addition, their profits are being taxed away. All this leaves little money to put into new production lines.

But what of private capital? It is something that would not have been thought of five years ago. Today, however, fortunes are being made in Russia, and the new private sector is developing rapidly. So far, little of this new money is finding its way into factories, machine tools, and the rest. One can borrow money in Russia. But, with high inflation a fact of life, no one will lend money for longer than a year; half of all loans are for three months or less. One does not use that kind of money to make an investment in equipment with a five-year payout or a twenty-year life. Instead of going into hard assets, money flees inflation by going into arbitrage, speculation, foreign currency, conspicuous consumption, or Swiss bank accounts.

Russians do own large amounts of dollars—tens of billions of them. Although no one really knows for sure, it is estimated that Russian "entities" other than the government may hold as much as $30 billion to $40 billion outside the country.[3] Some estimates are much higher. Inside the country, the dollar has become the second currency, with many billions of dollars in circulation. On a Sunday morning, at the Izmailovo open-air flea market on the outskirts of Moscow, the common currency is dollars, whether the transaction concerns paintings, antiques, *matryoshka* dolls, or T-shirts with Lenin's face superimposed over McDonald's golden arches. Some of the dollars in circulation are being put into construction, mostly of luxury or "middle-class" housing, which is beginning to boom on the outskirts of Moscow. But, for the most part, Russia's hard-currency capital is not being invested in long-term projects any more than foreign capital is.

Investment credits from foreign governments and aid from international agencies like the World Bank and the European Bank for Reconstruction and Development can help to fill the gap, but only up to a limited point. In the long run, only private investment can supply the necessary sums to make a real difference.

Prospects for investment are very scenario dependent. Under Muddling Down, Russia continues to face a crisis of investment. It cannot mobilize domestic sources, and the uncertainty and insecurity, as well as the lack of legal and financial foundations, impede foreign investment. In the Russian Bear, domestically generated investment is constrained. What investment there is overemphasizes heavy industry and military goods, thus retarding the economy's development. There is little role for foreign investment. Two-Headed Eagle does represent an effort to rebuild and modernize the economy, but domestic investment is bureaucratically directed. Owing to its politics, Two-Headed Eagle has to devote a disproportionate share of its resources to propping up the inheritance from the Soviet past. Foreign investment has a limited role, but a good deal of that money goes into resource development.

The Long Good-bye and *Chudo* are both more market-oriented in investment, as in other features. Long Good-bye witnesses large-scale investment by Japan and others in the Russian Far East for resource development, as well as ports and transportation. Russia's northwest becomes a focus for Scandinavian and German investment. Local and regional authorities encourage foreign investment as a way to tap into the global economy and, even more important, to maintain employment.

Chudo represents the sharpest break with the past and the most rapid development of the Russian economy. Domestically generated capital goes right back into investment that meets the huge pent-up demands of Russian society. Overseas capital returns home, seeking opportunities. Significant foreign investment takes place, not only in resources, but also in manufacturing and services, oriented to both Russian and global markets. Much of this investment is in partnership with Russians, thus contributing to the broader development of the Russian economy.

The differences among the scenarios are not only in economic organization, but also, of course, in their attitudes toward the outside world. The Russian Bear and Two-Headed Eagle are nationalistic, the first virulently so. Both have a deep sense of grievance; the Russian Bear is overtly hostile to the outside world, while the Two-Headed Eagle is potentially antagonistic.

Chudo, however, represents a Russia that is becoming integrated into the global economy. That means that, in contrast to Russian Bear and Two-Headed Eagle, it has another resource it can tap into, if the ideologies and anti-Semitism of the extremists can be held at bay. This is the "overseas Russian" population, particularly those who have been among the Jewish or part-Jewish émigrés who have left Russia since the early 1970s. They have acquired the skills of a capitalist economy. They also have the Russian language, attachment to Russian culture, and intuitive understanding of the economic system out of which Russia is emerging, as well as the personal links back to Russian enterprises and research institutes. They could play a role somewhat analogous to that played by the "overseas Chinese," who have brought skills, market links, and capital to mainland China and have been a strategic factor in China's current economic miracle. This may seem unlikely now, even far-fetched, but could become significant under *Chudo,* helping to close the gap between the Soviet past and the Russian future more speedily.

One way or another, unless investment recovers soon, Russia's position as an industrialized nation is at risk, and it will find its transition even more perilous and difficult than appears to be the case today.

Our scenarios suggest that Russia may face significant political costs in mobilizing capital. What does this mean? If Russian growth is sluggish, then the only way to step up investment from internal sources is to cut back on what goes into consumption. That would mean, for instance, cutting spending on health and education and reducing subsidies for food. But such action would require extensive government intervention, which could be highly unpopular. The only way to escape from this unpleasant prospect is by achieving rapid growth. But that requires substantial investment to get growth started in the first place. This is where foreign investment comes in.

THE RETURN OF FOREIGN INVESTMENT

Enormous attention has been given to possible foreign investment opportunities in Russia ever since Gorbachev first authorized it in 1987. Yet the fact is that foreign capital has not yet flowed. Total Western investment in Russia is around $2 billion.[4] Whatever the future of Russia, foreign investment will hardly be a factor, unless the obstacles to it can be surmounted. Indeed, at this particular moment, there is far more capital flowing out of Russia than moving in.

Of course, it is important to remember that as recently as 1987 there was no foreign investment in Russia at all, and there had not been any for half a century. The last time foreign investors were welcomed to Russia was during the 1920s when Lenin, presiding over a nation ruined by civil war, launched the New Economic Policy, a tactical

269

retreat from socialism. Armand Hammer (described by Lenin as "a little path to the American 'business' world" that "we should use . . . in every possible way") made money investing in a pencil factory, the proceeds from which he turned into Russian art. Averell Harriman, the son of an American railway magnate and later U.S. ambassador to Moscow, invested in a manganese concession in the Soviet Union and lost money, but chalked it up to experience.[5] When Stalin consolidated his power and launched the First Five-Year Plan at the end of the 1920s, the window for foreign investment closed.

In the seven-decade-long experiment in totalitarianism that was imposed on them, the Russians built a world that was in many ways as remote as the other side of the moon. For all but a handful of Russians, there was no contact with foreign businessmen, no experience of foreign business, and above all, no knowledge of the world of money, investment, taxation, and risk.

In light of this heritage, the Russians have covered a lot of ground very quickly. Starting from nothing, the beginnings have been laid for a legislative framework and a fiscal system. Tens of thousands of Russians and Westerners are debating investment issues every day. Russians can now read publications with names like *Kommersant* ("Businessman") and *Finansovye Izvestiia* ("Financial News"). The ruble can be converted into dollars.* And anyone who has been in Moscow and St. Petersburg in the last three years knows that it is now possible to do business in Western-style circumstances, to open a Russian office, to travel reasonably freely around the country, and to phone and fax back to Western Europe, Japan, and the United States—although there is still apt to be some extra "company" listening in on the line.

Japanese Business: Careful and Cautious

Japanese businessmen are among the most cautious when it comes to Russia. The Northern Territories, though small in population and size, stand as formidable political barriers. But the economic obstacles are considerable as well. Japanese companies were among the most active of all foreign business in the Soviet Union in the 1970s and 1980s, and they generally ended up with losses and credits that remain unpaid to the present day. Major Japanese companies are, for the most part, ex-

---

* Although at a rate that appalls the Russians. Until the collapse of the USSR, the official exchange rate was $1.50 for a single ruble. The exchange rate is now around 3,000 rubles per dollar.

tremely careful because of the political instability, the economic uncertainty, and the rapid rise of crime. "Skeptical" is the word often encountered. Smaller trading companies with left-wing connections that specialized in the Soviet Union have lost their constituencies within Russia, have been hit hard by the trade debts, and in some cases have simply gone out of business.

Total trade turnover between Japan and Russia today is about $4 billion. The Russians are exporting raw materials and importing manufactured and consumer goods. There is a brisk business in shipping used cars from Hokkaido and Nigata to Vladivostok, where these second-hand Japanese cars are shipped to the rest of the former Soviet Union; but the size of this trade is unclear since the cars fall under the customs classifications of "scrap"! About 150 Japanese-Russian joint ventures are in operation in the Russian Far East. Most are small. A few large projects are in various stages of development, of which the Sakhalin gas projects, in collaboration with American companies, are the most prominent. (Western companies have been interested in developing Sakhalin's resources at least since the early 1920s). Because of the perceived risk and the tensions in relations, there is a desire to do some of the big projects in collaboration with U.S. firms and American government support.

Although there are wide discrepencies in estimates of total foreign investment, Japanese direct investment in Russia appears to be about $100 million, compared to $400 million for the United States.

The Japanese government is providing various forms of aid and credits to Russia as part of the general approach of the G-7 countries, including a $700 million credit to Gazprom. But an overall umbrella of official Japanese-Russian cooperation, which would facilitate trade and investment, may be contingent on one of two developments: either a resolution of the Northern Territories issue, or, conversely, a fear that grips the entire G-7 that Russia is spiraling down into a deep economic crash that will have dangerous global repercussions.

For Russians in the Far East, Japan is a natural trading partner, bringing capital, technology, and markets. "Like everyone in the world, we admire Japanese technology and business acumen," a professor of management in the Far East recently observed. But the Russians are far from developing an economic strategy for the region, nor do they have the kind of cooperation among their various authorities that would facilitate trade. The formerly closed cities of Vladivostok and Khaborovsk are now open—and that means open to Asia. But the

Russians themselves are unsure as to how to proceed. One Russian businessman caught the edge when he said, "We're trying to learn to dance with the Asian tiger without getting swallowed up by it."[6]

LAYING THE FOUNDATIONS

Yet, by any commercial standards, the obstacles to investing in Russia are among the highest in the world. The most basic things are very difficult, or even impossible—such as establishing who owns a property or business that a Western business might be interested in acquiring, or figuring out who actually has the right to sign a contract or issue a license. Russia has substantial technical know-how, heretofore bottled up in research institutes, that could be commercialized globally, but it is not at all clear who actually controls the rights to this information. Foreign investors are barred outright from owning certain kinds of property, such as oil resources in the ground. Technical and financial data provided by the Russians are frequently unreliable. Concluding a deal requires lengthy high-level negotiations.

"It's turned into a quest," is the way one American businessman described the two and a half years he's spent trying to put together a joint venture with Russians. "It's like trying to do business with a federal agency that doesn't have any rules or procedures or any compelling reasons to come to a conclusion. They really don't understand how important crossing key milestones is. On our part, it has taken us a long time to appreciate the significance of the internal structures on the Russian side. What we've learned is that for the Russian partners, taking care of all their internal people, getting all the approvals and consulting all the people that need to be consulted, is the most important thing. The reason is that, up to now, everything they get—their food, their apartments, their cars, their careers—all of it is related to these government bureaucracies. To depend, instead, on a Western businessman who flies in once a month with dollars is much too risky.

"It's also very difficult to find out who has authority to do things. Your Western lawyer tells you that you have to have a clear path of ownership. But there's no way that's going to happen. All that you can deliver is who has clear authority to use it. It's not a question of who owns an asset, but who controls it."

In the West, it is assumed that a contract, once signed, is a contract and thus enforceable. This concept of "sanctity of contract" appears exotic to many Russians, as does the notion of "conflict of interest."

Taxes are high; worse, they are apt to be changed at a moment's notice. For instance, the economics of oil projects in Siberia were abruptly changed, and much for the worse, when the government slapped on a five-dollar-a-barrel export tax, which was applied retroactively to projects already up and running. The Russian banking system is chaotic, although the best banks are improving rapidly. There are now thousands of quasi-private banks, unregulated and overextended, that survive on their wits rather than on their assets.

When laws or regulations change, there is no central source to which the investor can refer to find out what is happening. Bills frequently go unpaid. Corruption is a plague. In the event of a dispute, there is no reliable path for legal redress. Russian politics are unstable, which means that a permanent cloud of uncertainty hangs over every deal. And the mafia threatens the entire economy. It does not discriminate: kiosk operators, Russian bankers, and Western businessmen have all been summarily murdered for failing to respond to mafia demands, or simply for getting in the way. The rise of criminality runs as a growing concern through all Russian-Western business relations.

One type of obstacle that should fade in the future is simply due to mutual unfamiliarity. For years, Soviet media and propaganda dished out a steady diet of vindictiveness and caricature—portraying the predatory foreign capitalist as the cartoon character in top hat and tails. Russians have been quick to perceive the irrelevance of this picture. Many Russians have already become conversant with international business practices, learning to choose the right foreign partner and to recognize a good or bad deal when they see one. They are also learning the Western business "language" of tax, project finance, risk assessment, and law. Meanwhile, foreign businessmen are adapting to the Russian market and are coming to understand the unsettled circumstances in which Russian managers have to work.

Mutual understanding, however, will not be enough. Foreign investment on a large scale will not proceed until the foundation is in place; and the basis for such investment—clear property rights, stable tax laws, and the like—is still missing. The authorities will have to deliver physical security.

Getting this foundation in place is very difficult because it is at the center of a high-stakes political battle on the Russian side. Take, for instance, property rights. They need to be clarified so that Western investment can go ahead. But that puts the foreign investor right in the middle of the struggle for authority and control between the federal government and the regions, between state enterprises and would-be private firms, and between Russians and other ethnic groups. Taxes and export quotas are equally contentious. Who levies the tax? Who gets the money? Who gets to change the taxes whenever they want? Such fiscal questions pit the regions against the federal government. Getting these types of matters resolved will involve protracted struggle.

Nevertheless, in a few years, these issues are likely to have been settled by the Russians with compromises that allow laws and regulations to be written. It will take longer before foreign investors are confident that they have access to the protection of courts, full and current information about government policies, and stable tax regimes. But the chaos of recent years will have given way to a more predictable business environment, which will be required in order for businessmen to commit large sums of money.

"NOT A DEAL IN THE DECK!"

But that does not mean that the doors of Russia will then be open to a flood of investment from the outside. For there is a more fundamental point: It is far from clear that Russians want foreign investment on a large scale. Indeed Russians' ambivalence on this fundamental point, and their consequent reluctance to make commitments, have also held back foreign investment.

The Russian feeling is understandable. Try as they may, it is difficult for foreign businessmen not to appear to Russian eyes as carpetbaggers descending on a defeated country. The very presence of even the most tactful foreign investor is a reminder to Russians of shortcomings in their current situation. Moreover, in the great majority of cases, foreign investors have come, seen—and left without making a deal. And so, despite its own ambivalence, the Russian side feels spurned.

Igor Pugachev, a former defense-industry executive who now heads a conglomerate that produces oil-field equipment, complained in a recent discussion about the many fruitless meetings he has had with delegations from Western companies. To make his point, he pulled out of his desk a six-inch stack of Western business cards. "Look at that," he said, shuffling them with a practiced hand. "Not a deal in the deck! What a waste of time!"

One can also hear Russians complain, no less than Westerners, that negotiations drag on forever and that the other side is unpredictable;

Russians add that foreigners take advantage of their unfamiliarity with foreign ways. Westerners will often remark on their difficulty in coping with the lunch that includes multiple toasts of vodka. But the single worst ordeal, from the viewpoint of at least some Russians, is the custom of the Western cocktail party. "They stand you up, ply you with liquor, and give you nothing to eat," said one Russian businessman. "At least we Russians eat when we drink; that way we don't get so drunk."

CONFLICTING GOALS

The ambivalence about foreign investment has deeper roots, reflecting the fact that there are conflicting goals on each side of the table. From the moment they opened the door to the first joint ventures, the Russians' policy on foreign investment has been aimed at escaping from exclusive dependence on raw materials, opening up foreign markets to their manufacture, getting technology and capital—and keeping operational control.

In many cases, the Western companies want just the opposite. They want to invest primarily in raw materials for export, gain access to the Russian domestic market, and limit technology transfer so as to avoid creating future competitors. They seek to minimize direct outlays of capital and to contribute management skills, where possible, rather than capital or technology. They also want operational control.

Control is the central issue. Russians welcome Westerners as lenders, as portfolio investors, as minority partners. But a controlling share of equity? That is another matter. As a Russian official put it, "What would you think if planeloads of Russians arrived in the U.S., all saying, 'Hi! I want to own you!'?"

These are common issues in foreign investment in third-world or newly industrializing countries. But the Russians do not consider themselves to belong to either category. Indeed, they have greeted the foreign failure to invest with pained surprise, and there is enough residual suspicion left over from the Cold War for many Russians to wonder whether there isn't a conspiracy to hold Russia back, to keep it in the position of a raw-materials supplier. A recent statement on foreign policy, signed by Yeltsin in the spring of 1993, identified one of the threats to Russian national security as anything that "weakens the basis for the economic autonomy of Russia, or pushes it further into the role of supplier of fuels and raw materials to the world economy, or contributes to degrading the industrial and technological capacity, squeezing it out of foreign markets, or denying it state-of-the-art technologies."[7]

Of course, these attitudes are not held by all Russians to the same degree. The ambivalence that the Westerner encounters depends on whether one is dealing with a government official or a private entrepreneur, and on which part of the economy is involved. In some fields, such as chemicals, Russian officials have relied on foreign technology for so long that they take it for granted. In the defense sector, foreign investment is new and is frequently regarded with suspicion whose roots go right back to the Cold War. The exception is the aircraft industry, where Russian manufacturers have greeted foreign partners with enthusiasm and are already dreaming of the international market for their Tupolev 204s and Ilyushin 96m's.

TELECOMMUNICATIONS

In telecommunications, the private sector is racing ahead in partnership with Western firms, while government agencies are trying to play catch-up with technologies that have already bypassed them. This is a perfect example of how foreign investment can help speed Russian economic recovery and, indeed, of how the transition is working in practice. In its current state, telecommunications, like roads, constitute one of the biggest single barriers to economic development in Russia. Russia has about twelve phone lines per hundred people, compared to thirty-five for Spain and fifty-six for the United States. Some estimate that it will take $10 billion just to bring Moscow up to Western European standards. The cost for the entire country may be $60 billion.

Telecommunications are centrally regulated by the federal Ministry of Communications. All the cables, switching, and radio relay stations are owned by Intertelekom, a government corporation—soon to be privatized, though the Russian government will remain the controlling shareholder. So, in principle, telecommunications are a monopoly of the federal government.

But certainly not in practice. Russian cities and provinces are seeking to seize opportunities in the high-value end of the business. The Moscow City Telephone Network has created over ten joint ventures with foreign companies to provide specialized services to foreign and private business in Moscow. These range from international telephoning by satellite and data-transfer systems to cellular telephones. Even the Moscow subway has gotten into the act; working with Western partners, it is laying fiber-optic cables in its subway tunnels. Other cities and provinces are proceeding in the same way. The military space command is negotiating with Western partners to use military technology to set up international earth-satellite phone services in provincial cities. But Intertelekom, the government company, is not standing still either. Working with Danish partners, it has built an eight-hundred-mile underwater cable from Copenhagen to St. Petersburg and is now about to build a line from the Russian Far East to Japan and South Korea. It is also trying its hardest to deny any licenses it can to its new competitors.

RULES OF THE GAME: START WITH A TOE

Although it has only been two years since the Soviet Union disappeared, Western investors have gained enough experience for guidelines to emerge. Certainly, Russia is a big market and a big economy, and companies need to recognize that there is a big risk in not being part of it. On the other hand, companies should only go in for the long term; the risks and uncertainty are too great to count on short-term returns. This is one market where the cliché of "putting a toe in the water" makes great sense. Other rules have also emerged: Start small. Find Russian partners in whom one has confidence, and then let them take the lead in the Russian business environment. Be a good citizen of the community. (Some companies have found themselves flying in disposable syringes and other medical supplies to distant parts of the country.) Try, first, to go directly to the enterprise and establish the basis for a relationship there before going to the central government. Try to supply the joint venture with supplies paid for in rubles, and use rubles to expand when it comes time to expand the business. And don't expect anything to happen quickly.

THE PRIZE: OIL

Of all investment opportunities, oil is the glittering prize for foreigners. At the same time, if there is any sector that could have a catalytic effect on the economy, it is oil. But in no other sector does the prospect of foreign investment do more to arouse complicated emotions and resentments against Western participation. Oil, together with natural gas, generated about $19 billion in hard currency earnings in 1993. The significance for the economy is very large. That sum is twice the total governmental budget deficit (at the current inflationary exchange rates, to be sure). Expanding, or at least maintaining, those export earnings is critical for the capital-starved nation. And yet at the very time when it could contribute so significantly to the transition, the Russian oil industry is gripped by a very serious crisis that threatens to reduce, not augment, the export earnings—and thus the funds available for investment.

As recently as five years ago, the Soviet oil industry was the hermit of the oil world. Though it was the world's leading producer, at nearly 12.5 million barrels per day, it was also isolated and secretive, depending almost entirely on its own technology, much of which was twenty or even thirty years out of date. Oil reserves—how much was estimated to be in the ground—had been a state secret since Stalin's day. Westerners heard rumors that all was not well; notwithstanding, both output and exports had been on the rise.

In retrospect, 1988 was the turning point. That year, output reached its peak and then began to fall, and it has been dropping quickly ever since. Of the 12.5 million barrels a day produced by the Soviet Union in 1988, 11.5 were in Russia. Today, Russian production has fallen by 5 million barrels a day, to 6.5 million barrels a day. It is an enormous drop. To get it into perspective, the fall in output is greater than the total production of any OPEC country except Saudi Arabia! But also in 1988, the Soviet Union was beginning to open up again to Western investors for the first time in a half century. In short, 1988 marks the beginning of both the acute crisis and the new opportunity in what had been the world's largest oil industry.

The free fall in the Russian oil industry is the result of poor, outdated technology and oil-field practices, compounded by the collapse in investment and the disruptions that have come with the breakup of the Soviet Union. Stabilizing Russian oil production at its current level to the year 2000 would require upwards of $50 billion. Otherwise, output could fall from its current level to as low as 4 million barrels a day, which would be a disaster for Russia. To bring production back to the levels of the late 1980s would require another $50 billion to $70 billion. Oil and gas seem to be the single most important key to the reconstruction of the Russian economy.[8]

At the same time, Russia needs to be alert to the "curse of oil": the dangers of overdependence on this natural resource for modernizing the economy. Many countries have learned how excessive reliance can block and even set back more thoroughgoing modernization and reform and, directly or indirectly, damage other sectors of the economy. Mexico painfully learned that lesson in the late 1970s and early 1980s. So, ironically, did the Soviet Union in the last years of Brezhnev.

Almost all large and middle-sized Western oil companies, and some small ones, now seem to have a "Russia Team" that has crisscrossed the former Soviet Union. Every region and nearly every field and prospect seems to have been visited. The Western companies have purchased detailed geological data (unthinkable even four years ago), formed joint ventures and signed production-sharing agreements with Russian and other companies, and established offices in Moscow and other cities. Some thirty joint ventures are already producing and exporting oil, though on a small scale, and several others are exporting refined products, condensate, and waste oil, as well as smaller volumes of crude.

Western companies, applying their technology, have concluded that Russia's oil reserves are much larger than had generally been suspected, indeed on the scale of a large Middle East producer's—though nowhere near as cheap and easy to produce as Middle Eastern fields. They have also learned that many Russian oil people are highly capable and well-trained professionals, who can be effective partners for Western companies.

Yet Western companies have found it very hard to make headway on the oil front in Russia. They have spent a lot of money, on the order of two billion dollars, investigating the Russian oil potential and trying to negotiate deals. That is about as much as the total foreign capital presently invested in Russia. And this two billion dollars has been spent before the major companies have begun investing serious capital in actual projects. If they persevere, they can look ahead to several years during which more of their money will go down Russian wells than will come up.

Even so, Western activity in Russian oil fields has begun to gain speed. Much of it is aimed at the thirty thousand or so wells that are not working "for want of a nail"—or, to be more precise, a drill bit or pump. Many small service companies are carrying out "workover" deals under contract, refurbishing these wells for modest profit. Including both joint ventures and workovers, Western companies are adding perhaps 300,000 barrels per day to Russian production.

But few of the larger projects have gotten beyond the "protocol" stage, and fewer yet have progressed beyond the early stages of feasibility studies. Progress in other republics, principally Kazakhstan and Azerbaijan, has been only slightly more rapid. Taken together, Western projects are unlikely to be producing more than a million barrels per day by the year 2000 in the entire former Soviet Union, at least if present trends continue, and most of that will be outside Russia.

If progress has been slow, it has not been for lack of persistence, energy, and ingenuity. Western companies have tried every strategy imaginable: They have worked from the top down and from the bottom up; they have sought joint ventures or production-sharing contracts or some other form of collaboration. They have dealt with the geologists, courted the gas monopoly, Gazprom, worked the legislative committees, shuttled between Moscow and the provincial capitals, talked to the oil directors, tried to negotiate tax holidays. Or tried simply to rely on a handshake. None of these methods has worked very well. Penetrating the Russian oil market, it turns out, has been like trying to drive down an unknown road without a map in the midst of an earthquake.

Oil investment has been held back by the same general problems as other Western investment, including the critical questions of whom you deal with and who has the authority and will risk signing a deal. But the conflict over objectives and outlook is perhaps greater in the oil industry than in any other.

THE RUSSIAN "OIL GENERALS" VERSUS THE WESTERN OILMEN

Consider the case of the director general of a Russian oil company in western Siberia, where most of the oil and gas is produced. The "oil general," as he is called, owes his success to his toughness, his ability to "make do" without supplies, his network of friends in higher places. But what has counted above all is his ability to deliver the one thing that counted under the old system: making the annual oil production target, regardless of cost or obstacle. That is what the old system was all about—meeting the quota. The oil general is proud of his past achievements and humiliated by the present chaos. He may have traveled recently to Houston or Prudhoe Bay, but he has little experience of the outside world and little knowledge of the workings of the international oil industry or of the oil companies that are courting him.

During the first year or so following the collapse of the Soviet Union, the general floated in a legal and political void. He had no owner, no board, and no equity, and his position as general director gave him no rights. A Western partner was, in these circumstances, more of a complication than a savior: Making a deal with a foreign company brought unwelcome publicity, hordes of government auditors, heightened demands from local politicians, and suspicion that the Russian oil general was making an illegal fortune. Moreover, the larger the Western oil company, the more difficult it was to control.

It is hard for foreign and Russian oilmen even to understand how different their worlds are. The Russian oilman comes from a world of bureaucratic bargaining, in which the object of the game was not to maximize after-tax profits or market share, but to gain as low an output target as possible to make it easier to attain. Taxation was not an issue; profit was a paper item of interest only to planners; the law was something that minor academics worried about; and economic justifications were largely a matter of massaging the numbers to produce the right political result.

When Western oilmen first began appearing on the scene, their Russian colleagues looked at them with eyes trained by a lifetime of anti-Western propaganda about greed and exploitation. What Russian oilmen have only begun to fathom is that their Western counterparts live in a world that is vastly different from that of the "capitalists" of the Soviet imagination. Today's Western oilmen are specialists in the complex business of tax law, corporate finance, painstaking project analysis, and calculation of political risk—all concerns that are still quite new to their Russian colleagues. They are also quite different from the typical personality to be found in the Russian oil business.

The two cultures do share one common foundation: the discovery and production of oil. On a scientific and engineering basis, they understand one another; but in every other respect they start from different planets. Consequently, Russian oilmen have had great difficulty understanding the Westerners' seeming obsession with law, taxes, and economics, their apparent determination to cut every deal to the bone as though it were to be the last, and the strange internal constraints the Western companies invoke at every turn to justify doing things their way. Westerners, for their part, have been baffled by the Russians' seeming indifference to those same crucial issues, and suspicious of the Russian insistence that if the Western side would only take the plunge, trust and friendship would carry the partners through.

RUSSIAN "MAJORS" AND INDEPENDENTS?

But something new has now come into the picture. Russian oil generals have begun to realize that they could be the owners of the "producing associations" they previously held in trust for the state. They could turn these associations into large integrated oil companies—"majors," to use the vernacular of the industry—and eventually, they hope, compete with the established majors like Shell and Exxon in the international marketplace. They intend to go "downstream." In the process, they would make themselves into international capitalists.

Someone who had begun to see such possibilities even before the breakup of the Soviet Union was Vagit Alekperov, an Azerbaijani national, who rose through the Siberian oil industry to become, in 1990, deputy oil minister of the USSR. By then, he was already planning a company called LUK-Oil (the initials stand for three of the Siberian oil associations). Alekperov spent two years cementing alliances with refiners and developing an oil trading and distribution system, turning the original upstream production company into an integrated oil company. Today LUK-Oil is a public joint-stock company. It produces about one million barrels per day. On paper at least, this makes it potentially one of the largest private oil companies in the world in terms of production (although for the moment the Russian government retains a controlling block of shares). It could, within a matter of years, become a major force in the world oil industry. A half dozen other integrated companies have followed, with new ones continuing to appear. So far, they are all led by oil generals.

As their status has solidified, the generals have begun to deal more confidently with Western companies, but also with a growing sense that they, too, can be significant players. This has made them, if anything, even more reluctant to surrender control to outsiders. This attitude is particularly striking in the case of the western Siberians, who have not forgotten that until very recently they were the world's leading oil producers. Oil companies in other regions of Russia have been much more hospitable to Western investment.

Smaller players have also taken advantage of the Soviet crack-up to break away and seek their own fortunes. Geological organizations, former subsidiaries of oil-producing companies, and even private local entrepreneurs have formed companies of their own. These companies are much more interested in foreign investment. They are the "independents" of tomorrow, whose partnerships with Western investors may one day lead to a new generation of large private oil companies in Russia.

One such company is Sinco, led by Sergei Shafranik, the younger brother of the Russian minister of fuel and power. Shafranik started with five small fields in western Siberia that had been pronounced noneconomic by the local oil and gas association. Shafranik proved the association wrong. Sinco's production is rising rapidly. Its Western connections make Sinco a trailblazer; it is 30 percent owned by Australian and other foreign investors. It contracted for a Canadian company to build a pipeline to connect its field to the Russian pipeline network. The pipeline was completed in record time.

Sinco could become a giant in its own right. It claims 1.7 billion barrels in proven reserves, putting it in about the same class as Amoco and Elf Aquitaine and ahead of Conoco and Phillips. There are a dozen similar companies in Siberia's Tiumen province alone.

"HOW CAN WE NOT GO AHEAD?"

Western investment in the Russian oil industry will grow. But the pace will be determined by a number of considerations. One is the speed at which the new Russian oil companies succeed in financing their own investment. The second is the degree to which a sufficient legal and contractual foundation for investment is established. The third concerns attitudes. Oil always seems to be a special case around the world, the "patrimony," intimately tied up with the nation's identity. And oil in Russia is very caught up with the "drive for identity" that is discussed in the "Building Blocks" section of this book. Some Russians want loans from the West, but that is all. They think that the defense industries can quickly be converted to producing the urgently needed up-to-date oil equipment. They say that they do not want to be "colonized," and argue that they can build up their domestic industry speedily. What may not be clear to them is that the market for oil investment is competitive; companies have to choose among Russia, Africa, Latin America, and Southeast Asia, as well as the other newly independent republics, notably Azerbaijan and Kazakhstan.

Yet the prospect of a further collapse in Russian oil output is real—and dire. It is very hard to see how the Russian industry can be turned around without a partnership between Russians and foreign companies. As a member of a Russian commission reviewing one Russian-American oil proposal put it, "This project will bring us forty billion dollars in foreign earnings over the life of the project that, otherwise, we would not have. We need that money. How can we not go ahead?"

GOING HOME AGAIN

Energy is just one part of the economy for which foreign investment is a central question. Whatever the sector, investment can come from the government, particularly in a Two-Headed Eagle scenario. It can be generated by businesses operating in Russia, especially in *Chudo*. Or it can also come from another source: the billions of dollars that Russians themselves are holding beyond their borders. This is usually described as "capital flight." But, if the experience of Mexico and other Latin American countries is a good guide, it might better be called "capital hover"—the money is hovering off shore, waiting for a more inviting economic environment at home. In Latin America, for instance, tens of billions of dollars of capital flight has shifted into "capital return," in response to policies in many countries that are now more favorable to private property and investment. With the first glimmers of the economic miracle of our *Chudo* scenario, with greater clarity in laws and taxes, and with greater confidence that inflation is under control, Russian capital flight would start going home again to Russia. And that could be a far more powerful stimulus than most would anticipate today.

But even capital return will not be enough. Foreign business, too, searching for economic opportunities, will have to help finance economic growth in Russia, as was the case in the United States a century ago. It is not going to be an easy business under any circumstances. Making it even more complicated is the fact that long-term success or failure will be affected by the overall relations with the Western world. And that is the subject to which we now turn.

18

Russia and the West

In Moscow in February of 1946, George Kennan, the chargé d'affaires in the American embassy, was laid up with a collage of winter ailments —cold, fever, sinus, tooth trouble, and the side effects of sulfa drugs taken for these various ills. What remained of America's and Britain's wartime alliance with the Soviet Union was fast disappearing. Moscow was once again in the grim grip of Stalinism. Bedridden, Kennan found himself brooding on what he saw as the naïveté of American opinion toward the Soviet Union—the assumption that it would be easy to get along with "Uncle Joe" Stalin—and on the rootless quality of American policy toward that terror-driven nation. Despondent and convinced that protracted trouble was ahead, Kennan dictated an eight-thousand-word telegram back to Washington.

"We have here," he said, "a political force committed fanatically to the belief that with the U.S. there can be no permanent modus vivendi, that it is desirable and necessary that the internal harmony of our society be disrupted, our traditional way of life be destroyed, the international authority of our state be broken, if Soviet power is to be secure."

Widely distributed in the U.S. government, the Long Telegram, as it was to be known, became the most famous dispatch in the history of the U.S. Foreign Service. For it coalesced the conviction among senior American officials that a new struggle was beginning, this time with the Soviet Union.

The next year, back in Washington, Kennan wrote another essay, which appeared in the journal *Foreign Affairs* in 1947 under the title "The Sources of Soviet Conduct." Owing to the fact that he was director of policy planning in the State Department, Kennan published the article under the pseudonym "Mr. X." His authorship was quickly revealed. Nevertheless, the article, the most famous that *Foreign Affairs* ever published, would be known evermore as the Mr. X Article.

"FIRM CONTAINMENT"

By the time the article was in press, the struggle with the Soviet Union had already become explicit with the enunciation in March 1947 of the Truman Doctrine, meant to keep Greece and Turkey from falling to Communist forces. The Truman Doctrine was quickly followed by the Marshall Plan, the much larger aid package aimed at revitalizing the Western European economies in the face of expansionist Soviet power. In the Mr. X Article, Kennan warned that the struggle would be protracted. He coined the term "containment" to describe how the West should respond—"with a policy of firm containment, designed to confront the Russians with unalterable counter-force at every point where they show signs of encroaching upon the interests of a peaceful and stable world." He also held out the prospect that the Soviet Union "bears within it the seeds of its own decay," and that containment would promote tendencies that would eventually result in "either the break-up or the gradual mellowing of Soviet power."[1]

All this happened before the Berlin blockade and the division of Germany and Europe, before the Soviets exploded their first atomic bomb, before the Communist victory in China, before the Communist North Koreans crossed the 38th Parallel, starting the Korean War. But, by 1947, the confrontation had already become known as the Cold War.

"The business of dealing with the Russians is a long, long job," Secretary of State Dean Acheson had predicted at the end of 1947.[2] Stalin died six years later, in 1953. Thereafter, periods of détente alternated with periods of tension and crisis; but, whatever happened, it seemed that the essential confrontation would indeed continue to last, as Acheson had foreseen, for a "long, long" time.

The extended and bitter rivalry of the Cold War became the architecture of forty years of world politics. As events turned out, the war was not always cold. There were two major hot wars—in Korea and Vietnam—and many smaller wars, proxy wars. Trillions of dollars were spent on defense, and technology was pushed to deliver the potential for ever vaster and more sophisticated destruction.

But when the Cold War finally did end in the late 1980s, it happened in a way that fit the formula that George Kennan had enunciated in his Mr. X article four decades earlier. The Soviet system succumbed to its cynicism, its loss of confidence, and to its own internal weaknesses and decay.

"A NEW ERA"

At a summit off the coast of Malta in 1989, remembered as much because so many people got seasick as for what it accomplished, Soviet president Mikhail Gorbachev announced the change: "The world leaves one epoch, of cold war, and enters another epoch. It's a central drama of contemporary history."

After the summit, President Bush was asked his reaction. "The emotional part of it is hard for me to describe because I'm not the most articulate emotionalist," he replied. But, he added, "We stand at the threshold of a new era."[3]

What is to be the nature of that new era? For most of the last three quarters of a century, with the brief exception of the four-year alliance against Hitler, Russia and the West have regarded each other as enemies. Now that the Communist system and the Soviet empire are gone and Russia has returned as a nation state, the whole basis of Russia's relationship to the West is fluid and undefined. There is hope, a sense of optimism, of potential in the aftermath of the Cold War confrontation and the winding down of the balance of terror. The threat of nuclear warfare and atomic annihilation, which hung over every person on the planet, has greatly receded.

But there is also the fear that the opportunity for a more stable and peaceful world may be lost, may drift away. And there is also skepticism that the hope will turn out to have been only an illusion all along, and new dangers and new evils will emerge out of the ruins of communism. Some fear that geopolitics is inescapable. In their view, Russia's strategic location, its military capabilities, and its traditions—and the instability, rivalries, and power vacuums on its borders—all these will inevitably carry it back to an aggressive path of expansionism.

Yet Russia and the West do have a historic opportunity to build a new relationship, founded on a growing range of common interests. "The West," of course, is a figure of speech, denoting the community of industrial nations that are attached to democracy and liberal values and that are knitting the world together into the global village of transnational communications, services, trade, and finance. This is the community of the West that Russians call "civilized."

The word "civilization" has become the most powerful code word in Russia today. To Russians, it is a word with a very specific and positive meaning. Civilization is the goal. The word connotes Russians' struggle to reject and escape the totalitarian past, and their ambition to adopt the ways of liberal countries and the standard of living that goes with it. "Civilization" is the choice of many Russians today—though certainly not all.

Here is the historic opportunity—that Russia will indeed join the "civilized" West, at a time when the West will need the talents and cooperation of "civilized" Russia in pursuing common interests and meeting global risks. But this community of interests is no more than a potential. The chances of making it real depend very much on the kind of Russia that emerges in the coming years. This exploration in scenario planning is meant to provide a structure for thinking about that future. And that includes the question of the role of the West.

THE BOUNDS OF THE POSSIBLE

What can the West do to help bring about the kind of Russia with which it can be in partnership?

The first step is to be realistic. There are definite limits to the West's ability to influence Russia directly, at least through government policies. However, the recent elections reinforce Russia's sensitivity to the perception that the West is treating Russia as a suppliant rather than an equal. The December 1993 election sounded an alarm bell to the West. To some, it meant that the West must handle its relations with Russia more judiciously than in the previous two years. Others saw in that election, as well as in military moves in the Near Abroad, indications that Russia could be embarked on an expansionist course, one in which it would again seek direct or indirect control over its neighbors.

Yet, when stepping back, one sees that the influences of the West on Russia in the rest of this decade and into the next will be manifold, multi-dimensional, sometimes unintended, and unpredictable. The influences will take many more forms beyond what passes between government and government. There is the influence of the Western businessman who establishes a successful joint venture with a Russian enterprise that begins to export to global markets—and preserves Russian jobs in the process. There is the influence of the American company that hires a dozen Russian managers and brings them to the Midwest for six months of training. There is the influence of Western technology on everything from oil exploration to telecommunications. There is the influence of the professor teaching accounting in a business school in the Urals. There are the pervasive influences of music and film and style, and the unsavory influences of sensationalism and pornography. And there is the fundamental influence that comes as electronic communications provide for the instant exchange of information that will anchor Russia in the world economy.

What happens beyond Russia's borders will also have a strong impact. If the world economy grows strongly over the next two decades, the result will be a more favorable environment for foreign investment in Russia, and for Russian exports. If the global economy is weaker, then that will make Russia's situation more difficult, by reducing the flow of foreign investment and raising the barriers to its exports.

Events occurring outside Russia as well as within, of the kind we have already described in the surprises, will influence the Russian economy and diplomacy. The countries of the former Soviet bloc and the Near Abroad are themselves not ciphers; their stability and behavior will affect those of Russia. These are states that are in the process of finding their own identities and bolstering their own independence. Their evolution, their complaints, and their clashes could change Russia's course.

While outside influences will affect Russia, strong reactions against the widespread intrusion of the West will also develop. The modern-day Slavophiles, the Eurasianists in foreign policy, their opposite numbers in culture and the arts, and the angry and the resentful—all these will resist the Western influences and seek to stem them.

Ultimately, of course, Russia will make its own history. The triple shock wave that hit Russia—the collapse of the Soviet political system, the collapse of its economy, the implosion of its empire—is so powerful that internal forces will dominate. The evolution of Russian politics will be a Russian game, played mostly by Russian players, and largely over Russian issues. The economic transformation of Russia will be shaped mainly by its internal politics. Success is not guaranteed. Gorbachev tried, through perestroika, to unleash Soviet energies and Soviet capital—and failed. The main issue now will be whether Russians can create economic and political institutions that will unleash

Russian energies and capital. In the end, the Russians will have to do the job themselves, because the Russian recovery will require capital far beyond what foreign governments or Western companies and financial institutions can provide. Moreover, bad choices made within Russia can overwhelm whatever aid the West can deliver. For instance, a wrongheaded, half-baked currency reform or expanded credits to uneconomic industrial enterprises can undo a year's worth of Western support of Russian economic stabilization.

The West's attractiveness as a model of growth and a source of ideas and culture will depend on how the West handles its own internal problems—from unemployment, to crime and violence, to disunity and social decay. Over the last twenty years, the global ideological pendulum has swung, not only away from socialism but also away from state control and nationalized industries, toward free markets and privatization of economic activity.

The pendulum could swing back around the world, particularly if free markets do not deliver "the goods"—that is, widely shared economic growth. Or corruption, concentration of wealth, and conspicuous consumption could become too flagrant. These are the dangerous three "C's," which can undermine the commitment to the market and rejuvenate the opposition to capitalism. If other ideological yearnings collide with the market, there could then be some sort of renewed interest in collectivist solutions, if not outright socialism. Moreover, Russians will increasingly have competing models to choose from. China and the entire Pacific Rim, though they may worry Russians, will also attract them, especially since they represent mixed economies in which the state plays a strong economic and political role.

IMPROVING THE ODDS

At the same time, it will be difficult for Western democracies to apply a clear and consistent diplomacy to events around the world. The information revolution, the multitude of problems competing for the attention of Western publics, the lack of a Cold War focus—all these strain the ability of politicians and statesmen to think in long-range terms. The electronic age turns every incident into a crisis, and governments are forced to respond. This feature of contemporary politics will raise tensions if and when new violence breaks out.

The area that will be especially trying for Western diplomacy will be tension and conflict between Russia and the other successor states. The nature of the divorce among the former Soviet republics has left acrimony over the division of property, many very sore points, and much anger and resentment.

Certainly, broad elements in Russia regard the Near Abroad as a Russian sphere of influence and will try to reassert that influence. The strong showing of the extreme right in the December 1993 election has resulted in a more nationalist stance across the political spectrum, as well as increased criticism of the United States and the West. Some believe, as previously pointed out, that the break-up was a foreign plot to weaken Russia. They will castigate Western involvement—"meddling"—on their borders, and will seek to eject it. The ethnic cast of the division means that there will be a strong tendency to conflict, especially involving the 25 million Russians in the other republics. If the economic situation in the former Soviet Union does not improve, ethnic tensions will increase, reinforcing security tensions. The interaction of these issues could be explosive. As already observed, the biggest risk is in Russian-Ukrainian relations, and the consequences could be most serious.

The testing of Russian relations with the West has yet to come. Such a test may well arise with armed conflicts within the borders of the former Soviet Union, as we describe in the Two-Headed Eagle and Russian Bear scenarios. Moscow may conclude that its fundamental security is threatened either by secessionist moves within its territory or by conflicts along its borders, into which it is thus drawn. Extremists may fan such sentiments. This is when the possibilities for misunderstanding between Russia and the West, and for confusion in Western policy, become very high. There will be calls in the West for involvement in one form or another, or for the suspension of aid or the imposition of trade sanctions. But such responses need to be measured carefully against the possible effects within Russia. It will be a very critical moment. Thinking through such possibilities early—and trying to create the institutional structures in advance to mitigate such conflict—would be very constructive for all concerned.

While recognizing the limits, Western policies can nevertheless bolster Russia's future course toward democracy, a market economy, and cooperative relations in the world community. One might simply call this effort improving the odds.

There are four major ways in which Western policies can help improve those odds of a favorable outcome in Russia by 2010. The first is in aid and trade. The second is to give priority to developing joint structures to pursue arms control and manage potential flashpoints. The third is to focus on catalyzing Russian democracy and the market through programs with high leverage on Russian attitudes and skills. The fourth is to extend to Russia participation in the Western community of nations.

AID AND TRADE: A "STRATEGIC ALLIANCE WITH REFORM"

Western aid cannot "save" Russia. There is not enough money in the West and, in any event, the aid would be difficult to deploy effectively, even if the funds were available. Only Russia can build its new economy. But Western aid can help facilitate the process, by supporting the transition at critical points, diffusing technologies and skills, and helping to buffer the effects of the disruption of traditional trade and economic links. Keeping the aid in proper focus is important not only for the donors, but also to avoid skepticism and cynicism among Russians. Billions and billions of dollars of aid have been announced; only a fraction has been disbursed, and, in any event, many of the billions are not really direct aid, but debt relief, export credits, or stabilization funds.

Unless high inflation is reined in, the Russian economy is going to have great difficulty recovering, and instability will be the order of the day. To tackle inflation will require the kind of tough economic policies on the part of the Russians themselves that are described in *Chudo*. But Western aid can help by providing stabilization facilities to support continuing reform. That is the type of aid that can help on the macroeconomic level.

At the same time, there is a major role for aid at the micro level—at the level of the firm, the town, the university. This may be to provide critically needed capital that a company needs to expand production, or to fund "county agents" who can deliver technical assistance to farmers, or to provide marketing advice for a start-up biotechnology firm and supply Russian-language instructional materials on business practices to a teaching institution. This kind of help needs to be delivered, as much as possible, regionally and locally, to the people who will use it. Some of this assistance will be in a middle area between outright grants and traditional loans. Government aid can also be leveraged with private-sector programs.

This kind of approach is embodied in the Clinton Administration's aid programs. The objective of these policies is to promote American interests in building a safer and more stable and productive world through what Strobe Talbott, U.S. Deputy Secretary of State, describes as "a strategic alliance with post-Soviet reform."[4]

Aid is a bridge, perhaps over a five- to seven-year period. But trade and investment are the future. The new Russia will need to be able to earn a living in the world economy, and that means having the opportunity to export. But there are—and will be—many obstacles.

Some of the Cold War restrictions on trade have already been removed. In April 1994, CoCom, the Coordinating Committee that enforced Western technology controls against the Warsaw Pact, went out of business. Some controls remain, however, especially those designed to curb the proliferation of nuclear weapons. Further liberalization of trade will not be easy. As it is, in Muddling Down the Western world could be flooded by exports from a Russian economy in which domestic demand is collapsing faster than production. Russian exports of aluminum, nickel, and other metals have already depressed world metals markets. With vast unused industrial capacity, Russian industry could soon be exporting many more products to the rest of the world. To protect domestic industries, Western governments will be tempted— or pressured—to invoke tariffs, quotas, import ceilings, voluntary restraints, and antidumping procedures, particularly given the distortions from the collapse in value of the ruble. (At current exchange rates, top Russian professionals earn the equivalent of twenty dollars a month.)

Currently, provisions of U.S. trade laws that deal with what are called "nonmarket economies" (a euphemism for communism) raise tariff barriers against Russian products. The European Community has a host of protectionist restrictions that will exclude Russian exports. Many of these exclusions can be turned around so as to give access to Western markets for "economies in transition." When it comes to trade, European countries and Japan will have to think of Russia as more than a source of raw materials.

Protectionism and market access are not yet on the agenda between Russia and the West, but will be in the years ahead, especially as Russia does recover economically. Boris Yeltsin tried to raise the matter at the Tokyo Economic Summit. "In response to my energetic urging," he said afterward, "they answered, 'Yes, yes, we understand, but it is difficult to solve this problem.' " The answer will not necessarily grow any easier in the future. Aid is important to facilitate the transition.

But closing the door to trade will threaten the economic revitalization that the aid is supposed to help jump-start, and will damage longer-term relations between Russia and the West.[5]

COOPERATIVE SECURITY

A consequence of the breakup of the Soviet bloc and the Soviet Union is that Russia is now thrust far away from Europe and is thus more removed from the West geopolitically than it has been in two centuries, at the very time when it has become intellectually and emotionally closer than ever before. Geography and history both speak loudly: It is virtually inevitable that the countries of Eastern Europe, plus Ukraine, will look to the West and to one another for defense against their giant neighbor to the east. The greatest single threat to friendly relations between Russia and the West is the strong likelihood of renewed tension on the borders of western Russia.

It is entirely possible that events to the east and south will draw Russia's attention away from its western borders, thus defusing potential tensions there. The rise of China and of the Pacific Rim, political Islam, the economic power of Japan—these may emerge among the principal challenges to Russian diplomacy.

But, in the meantime, the West can move vigorously to associate Russia in multilateral security arrangements that encourage it and the other ex-Soviet states to look beyond their own borders, and to do so in partnership with both Eastern and Western Europe. Such arrangements would promote "cooperative security" by reducing reasons to fear surprise attack, by increasing "transparency" in terms of military capabilities and spending, by explicitly emphasizing "defense" over "offense," and by encouraging democratic control over military forces.[6]

The NATO Partnership for Peace—which involves joint military exercises, joint consultations and a variety of contacts short of actual membership—is a step in this direction. But, since most Central European nations would like full membership in NATO while Russia views their accession with great suspicion, there will be limits to the degree to which the West can be involved in cooperative security with all the countries of the former Soviet bloc.

But the first priority for Russian-Western diplomacy remains arms control and nuclear safety. Comprehensive monitoring of the dismantling of nuclear warheads should be placed on a reciprocal basis, as the programs need to be further implemented to control arms and promote the safe disposal of nuclear materials. As for nuclear safety, since it is most unlikely that Russia will be able to decommission its graphite-cooled reactors, the West should come to grips with the problem of improving safety both through training of operating personnel and through better controls.

CATALYSTS AND LEVERAGE

The West can help to improve the odds for Russian economic recovery and progress toward the market by focusing on a limited number of "catalytic" programs, in which relatively small investments can have large effects. Some private groups are pointing the way. The International Science Foundation is trying to preserve the integrity of science in Russia and the rest of the former Soviet Union by supporting scientists in the face of the disappearance of local funding. Public as well as private programs along this line could help the teachers, doctors, and the like who have been impoverished by the recent changes. Their political and economic commitment will be essential to the transition, and their demoralization would be a tremendous handicap.[7]

A major vehicle through which the potential community of interests between Russia and the West can be turned into reality is education. The most famous Russian exchange student, of course, was Peter the Great, who, at seven feet tall, went to work for nine weeks in 1697, not altogether anonymously, as an apprentice carpenter in the Dutch shipyards. But unlike China and Japan, Russia has never sent large numbers of its citizens to the West to study. Turkey has brought several thousand students from the Central Asian republics to study in Turkish universities. This is more than the total number of Russians in American universities.

Now that Russia has authorized its citizens to travel freely, the United States and other Western countries could seek to bring at least that number, and preferably many more, to study in Western high schools and universities each year. As much as possible, there should be multiyear programs. Experience proves their value. Exchange programs that brought Japanese and German students to the United States in the 1950s and 1960s helped forge critical and durable transatlantic relationships.

Another prime example is programs that help Russia manage money in all its aspects. Strong financial, budgetary, and banking systems are crucial to any prospects for a market in Russia. Though progress has not been easy, Western governments should continue to support efforts to help the Russians improve their tax system, balance their budget, update their accounting systems, and the like. In this area, too, training programs are vital, and a major effort has already begun. Similar programs for professionals from other sectors can also serve to propel progress.

MEMBERSHIP IN THE CLUB

If Russia is to be a partner with the West, then Russia will have to become a member of the club. The West must admit Russia without waiting to see whether it will become a "better" or "fitter" partner. It cannot hold out the prospect of collaboration as a reward for "better behavior." No proud people will tolerate being made to wait at the door, as the Russians are being asked to wait today. As Boris Yeltsin put it so revealingly after the G-7 summit in Tokyo in July 1993: "You understand, there was not this atmosphere of a student being taught by teachers . . . but one of equality and mutual respect."[8] In light of criticism and contention over aid, Western financial institutions are rethinking their approaches and policies toward Russia.

Since the December 1993 election, there has been increasing debate within the United States about how much aid should be given to Russia, as well as about the overall direction of U.S. policy. If the situation in Russia does not improve, or if Russia becomes more nationalistic, then America will be increasingly reluctant to be involved, as will Japan and other major countries.

There is no denying the constraints involved, and the West is likely to be uncomfortably limited and divided in dealing with Russia's problems. But one thing the West can and should do is bring Russia, to the degree possible, into the political arena where lending and trade policies are fought out. This is a critical time, before attitudes, policies, and alliances begin to jell. We are at a point of the kind that a historian once called one of those sensitive moments in history.[9]

RUSSIA 2010

Throughout this book we have described the events in Russia today as a revolution. But revolutions come in all shapes and sizes. Some revolutions become radicalized and run amok, devouring their own children; some do not. Some provoke a fearsome reaction. How will the revolution turn out in Russia? Since no one can know, the scenario method is designed to generate a spectrum of plausible pictures of the future. They include radical outcomes—civil war or authoritarian dictatorship. But the scenario analysis also shows that there are strong forces pushing Russia down a middle path toward less extreme outcomes.

The reason is that several key elements are missing to make a radical revolution in Russia. There is no deep ideological divide in Russia today, as there was in 1917. Instead, there is a striving for "civilization." The people of the Russian Federation are predominantly Russian and Orthodox, especially in the industrial and urban core of the country. The population is relatively old. (The truism that people generally become radical young is borne out by the evidence. The average age of the leading Bolsheviks when they took power in 1917 was thirty-six; the average age at which they became Bolsheviks was seventeen.)[10] There are—at least currently—no deep divisions among classes. Indeed, there are hardly any classes at all. The new class of private entrepreneurs overlaps with the former class of apparatchiks, so that the two are becoming barely distinguishable. These groups are more likely to fuse than to fight.

Other former Soviet republics may follow more violent paths. Some already have. But for the new Russian revolution, there are powerful countervailing forces to the full cycle of upheaval and bloodshed.

From our scenarios, then, emerges a set of conclusions:

Russia in 2010 will not be Communist (even though former Communists and even neo-Communists will play leading roles). There will be no return to the dictatorship of the Communist party or to the command economy, and therefore no return to the Cold War as we knew it. Russia will not be a global security threat in the way that the Soviet Union was. The bases of antagonism—arising from Soviet ideology, expansionism, and totalitarianism—are gone.

But what does happen in Russia will have great impact, one way or another, on the stability of Europe, Asia, and the Middle East, and will affect the United States. A Time of Troubles in Russia that veers toward chaos would send shock waves through the economies of Western Europe, reverberating out to the rest of the world. The Gulf crisis caused the confidence of consumers and financial markets to plummet, making the economic downturn worse. The effects on confidence of chaos in Russia—and uncertainty about its nuclear weapons—could be far greater. A *Chudo* in Russia, on the contrary, would mean growing markets for Western exporters and growth in the world economy.

Despite the currently widespread expectation in the West that Russia is fated to break up, there will be contrary pressures toward unity, although these forces are less apparent today than the more divisive tendencies. Ultimately, the unifying forces in Russia could well prevail. Even our Time of Troubles scenario includes, by 2010, a "regathering of the Russian lands."

For much of the next generation, Russia will be preoccupied with its internal problems, but there is enough potential for economic recovery so that the country will bounce back from its currently weakened state. In that case, Russians will be recovering their self-confidence and their ambition as a great nation. By 2010, if not well before, Russia will be returning actively to the world stage as a major player.

Problems with the Near Abroad are a virtual certainty under all scenarios. This likelihood requires special emphasis, because it is the most dangerous aspect of the next twenty years, both for the internal prospects for democracy in Russia and for Russia's relations with the West. But time is of the essence here: The longer confrontation can be delayed, the greater the chances will be that peaceful relations can be devised. One should not underestimate the determination of most Russians, Ukrainians, and their neighbors to avoid bloodshed.

Even with *Chudo,* Russia will still have a long way to go to be a prosperous country by 2010. If there is an economic miracle, it will emerge as a miracle for some people, some sectors, and some regions, with high inequalities. But the Russian economy could be growing strongly, with the realistic prospect of prosperity ahead. Russia will have begun to develop its own variant of Capitalism Russian-Style.

HOPE AND HISTORY

"We were so full of hope."

Again and again, one encounters that refrain from reformers in the former Soviet Union, as well as Eastern Europe, as they look back to the exultation that they felt in 1989 when the Berlin Wall came down and communism collapsed in Eastern Europe. They contrast it to the disillusionment and even despair they feel now, faced with the dislocations and hard times, the multitude of problems and painful choices, that come with the passage out of the Communist era.

The grim reality of the morning after has indeed dispatched the optimism. Communism slipped away in the night, with relatively little bloodshed at the end, at least so far, and when measured against what might have been the result. But it left its former quarters in very bad shape and left behind a very big bill that has yet to be paid. Owing to the way unification was implemented, to bring what had been East Germany up to Western standards will cost the German government $140 billion a year for ten years—a trillion dollars or more altogether. But eastern Germany already had a higher standard of living than Russia and had but sixteen million people, only a tenth of Russia's population. Given the price tag for East Germany, there is really no point in trying to calculate what the cost of Russia's transformation will be.

Yet, if the optimism went too far at the end of the 1980s, so now has the pessimism. What has happened, and is happening, is after all, amazing. The risks and dangers are there, certainly, but so are grounds for cautious optimism. But even if one judges that the odds are poor, even if one's reaction to current realities and the scenarios makes one a pessimist, both history and interest impose the obligation to engage.

The future is contingent, not foreordained. Many forces will converge to give it its distinctive shape. That is why we have approached the subject through these scenarios. We are at another time of beginning; which, despite all its risks and difficulties, is so much more promising than the grim prospect that George Kennan foresaw in 1946 as he composed the Long Telegram from his sickbed. The scale of this new beginning is so great that it is almost as though the twenty-first century has already begun. In *Russia and the West Under Lenin and Stalin,* which he wrote in the 1950s, Kennan describes "international life" as including "nothing final in point of time, nothing not vulnerable to the law of change."[11] In that spirit, we chose 2010 not as an endpoint, but rather as a convenient point of observation, both of Russia, and of Russia and the West, in the new century.

For, in the year 2010, Russia will still be in the middle of its transformation, still in the midst of building a life after communism and of rejoining its history to that of the world. This is a matter not of years, but of generations.

We do believe that all the scenarios end up with some version of Capitalism Russian-Style, but that the character of that particular brand of capitalism will depend upon the pathway to it. And we cannot say by which path Russia will reach it. We cannot say whether Russia will arrive by a more benign, democratic path of Muddling Down, or by the more tightly controlled administrative path of Two-Headed Eagle. We cannot say what crises will shake Russia along the way.

What we can say is that there is a road, and that there are strong forces pushing Russia down it. They are the forces unleashed by the collapse of the old system, which prevent a return to the command economy; by the rise of private enterprise and private property in Russia; by the daily growth of the importance of money in Russian life; and by the rapid breakup of state property, which is occurring before our eyes. To these must be added the impact of ideas—the virtual disappearance of Marxism as an intellectual force, both in Russia and the rest of the world, and the dominance of the ideas of the market and private enterprise throughout the world. The intellectual turn is profound and far-reaching: In the 1930s, the failures of the market system made many people into adherents of Marxism and believers in central planning. Today, the dynamism of the market and the failure of central planning make them into believers in the market.

We cannot say whether Capitalism Russian-Style will be more liberal or more conservative, more democratic or more authoritarian, more imperialistic or more cooperative. That will depend on the road by which Russia reaches 2010. It will also depend on the degree to which what might be called civic virtue can develop, and the extent to which corruption and crime can be kept in check. In any case, Capitalism Russian Style will not look like American-style capitalism, or European-style, or Asian-style, or Latin American–style. It will be Russian, built by Russians, shaped by Russian experience and traditions, responding to Russian interests and constraints, and serving Russian interests. Russia's path to capitalism in the twenty-first century does not, however, start from nowhere. Rather it marks Russia's return to a journey that it abandoned, under duress, in 1917.

By 2010, the post-Soviet transition will be far from complete. Russia could well run off the road in the meantime, once or more than once. But a democratic Russia is possible; a nonimperial Russia is possible. A capitalist Russia seems almost certain.

Appendix

Newly Independent States of the Former Soviet Union

State	Territory (square miles)	Population
Russian Federation	6,592,692	149,299,000
Kazakhstan	1,049,039	16,947,000
Ukraine	233,206	52,103,000
Turkmenistan	188,418	3,856,000
Uzbekistan	172,588	21,301,000
Belarus	80,154	10,263,000
Kyrgyzstan	76,834	4,506,000
Tajikistan	55,213	5,272,000
Azerbaijan	33,591	7,146,000
Georgia	27,027	5,476,000
Lithuania	25,174	3,736,000
Latvia	24,942	2,702,000
Estonia	17,413	1,581,000
Moldova	13,127	4,372,000
Armenia	11,583	3,504,000

Notes

CHAPTER 1: "THE WORLD BEHIND THE MIRROR"

1. On the risks and opportunities, see James Schlesinger, "New Instabilities, New Priorities," *Foreign Policy*, Winter 1991–1992, pp. 3–24.
2. George F. Kennan, *Memoirs 1925–1950* (New York: Pantheon Books, 1967), p. 527.
3. For Pearl Harbor, see Roberta Wohlstetter, *Pearl Harbor: Warning and Decision* (Stanford: Stanford University Press, 1962). On the Japanese Prime Minister, Martha Ann Caldwell, "Petroleum Politics in Japan: State and Industry in a Changing Policy Context," Ph.D. dissertation, University of Wisconsin, 1981.
4. *Public Papers of the Presidents of the United States: Jimmy Carter, 1977*, book 2 (Washington, D.C.: GPO, 1978), pp. 2220–21.
5. Anthony Eden, *Full Circle: The Memoirs of Anthony Eden* (Boston: Houghton Mifflin Co., 1960), p. 520.
6. Nicholas X. Rizopoulos, "A Third Balkan War?" *World Politics Journal*, Summer 1993.
7. On IBM, see Daniel Bell, "Downfall of the Business Giants: As American Capitalism Changes," *Dissent*, Summer 1993, pp. 316–23; Charles H. Ferguson and Charles R. Morris, *Computer Wars: How the West Can Win in a Post-IBM World* (New York: Times Books, 1993); and Paul Carroll, *Big Blues: The Unmaking of IBM* (New York: Crown Publishers, 1993).
8. U.S. Congress. Senate. Select Committee on Intelligence. *Nomination of Robert M. Gates to be Director of Central Intelligence.* 102nd Congress. 1st session. (Washington, D.C.: GPO, 1992), vol. 1, pp. 579–80.
9. The two original thinkers who led the development of scenario planning

at Shell were E. V. Newland and Pierre Wack. A major emphasis in scenario planning is on the learning process. Newland, Wack, and their colleagues were in the first instance concerned that so strong was the impact of the previous decade on the minds of senior managers, change might be upon these managers before they could recognize it. Thus, the planners sought to develop an alternative to conventional forecasting, one that would change the managers' "microcosm"—their mental images and assumptions about the future—and make them more receptive to different views and indicators of change. Newland is now a senior consultant to CERA, specializing in scenario planning. On Shell's experience in scenario planning, see Pierre Wack, "Scenarios: Uncharted Waters Ahead," *Harvard Business Review*, 63:5, September-October 1985, pp. 72–89; Pierre Wack, "Shooting the Rapids," *Harvard Business Review*, 63:6, November-December 1985, pp. 139–50; Arie P. de Geus, "Planning as Learning," *Harvard Business Review*, 66:2, March-April 1988, pp. 70–74; Peter Schwartz, *The Art of the Long View* (New York: Doubleday, 1991). On the limitations of economic forecasting, see Robert Stobaugh and Daniel Yergin, *Energy Future: Report of the Energy Project at the Harvard Business School* (New York: Vintage, 1983), pp. 309–42.

10. The "Greening of Russia" effort was conceived and led by Peter Schwartz, a successor to Newland and Wack and a leading scenario planner. He had been stimulated to ask the "what if?" questions by clues he had picked up in Hungary, and then creatively directed the scenario development. The only practicing Sovietologist on the Shell team was Angela Stent, a professor at Georgetown and CERA senior associate—and a contributor to *Russia 2010*. As with other scenarios, the "Greening of Russia" was not an academic exercise; it influenced strategy. See Schwartz, *Long View*.

Scenarios on South Africa's future provided a significant "learning experience" that changed many minds in South Africa in the late 1980s. See Clem Sunter, *The World and South Africa in the 1990s* (Pretoria: Human & Rousseau Tafelberg, 1987). The importance of the economic context for successful political transitions is developed in subsequent scenarios in Bob Tucker and Bruce R. Scott, *South Africa: Prospects for Successful Transition: The Nedcor Old Mutual Scenarios* (Kenywa: Juta & Co., 1992).

11. Cambridge Energy Research Associates, *Russia and the Former Soviet Union to 2010: Energy Strategies Risks and Opportunities* (multiclient study, 1993).

CHAPTER 2: THE NEW RUSSIAN REVOLUTION

1. Robert Campbell, quoted in Gregory Grossman, "Gold and the Sword: Money in the Soviet Command Economy," in *Industrialization in Two*

Systems: Essays in Honor of Alexander Gerschenkron, Henry Rosovsky, ed. (New York: John Wiley & Sons, 1966), p. 217.

2. David Remnick, *Lenin's Tomb: The Last Days of the Soviet Empire* (New York: Random House, 1993), pp. 148–49. Also see Robert Kaiser, *Why Gorbachev Happened, His Triumphs and His Failures* (New York: Simon & Schuster, 1991.)

3. Speech to XIX Party Conference, *Pravda,* July 2, 1988.

4. Michael R. Beschloss and Strobe Talbott, *At the Highest Levels: The Inside Story of the End of the Cold War* (Boston: Little, Brown & Co., 1993), p. 62.

5. Dmitri Volkogonov, *Stalin: Triumph and Tragedy* (Rocklin, CA: Prima Publishing, 1992), p. 310.

6. Hedrick Smith, *The New Russians* (New York: Avon Books, 1991).

7. Yeltsin in Boris Yeltsin, *Against the Grain: An Autobiography*, translated by Michael Glenny (New York: Summit Books, 1992); Gorbachev in *The Washington Post*, December 26, 1991, p. A27.

8. Yeltsin, *Against the Grain*, pp. 23–25.

9. Yeltsin, *Against the Grain*, p. 243.

10. On the sources of Russian inflation, and dealing with it, see Jeffrey Sachs, "Prospects for Monetary Stabilization in Russia," June 1993, mimeograph.

11. *Finansovye izvestiia*, no. 37 (July 10–16, 1993); *Moskovskie novosti*, no. 35 (29 August 1993); Maxim Boycko, Andrei Shleifer, and Robert W. Vishny, "Privatizing Russia," August 1993, mimeograph; Anders Aslund, "Russia's Success Story," *Foreign Affairs,* vol. 73, no. 5 (Fall 1994), pp. 58–71.

12. Authors' interview with Evgenii Yasin, May 1994.

CHAPTER 3: THE BATTLE FOR POWER

1. Isaac Deutscher, *Stalin: A Political Biography* (New York: Oxford University Press, 1966), p. 620.

2. *The Washington Post*, May 17, 1993, p. A15.

CHAPTER 4: THE BIG ENGINE THAT COULDN'T

1. Janos Kornai, *The Socialist System: The Political Economy of Communism* (Princeton: Princeton University Press, 1992).

2. *Izvestiia*, March 26, 1994.

3. Joseph Berliner, *The Innovation Decision in Soviet Industry* (Cambridge: MIT Press, 1976).

CHAPTER 5: THE IMPLOSION OF EMPIRE

1. See Samuel Huntington, "The Clash of Civilizations," *Foreign Affairs*, Summer 1993.
2. S. Frederick Starr, *Red and Hot: The Fate of Jazz in the Soviet Union* (New York: Oxford University Press, 1985).
3. Timothy J. Colton and Thane Gustafson, eds., *Soviet Soldiers and the State* (Princeton: Princeton University Press, 1990).

CHAPTER 6: PLAYERS AND PRIME MOVERS

1. John Webb, "Regional Russian Leadership Formation Process, 1987–1993: Four Case Studies," Ph.D. dissertation, Georgetown University, 1993.
2. Thomas M. Nichols, *The Sacred Cause: Civil-Military Security, 1917–1992* (Ithaca: Cornell University Press, 1993); Sergei Rogov, ed., "Russian Defense Policy: Challenges and Developments," a paper published jointly by the Institute of the USA and Canada of the Russian Academy of Sciences and the Center for Naval Analyses (Washington, D.C., February 1993), p. 20, 23.
3. Stepashin, a naval officer's son who rose through the ranks of the uniformed police, was chairman of the parliament's Committee on Defense and Security from 1992 to 1993. A brief biography appears in *Moskovskie novosti*, No. 10 (6–13 March 1994), p. A2. For a description of the reorganization of the FSK, see an interview with the former minister of security, Nikolai Golushko, in *Izvestiia*, February 3 1994. Background on the recent history of the KGB since Gorbachev can be found in Jeremy R. Azrael and Alexander G. Rahr, *The Formation and Development of the Russian KGB, 1991–1994* (Santa Monica, California: The Rand Corporation, National Defense Research Institute, 1993).
4. Amy Knight, "Russian Security Services Under Yeltsin," *Post-Soviet Affairs*, vol. 9, no. 1, January-March, 1993.
5. *Moskovskie novosti*, No. 14 (April 3–10, 1994), p. A6; *Interfax*, February 3, 1994.

CHAPTER 7: THAT THE GUARD NOT TIRE

1. Richard Pipes, *The Russian Revolution* (New York: Vintage Books, 1990), pp. 550–55.
2. *Izvestiia*, July 3, 1993.

CHAPTER 8: THE ROUGH ROAD TO THE MARKET

1. On the Russian "economic miracle" in the 1890s and again before World War I, Hans Rogger, *Russia in the Age of Modernization and Revolution, 1881–1917* (New York: Longman, 1983); Alexander Gerschenkron, *Economic Backwardness in Historical Perspective: A Book of Essays* (Cambridge: Belknap Press, 1962).
2. Alan Ball, *Russia's Last Capitalists: the Nepmen, 1921–1929* (Berkeley: University of California Press, 1987).
3. On the importance of "market skills" in privatization, based on Eastern European experience, see Kevin R. McDonald, "Why Privatization Is Not Enough," *Harvard Business Review*, May-June 1993, pp. 49–59.
4. *Izvestiia*, July 20, 1993.
5. Stephen Handelman, "In the Grip of Russia's Mafia," *New York Times Magazine*, January 24, 1993. See also, Stephen Handelman, "The Russian Mafia," *Foreign Affairs*, March–April 1994, pp. 83–96.
6. *RFE/RL Daily Report*, March 9, 1994.
7. On the status of women, see Angela Stent, "Women in the Post-Communist World: The Politics of Identity and Ethnicity," *World Policy Journal*, Winter 1993–94, pp. 65–71.

CHAPTER 9: MUDDLING DOWN

1. *Izvestiia*, August 27, 1993.
2. *Kommersant*, no. 33, August 26, 1993, p. 18; Jeffrey Hahn, "Attitudes Toward Reform Among Provincial Politicians," *Post-Soviet Affairs*, vol. 9, no. 1, January-March 1993, pp. 66–84.

CHAPTER 11: THE TIME OF TROUBLES: CHAOS AND REACTION

1. *Kommersant*, no. 33, August 26, 1993, p. 18; *The Economist*, September 4–10, 1993, p. 74.
2. *Izvestiia*, August 24, 1993.

CHAPTER 12: *CHUDO*: THE RUSSIAN ECONOMIC MIRACLE

1. On economic miracles, see Yutaka Kosai, *The Era of High Speed Growth* (Tokyo: University of Tokyo Press, 1986); Kazushi Ohkawa and Henry Rosovsky, *Japanese Economic Growth: Trend Acceleration in the Twentieth Century* (Stanford: Stanford University Press, 1973); Hugh Patrick and Henry Rosovsky, *Asia's New Giant: How the Japanese Economy Works* (Washington, DC: The Brookings Institution, 1976); *Postwar Economic Reconstruction and Lessons for the East*, edited by Rudiger Dornbusch, Wil-

helm Nolling and Richard Layard (Cambridge: The MIT Press, 1993); Shigeto Tsuru, *Japan's Capitalism* (Cambridge: Cambridge University Press, 1993); and Henry C. Wallich, *Mainsprings of the German Revival* (New Haven: Yale University Press, 1955).

2. On China's economic miracle see Dwight Heald Perkins, "Reforming China's Economic System," *Journal of Economic Literature*, vol. XXVI (June 1988), pp. 601–45; Kang Chen, Gary H. Jefferson and Inderjit Singh, "Lessons from China's Economic Reform," *Journal of Comparative Economics*, vol. 16, June 1992, pp. 201–25. For an insightful comparison of Chinese and Soviet economic reform, see Joseph S. Berliner, "*Perestroika* and the Chinese Model." Mimeograph. See also *The East Asia Miracle: Economic Growth and Public Policy* (Washington, D.C.: World Bank, 1993).

CHAPTER 15: SURPRISES

1. *Los Angeles Times,* February 10, 1994.
2. *Economist*, June 5–11, 1993.
3. Russian Federation Ministry of Foreign Economic Relations.
4. Murray Feshbach and Alfred Friendly, *Ecocide in the USSR* (New York: Basic Books, 1992).

CHAPTER 16: THE RETURN OF A GREAT POWER

1. *Hope Dies Last: The Autobiography of Alexander Dubček*, translated by Jiri Hochman (New York: Kodansha International, 1993), p. 212; Kádár quote in Zdenek Mlynar, *Nightfrost in Prague: The End of Humane Socialism* (New York: Karz, 1980), p. 157.
2. *Financial Times*, July 2, 1993.
3. Kravchuk quoted in *Japan Times*, September 6, 1993.
4. On Russia's relations with the Near Abroad, including the Caucasus, see Paul Goble, "Russia and Its Neighbors," *Foreign Policy*, Spring 1993, pp. 79–88; Thomas Goltz, "The Hidden Russian Hand," *Foreign Policy*, Fall 1993, pp. 92–116.
5. Sergei A. Karaganov, *Russia: The New Foreign Policy and Security Agenda: A View from Moscow* (London: Brasseys, 1992).
6. *Washington Post,* April 3, 1994.
7. Bakunin quoted in Angela Stent, *From Embargo to Ostpolitik: The Political Economy of West German–Soviet Union Relations 1955–1980* (Cambridge: Cambridge University Press, 1981), p. 1. Percentage of officials, T. G. Masaryk, quoted in Walter Laqueur, *Russia and Germany* (New Jersey: Transaction Publishers, 1990), p. 53.

8. James Placke, *Iran Resurgent*, CERA Report, 1992; *Political Islam*, CERA Report, 1993.

CHAPTER 17: WHO PAYS FOR THE PLOWSHARES? FOREIGN INVESTORS AND THE NEW CAPITALISTS

1. Russian Federation Supreme Soviet, Council of the Republic, Commission on Transportation, Communications, Informatics and Space. Data as of January 1, 1993.
2. Various sources on investment are contradictory, so these numbers should be taken as indicative of trends only. The share of GNP devoted to investment in the Soviet period comes from Goskomstat SSSR, *Narodnoe khoziaistvo SSSR v 1990 godu* (Moscow, 1991), p. 6. The current share of investment comes from Nikolai Petrakov in *Finansovye izvestiia*, no. 33 (1993), p. 4. The figures on decline between 1991 and 1992 are cited by Andrei Sizov, *Rossiiskaia gazeta*, February 10, 1993. Similar estimates can be found in A. Z. Astapovich and Leonid Grigor'ev, eds., *Foreign Investment in Russia: Problems and Prospects* (Moscow, 1993). On the other hand, official figures from the Russian government's Center for Economic Reform, as published in the authoritative *Russian Economic Trends: 1993* (number two), are much less dramatic. They show a 45 percent decline in investment over two years rather than one, Russian investment at 17 percent of GDP in 1992, and a stabilization in the fourth quarter of 1992.
3. Expert Institute, Russian Union of Industrialists and Entrepreneurs.
4. Russian Federation Ministry of Economics, April 1993, and other estimates.
5. Lenin quoted in Daniel Yergin, *The Prize: The Epic Quest for Oil, Money & Power* (New York: Simon & Schuster, 1992), p. 575; Averell Harriman, *America and Russia in a Changing World* (Garden City: Doubleday, 1971), pp. 2–8.
6. *Asian Wall Street Journal*, April 19, 1994.
7. Excerpts from the foreign-policy statement were published in *Nezavisimaia gazeta*, April 29, 1993.
8. Joseph Stanislaw and Daniel Yergin, "The Oil Shocks to Come," *Foreign Affairs*, September-October 1993. On the Russian gas industry, see Thane Gustafson, Vadim Eskin, and Alexander Rudkevich, *Gazprom's Dilemma: Too Much Gas or Too Little?* Cambridge Energy Research Associates Report, 1993.

CHAPTER 18: RUSSIA AND THE WEST

1. Kennan, *Memoirs*; "Mr. X," "The Sources of Soviet Conduct," *Foreign Affairs*, July 1947.
2. Acheson quoted in Daniel Yergin, *Shattered Peace: The Origins of the Cold War and the National Security State* (New York: Penguin Books, 1990), p. 5.
3. *New York Times*, December 4, 1989.
4. Testimony of Ambassador Strobe Talbott to the U.S. House of Representatives' Committee on Foreign Relations Subcommittee on Appropriations. April 19, 1993. Mimeograph.
5. *Financial Times*, July 10, 1993.
6. Ashton B. Carter, William J. Perry, John D. Steinbruner, *A New Concept of Cooperative Security, Brookings Occasional Papers* (Washington, D.C.: The Brookings Institution, 1992).
7. George Soros, the initial underwriter of the International Science Foundation, emphasizes the essential role of what he calls "active assistance" and "reinforcement" in *Nationalist Dictatorships versus Open Society* (New York: The Soros Foundations, February 1993).
8. *Financial Times*, July 10, 1993.
9. Herman Feis, *The Road to Pearl Harbor: The Coming of the War Between the United States and Japan* (Princeton: Princeton University Press, 1950).
10. Merle Fainsod, *How Russia Is Ruled* (Cambridge: Harvard University Press, 1963).
11. George Kennan, *Russia and the West Under Lenin and Stalin* (Boston: Little, Brown & Co., 1960), p. 398.

Acknowledgments

This work emerges out of and is part of the ongoing research program at CERA—Cambridge Energy Research Associates. And thus we are most grateful to our colleagues both for their own work and for supporting and contributing to this book.

We would like to express our deep appreciation to Joseph Stanislaw, CERA managing director and director of research, who leads CERA's strategic and scenario planning efforts, for his contribution to the development of this work and its overarching economic and political themes, for his probing insights and for sharing his thinking. And to James Rosenfield, CERA managing director, for his conceptualizing and motivating this project; for his clear ideas and support, and for bringing his keen sense of structure to bear on the framework of the book.

We are also very grateful to Angela Stent, CERA senior associate, associate professor of government at Georgetown University, and expert on Russian foreign policy, for her knowledge and criticism and for her substantial contribution to the section on Russia and the world. Some of her own current work on Russian foreign policy is the basis of chapter 16. She also asked the pertinent question, "Why not a *chudo?*"

We especially want to thank James Schlesinger, who gave generously of his time, trenchantly criticized the manuscript, shared his own insights and wealth of knowledge, and stimulated our thinking with his searching questions.

We thank those who advised and contributed to this work: Peter

Hauslohner, formerly of Yale University and the Policy Planning Staff in the U.S. State Department and an expert on Russian politics and society, for his criticism and his work on Western policy; E. V. Newland, CERA senior consultant and, for almost a decade, CERA's coach on scenario planning; Joel Hellman, CERA senior associate and assistant professor of government at Harvard University, for his detailed and careful analysis of the dynamics of Russian politics and constitutionalism; Todd Foglesong, of the University of Toronto, for his contribution on the evolution of the law; Laurent Ruseckas, CERA research associate for the non-Russian republics of the former Soviet Union, who coordinated our multiclient study and contributed to this book. We were greatly helped by Jennifer Long, doctoral candidate at Georgetown University, who worked with great dedication as research associate on this project, bringing her own valuable knowledge of Russian politics and reform to bear. Steve Haggett, as coordinator of our FSU Advisory Service, contributed to the necessary foundations of this venture. And our CERA colleagues in Moscow, Aleksey Reteyum and Vadim Eskin, helped in crucial ways.

We are also very grateful to Nicholas X. Rizopoulos, who incisively and with care critiqued the manuscript. Leonid Grigoriev read the manuscript as a participant, an international economist, a writer, and as a Russian citizen. Christopher Beauman shared perspectives from his work in international finance and economic transitions. Yukon Huang helped us with his grasp of the Russian economy and of the imperatives of economic development. Eugene Lawson shared with us his knowledge of foreign investment and economic relations between Russia and the industrial world. Harley Balzer helped us as a Russian intellectual historian engaged in helping to preserve Russia's current intellectual resources.

We owe a special word of appreciation to John Browne, who early on saw the need for better and focused understanding of Russia's future after communism.

We are very grateful to the following people for the opportunity to discuss this work and benefit from their perspectives, especially in the midst of their demanding schedules: Robert Strauss, Strobe Talbott, and Sir Brian and Lady Fall.

We want to thank the following people variously for their advice and help, for reading and commenting, or for ongoing dialogue—or some combination of all of the above: Hans Bär, Roger Beach, Joseph Berliner, Wilhelm Bonse-Geuking, Eric Brenner, Elizabeth Bumiller,

313

James Chace, Margaret Chapman, Howard Chase, Shelby Coffey, Herbert Detharding, Richard Dobson, Rondo Fehlberg, Ronald Freeman, Benjamin Friedman, Rafael Goldberg, Victor Gilinsky, Rose Gottemoeller, Thomas Hamilton, Nancy Hewett, Richard Hildahl, Steedman Hinckley, John Hines, Sir Peter Holmes, John Jennings, Catherine Kelleher, Robert C. Kelly, Andrey Konoplyanik, Vera de Ladoucette, Helmut Langangen, Kenneth Lay, Steve Lipman, Andrew Lowenstein, Clem Malin, Molly Meacher, Thomas Nichols, Robert Reisner, Thomas Richardson, Eugene Rumer, Ronald Stent, Samuel Stern, Hermann Tophof, John Webb, Steven R. Weisman, James Wyatt, John Wing, and K. S. Wu.

We want to thank those who worked on the CERA energy multiclient study on Russia and the former Soviet Union, which preceded this book in our research and provided one foundation for *Russia 2010*. In addition to some of those cited above, those from CERA included: Professor Raymond Vernon, CERA board director and professor emeritus, Harvard University; Simon Blakey, I. C. Bupp, Robert Ebel, Robert Esser, and James Placke. Many of them also read and commented on part or all of this book. Alexander Kollontai and Thomas Richardson also worked on that study. We thank Edward Jordan, CERA board director, for his advice and counsel.

Our special thanks to Sue Lena Thompson, who coordinated the entire process of publication and, as always, brought clarity and rigorous standards and dedication to the process. And to Maria Rodriguez, John Newton, and James Worsley, valued colleagues for many years on whose advice we rely.

At CERA, too, we are deeply in debt to Kath Fitzgerald, for helping to balance this book in what seemed to be a constantly changing field. And to Susan Nardone and Helen Sisley for expertly adding their contribution to this endeavor.

We are very grateful to others at CERA, who helped to make this book happen expeditiously, especially Heidi Eklund, who supervised production, Stephen Aldrich, Welton Barker, Alice Barsoomian, Jennifer Battersby, Teresa Chang, Michael Kelly, Roberta Klix, James Long, Daniel Lucking, Micheline Manoncourt, Philippe Michelon, Christine Nevius, Kevin Redmond, Amy Rowland, and Robin Weiss. We thank Robert Forget for the care with which he developed the maps, and Wes Shaffer, III at Berryville Graphics for the precision of his work under pressured conditions.

Many, many people in interviews and discussions shared their thoughts, experience, their hopes, and certainly their fears, with us, and we thank them all.

We certainly want to acknowledge the pioneers of scenario planning —E. V. Newland and Pierre Wack—and our friends and practitioners, Peter Schwartz and C. Napier Collyns. We much value the dialogue with all of them.

It was Kate Medina of Random House who was interested in the "history" of the twenty-first as well as the twentieth century and who made this book possible. We want to express our great appreciation to her. She saw the potential for this book, worked closely with us over every line, managed the process, and encouraged us throughout. She visualized how the book should come out and then made it happen.

We are very grateful to Amanda Urban of ICM for her considered judgment, her conceptualization of this work, her conviction and encouragement, and for ensuring that it would proceed.

At Random House, we also want to thank Harold Evans, Walter Weintz, Jonathan Karp, Susan Hood, Camille Capozzi, Gail Blackhall, Alex Siegel, Carol Schneider, Ivan Held, Andy Carpenter, Amy Edelman, Jolanta Benal, Andrew Ambraziejus, Brian Hudgins, and Benjamin Dreyer.

At Vintage Books we are very appreciative to Peter Dimock and to Martin Asher.

At Futami Shobo we are appreciative to Masami Ikeda. And we continue to be in the debt of the gracious Tachi Nagasawa of Japan UNI.

At Nicholas Brealey Publishing, we are very grateful to the innovative and clever Nicholas Brealey himself, who is re-engineering publishing. We also wish to thank Angie Tainsh and Liz Mason for their valuable assistance.

Finally, we thank Nil Gustafson and Angela Stent for their personal support and commitment and for their patience, on which we drew far more than anyone had anticipated.

We have thanked many people, but of course the responsibility for the book and the judgments herein is ours alone.

—Daniel Yergin
Thane Gustafson

Index

relationship with Germany, 7, 16, 242, 258–59, 263–64
Russian minority outside, 68–69, 97–98, 247–52
as successor of Soviet Union, 238, 240
triple transition of, 4–6, 13, 239, 289
Yeltsin as president of, 33, 47, 54
Russian Orthodox Church, 46, 67–68, 96, 200, 248
Russian Way bloc, 82
Rutskoi, Aleksandr, 36, 38, 79, 82, 148
Rybkin, Ivan, 80

St. Petersburg, 164, 167, 175, 192
Sakharov, Andrei, 3
Scandinavia, 252, 268
scenario planning, *xix-xx*, 8–9
CERA (Cambridge Energy Research Associates) in, *xx*, 11–12
Chudo Scenario, *xiii*, 15, 132, 177–94
conclusions from, 297–98
development of, 10–11
Muddling Down, 14, 131, 133–46, 188
objective of, 12
prime movers in, 74
surprises in, 10, 216–34
Time of Troubles, 14, 131–32, 158–76, 188
Two-Headed Eagle, 14, 131, 147–57
see also Capitalism Russian-Style; *names of specific scenarios*
Schlesinger, James, 9
secret police
and civil-military relations, 106–7
FSK, 13, 87–88, 107, 149, 219–20
influence of, 86–88
KGB, 7, 13, 23, 31, 52, 59, 71, 88
in scenarios, 149–50, 152, 170–74
Serbia, 49
service sector, 193

Shafranik, Sergei, 283
Shell, 10–11, 282
Shevardnadze, Eduard, 28, 244, 251
Shumeiko, Vladimir, 81
Siberia, 198–99, 261
in *Chudo* Scenario, 183, 192
oil projects in, 273, 280, 282
and potential capitalism in China, 224
purge in, 30–31
Sinco, 283
Singapore, 186
Slavophiles, 253
Smith, Adam, 110
social capital, 190, 191
socialism, 4, 23, 25–26, 46–47
South Russian Confederation, 166, 167
"Soviet internationalism," 68–69, 86
Soviet republics, *see* former Soviet republics
soviets, 77, 80–81, 85
Soviet Union
collapse of, 21–22, 28–33, 45–57, 60
foreign policy of, 242–44
map of former, *xvi-xvii*
as a superpower, 242–44
"whip and cake method" of control in, 49–50
see also Cold War; former Soviet republics; Russian Federation
stagflation, 137
Stalin, Joseph, 21, 23, 26–27, 30–31, 45, 64, 69, 165, 172, 229, 249, 259, 270, 285, 286
Stanislaw, Joseph, *xix-xx*, 12
START, 219, 256
State Duma, 39, 80, 81–82, 91, 255
state enterprises, 62, 76–77, 83, 113–15, *see also* privatization
Stent, Angela, 238*n*
Stepashin, Sergei, 87, 88
Strauss, Robert, 265
strike committees, 97
subsidies, 185, 205

ABOUT THE AUTHORS

DANIEL YERGIN, president of Cambridge Energy Research Associates (CERA), is an authority on international politics, energy, and scenario analysis. He is the author of *The Prize: The Epic Quest for Oil, Money, and Power,* a number one best-seller and winner of the 1992 Pulitzer Prize for general nonfiction. It also won the 1992 Eccles Prize for best book on economic themes for a general audience. *The Prize* was the basis of an acclaimed eight-part television series of the same name, a coproduction of PBS, BBC, and Japan's NHK. Dr. Yergin is the author of *Shattered Peace,* an award-winning history of Russian-American relations in the Cold War, as well as studies on East-West trade. He coauthored *Energy Future: Report of the Energy Project at the Harvard Business School,* which was also an international best-seller. He was a professor at the Harvard Business School and the Kennedy School of Government at Harvard. He holds a Ph.D. in international relations from Cambridge University, where he was a Marshall Scholar, and has a B.A. from Yale University. He is currently Chairman of the U.S. Government's Task Force on Energy Research and Development.

THANE GUSTAFSON, CERA director, heads its former Soviet Union (FSU) Advisory Service and prepares the *FSU Watch.* A leading expert on Russia and on business strategy, he advises companies on investment prospects in the former Soviet Union. He is also a professor of government at Georgetown University. He is the author of *Crisis amid Plenty,* a study of Soviet energy and the decline of the Soviet Union, which won the Marshall Shulman Award for best book on Soviet affairs in 1989. He is also the author of *Reform in Soviet Politics* and *Soviet Negotiating Strategy,* and coauthor of *Soviet Soldiers and the State* and *The Soviet Union at the Crossroads.* He taught at Harvard University, was on the staff of the RAND Corporation, and directed the Soviet studies program at the Center for Strategic and International Studies in Washington, D.C. He was a Fulbright Scholar in Russia and Ukraine, and is a frequent traveler throughout the former Soviet Union. Dr. Gustafson holds a Ph.D. from Harvard University and a B.S. from the University of Illinois. He is at work on a new book, *Capitalism Russian-Style.*

Cambridge Energy Research Associates—CERA—is a leading international consulting firm focused on energy, global economics and politics, and scenario and strategic analysis. The firm, founded in 1982, provides objective and independent advice to many companies, financial institutions, and governments around the world on a broad range of strategic and investment issues, as well as on planning. It operates from offices in Cambridge, Massachusetts, Paris, Oslo, Washington, D.C., and Oakland, California. Since 1985, it has conducted a number of scenario studies—on energy issues; on the future of Mexico, Latin America, and the Middle East; environmental prospects; economic, political, and social change in Europe; and privatization and the international economy. It also began its research and advisory services on the then Soviet Union in 1985. It launched its FSU Advisory Service in 1991.